MOON

SALT LAKE CITY & PARK CITY

W. C. McRAE & JUDY JEWELL

Contents

SALT LAKE CITY
& PARK CITY

Salt Lake City

Look for ★ to find recommended
sights, activities, dining, and lodging.

Highlights

★ **Temple Square Historical Tour:** Take a free 40-minute tour of Temple Square, the epicenter of Mormon faith, offering museums, public gardens, and eye-popping architecture. Whether you're a believer or not, you'll enjoy the spectacle (page 12).

★ **State Capitol:** Modeled on the U.S. Capitol, Utah's seat of government is grandly scaled and brimming with granite and marble. From the steps leading to the building, views of the city and the Wasatch peaks are breathtaking (page 17).

★ **Red Butte Garden and Arboretum:** An oasis of green in arid Salt Lake City, these gardens cover 30 acres. Two hundred acres of adjacent woodlands are laced with trails for hiking and jogging (page 20).

★ **Liberty Park:** This lovely park, with playgrounds, a lake, and lots and lots of manicured lawns, is also beloved for its Tracy Aviary, a bird zoo with falconry events (page 22).

★ **City Creek Canyon:** The most accessible hiking and cycling path in Salt Lake City starts right downtown and winds up in City Creek Canyon along a rushing stream running past wooded glens. Bring a picnic and enjoy an island of nature in the middle of the city's urban sprawl (page 30).

★ **Union Station Museums:** The cavernous Union Station is a glorious relic of Odgen's railroading past. It now serves as home to a clutch of interesting museums and collections (page 55).

★ **Antelope Island State Park:** Hike or bike to explore the curious natural history of the largest island in the Great Salt Lake (page 64).

★ **Golden Spike Visitor Center:** The first transcontinental rail lines were joined at this remote site in 1869; the visitors center and replica steam trains help re-create the epoch-making event (page 71).

★ **American West Heritage Center:** The living-history museum enacts aspects of the Logan area's rich human history, from Native American culture to homestead farming. Seasonal celebrations and ritual events make for a year-round series of festivals (page 74).

★ **Benson Grist Mill:** This perfectly preserved grain mill from the 1850s offers a fascinating glimpse into the agrarian life of frontier Utah (page 82).

I n 1847 the Mormon prophet Brigham Young proclaimed this site the "right place" for a new settlement. Today, many residents and visitors still agree. Modern Salt Lake City offers an appealing mix of cultural activities, historic sites, varied

architecture, engaging shopping, sophisticated hotels, and elegant restaurants. About 190,000 people live in the city, making it by far the largest and most important urban center in Utah, while more than one million people reside nearby in the city's sprawling suburbs.

Salt Lake City enjoys a physical setting of great visual drama. The city lies on the broad valley floor and terraces once occupied by prehistoric Lake Bonneville. Great Salt Lake, the largest remnant of that ancient inland sea, lies just northwest of the city. The Wasatch Range rises immediately to the east; these rugged mountains, including many peaks exceeding 11,000 feet, are cut by steep canyons whose streams provide the area's drinking and irrigation water. Just minutes from downtown, you can be skiing on some of the world's best powder in winter or hiking among wildflowers in summer. On the other side of the valley, to the west, Lewiston Peak (10,626 feet) crowns the Oquirrh Mountains.

Salt Lake City's strong sense of focus and purposefulness comes from a near-unique combination of attributes. It's a state capital, a major university center, the largest city for hundreds of miles, and the seat of a wealthy and powerful worldwide religion.

The early Mormons' pride in their City of Zion is clearly seen in the old residential districts, with their beautiful Victorian mansions, as well as the downtown area's ornate storefronts and civic structures. Few cities in the West retain such a wealth of period architecture.

PLANNING YOUR TIME

To see the sights in Salt Lake City requires at least three full days. Because the city is easily the most sophisticated place to stay and eat for hundreds of miles around (with the possible exception of Park City), it's also a comfortable and convenient hub for exploring the scenery and recreation of northern Utah.

Previous: Utah's State Capitol; TRAX light rail train. **Above:** Salt Lake Temple.

Salt Lake City and Vicinity

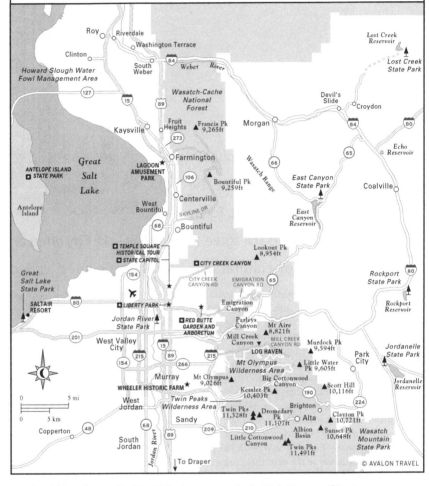

© AVALON TRAVEL

You could easily spend a day visiting just the Latter-day Saints museums, religious and historic sites, and administrative buildings that front Temple Square. Many people budget time to perform ancestry research while here—the church has extensive genealogical records and allows visitors to research family records free of charge.

A second day in Salt Lake City can be divided between visits to the state capitol and the nearby Pioneer Memorial Museum, plus a stop by the Utah Museum of Contemporary Art. Add in a picnic at Liberty Park and a visit to the Tracy Aviary, a bird zoo with live falconry displays, and you'll have a full and varied day. A number of hiking trails begin right in the city: City Creek Canyon and Red Butte Garden and Arboretum, for example, are within reach of almost any downtown hotel.

Day-trip options include Antelope Island State Park, a good destination for hiking and mountain biking (plan to spend half a day exploring this island in Great Salt Lake), and Park City, a historic mining camp now turned glittering world-class ski resort. Ogden's museums and old city center can also be visited as a side trip from Salt Lake City, but if you're heading as far as Logan to attend one of its many music and theatrical festivals, it's worth spending the night. Depending on the season, skiing or hiking in the Wasatch Mountains directly behind the city should definitely be a part of every traveler's itinerary.

HISTORY

Salt Lake City began as a dream—a utopia in which the persecuted Latter-day Saints would have the freedom to create a Kingdom of God on Earth. Their prophet, Brigham Young, led a first group of 143 men, 3 women, and 2 children to the valley of Great Salt Lake in July 1847. The bleak valley, covered with sagebrush and inhabited mainly by lizards, could best be described as "the land nobody wanted."

The pioneers set to work digging irrigation canals, planting crops, constructing a small fort, and laying out a city as nearly 2,000 more immigrants arrived that first summer. Tanneries, flour mills, blacksmith shops, stores, and other enterprises developed under church direction. Beautiful residential neighborhoods sprang up, reflecting both the pride of craftsmanship and the sense of stability encouraged by the church. Workers began to raise the temple, the tabernacle, and the other religious structures that still dominate the area around Temple Square. Colonization of the surrounding country proceeded at a rapid pace.

As the Mormons' earthly City of Zion, Salt Lake City came close to its goal of being a community devoted to God. Nearly all aspects of political, economic, and family life came under the influence of the church during the first 20 years.

The isolation that had shielded Salt Lake City from outside influence began to fade around 1870, but the city remained conservative and inward-looking until the 1970s, when its superlative access to recreation began to attract an influx of young non-Mormons drawn to skiing, hiking, and other outdoor activities. With business booming, Salt Lake City soon became one of the leading cities of the American West. As a measure of the city's new prestige, Salt Lake City hosted the 2002 Winter Olympics.

Sights

Although Salt Lake City is a sprawling urban area, the majority of visitor destinations are concentrated in an easy-to-negotiate area in and near the downtown core. Excellent public transportation makes it simple to forgo a rental car and just hop on the light rail or a bus.

TEMPLE SQUARE AND MORMON HISTORIC SITES

Easily Salt Lake City's most famous attraction, the **Temple Square** complex (between North Temple St. and South Temple St., 9am-9pm daily) has a special meaning for Mormons: It is the Mecca or the Vatican of the Church of Jesus Christ of Latter-day Saints. Brigham Young chose this site for Temple Square in July 1847, just four days after arriving in the valley. Nearby, Young built his private residences; the tabernacle, visitors centers, museums, and a host of other buildings that play a role in LDS church administration also line the streets around Temple Square. You're welcome to visit most of these buildings, which provide an excellent introduction to the LDS religion and Utah's early history.

Enthusiastic guides offer several tours of Temple Square, which covers an entire block in the heart of the city. A 15-foot wall

Temple Square

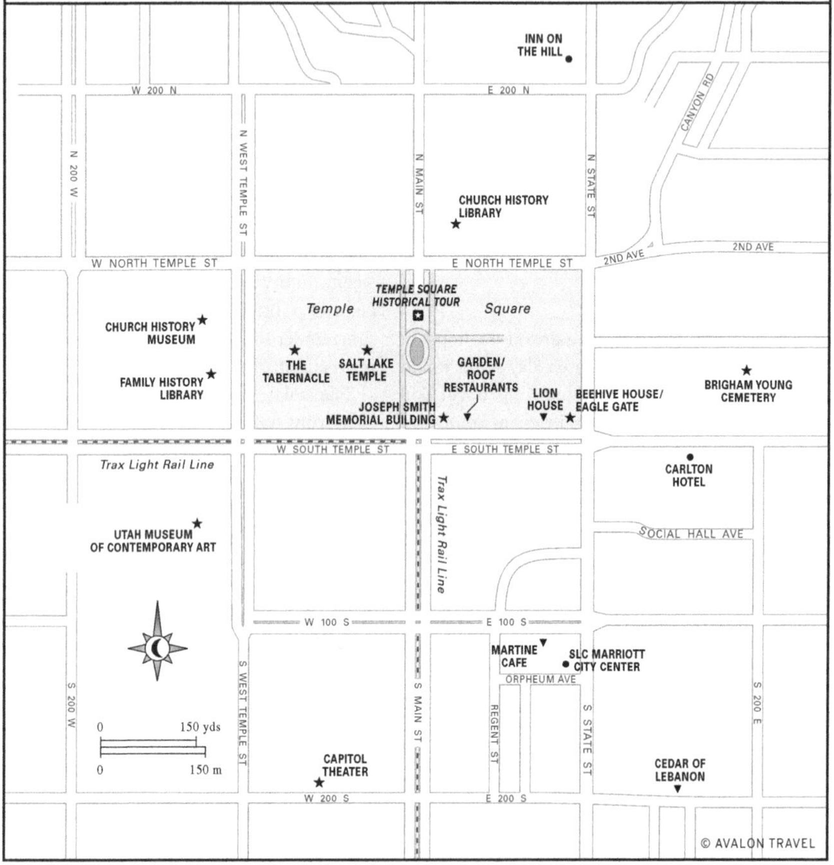

INN ON
THE HILL

W 200 N

E 200 N

CANYON RD

N 200 W

N WEST TEMPLE ST

N MAIN ST

N STATE ST

CHURCH HISTORY
LIBRARY ★

2ND AVE

2ND AVE

W NORTH TEMPLE ST

E NORTH TEMPLE ST

CHURCH HISTORY ★
MUSEUM

FAMILY HISTORY ★
LIBRARY

Temple

TEMPLE SQUARE
HISTORICAL TOUR ▣

Square

★   ★
THE   SALT LAKE
TABERNACLE TEMPLE

JOSEPH SMITH
MEMORIAL BUILDING ★

GARDEN/
ROOF
RESTAURANTS LION BEEHIVE HOUSE/
             HOUSE EAGLE GATE
                 ▼   ★
              ▼

BRIGHAM YOUNG ★
CEMETERY

W SOUTH TEMPLE ST

E SOUTH TEMPLE ST

CARLTON
HOTEL

Trax Light Rail Line

UTAH MUSEUM ★
OF CONTEMPORARY ART

Trax Light Rail Line

SOCIAL HALL AVE

W 100 S

E 100 S

S 200 W

S WEST TEMPLE ST

0   150 yds

0   150 m

S MAIN ST

MARTINE ▼
CAFE   SLC MARRIOTT
        ● CITY CENTER
ORPHEUM AVE

REGENT ST

S STATE ST

S 200 E

CAPITOL
THEATER ★

W 200 S

E 200 S

CEDAR OF
LEBANON
▼

© AVALON TRAVEL

surrounds the square's 10 acres; you can enter through wrought-iron gates on the south, west, and north sides. All tours, exhibits, and concerts are free. Foreign-language tours are also available—ask at the North Visitors' Center. Smoking is prohibited on the grounds.

★ Temple Square Historical Tour

Guides greet you at the gates of the square and offer an introduction to Salt Lake City's pioneers, the temple, the tabernacle, Assembly Hall, and historic monuments. The free 40-minute tours begin every 10 minutes during the summer season and every 15 minutes the rest of the year (usually 9am-9pm daily). Custom group tours can be scheduled in advance. Points of interest, which you can also visit on your own, include the Seagull Monument, commemorating the seagulls that devoured the "cricket" plague in 1848; a bell from the abandoned Nauvoo Temple; sculptures of Christ, church leaders, and handcart pioneers; an astronomy observation site; and a meridian marker (outside the walls at Main St. and South Temple St.) from which surveyors mapped out Utah. Although tour leaders don't normally proselytize, the

the skyline at Temple Square

The plan for Salt Lake City's temple came as a vision to Brigham Young when he still lived in Illinois. Later, Young's concept became a reality with help from church architect Truman O. Angell; construction began in 1853. Workers chiseled granite blocks from Little Cottonwood Canyon, 20 miles southeast of the city, then hauled them with oxen and later by railroad for final shaping at the temple site. The temple dedication took place on April 6, 1893—40 years to the day after work began.

The foundation alone required 7,478 tons of stone. The tallest of the six slender spires stands 210 feet tall and is topped by a glittering statue of the angel Moroni with a trumpet in hand. The 12.5-foot statue is made of hammered copper covered with gold leaf.

East of the temple are acres of manicured flower gardens with reflecting pools and fountains. This is a very serene vantage point to take in the temple's gothic beauty.

The Tabernacle

Pioneers labored from 1863 to 1867 to construct this unique dome-shaped building. Brigham Young envisioned a meeting hall capable of holding thousands of people in an interior free of obstructing structural supports. His design, drawn by bridge-builder Henry Grow, took shape in massive latticed wooden beams resting on 44 supports of red sandstone. Because Utah lacked many common building supplies, the workers often had to make substitutions. Wooden pegs and rawhide strips hold the structure together. The large organ pipes resemble metal, balcony pillars appear to be marble, and the benches look like oak, yet all are pinewood painted to simulate these materials.

The tabernacle has become known for its phenomenal acoustics, a result of its smooth arched ceiling, and its massive pipe organ is regarded as one of the finest ever built. From 700 pipes when constructed in 1867, the organ has grown to about 12,000 pipes, five manuals, and one pedal keyboard. Daily **recitals** (noon and 2pm Mon.-Sat., 2pm Sun.)

tours do give the guides a chance to witness their faith.

The Salt Lake Temple and Gardens

Mormons believe that they must have temples in which to hold sacred rites and fulfill God's commandments. According to the LDS faith, baptisms, marriages, and family-sealing ceremonies that take place inside a temple will last beyond death and into eternity. The temple is used only for these special functions; normal Sunday services take place in local stake or ward buildings—in fact, the temple is closed on Sunday.

Only LDS members who meet church requirements of good standing may enter the sacred temple itself; others can learn about temple activities and see photos of interior rooms at the South Visitors' Center. Non-Mormons are not allowed to enter the temple or its grounds. However, you can get a good look at the temple's east facade from the Main Street gates.

demonstrate the instrument's capabilities. The renowned **Mormon Tabernacle Choir,** 360 voices strong, is heard on the Sunday-morning national radio show *Music and the Spoken Word*. Visitors can attend choir rehearsals at 7:30pm Thursday evening or the broadcast performance at 9:30am Sunday (be seated by 9:15am); both are free.

Assembly Hall

Thrifty craftspeople built this smaller Gothic Revival structure in 1877-1882, using granite left over from the temple construction. The truncated spires, reaching as high as 130 feet, once functioned as chimneys. Inside the hall there's seating for 1,500 people and a choir of 100. The baroque-style organ, installed in 1983, has 3,500 pipes and three manuals; of particular note are the organ's horizontal pipes, called trumpets. The Salt Lake Stake Congregation once met here; now the building serves as a concert hall and hosts church functions.

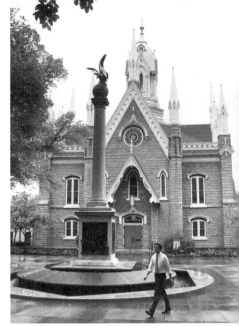

the Assembly Hall

North Visitors' Center

Wander around on your own or ask the ever-present tour guides for help. Exhibits focus on the life and ministry of Jesus Christ and the importance of ancient and modern prophets, including those from the Bible and from the Book of Mormon. An interesting scale model shows Jerusalem as it may have looked at the time of Christ. A spiraling ramp leads to the upper level, where *Cristus,* an 11-foot replica of a sculpture by Bertel Thorvaldsen, stands in a circular room with a wall mural depicting the universe.

South Visitors' Center

Two exhibits cover the building of the Salt Lake Temple and "Strengthening the Family." Exhibits on the main level include paintings of prophets and church history, a baptismal font supported by 12 life-size oxen (representing the 12 tribes of Israel) as used in temples, photos of the Salt Lake Temple interior, and a scale model of Solomon's Temple. Head downstairs to see replicas of the metal plates inscribed

with the Book of Mormon that Mormons believe were revealed to Joseph Smith in 1823. Ancient plates of Old World civilizations and stone boxes from the Americas are exhibited to support the claim that the plates are genuine.

Museum of Church History and Art

Brigham Young encouraged the preservation of church history, especially when he saw that Salt Lake City's pioneering era was drawing to a close. The **Museum of Church History and Art** (45 N. West Temple St., 801/240-4615, 9am-9pm Mon.-Fri., 10am-5pm Sat.-Sun. and holidays, closed New Year's Day, Easter, Thanksgiving, and Christmas, free) houses a collection of church artifacts that includes the plow that cut the first furrows in Great Salt Lake Valley. Perhaps the most striking piece is the gilded 11.5-foot statue of Moroni that crowned a Washington DC chapel from 1933 to 1976. Step outside to see the 1847 log cabin, one of only two surviving from

Salt Lake City's beginnings. The interior has been furnished as it might have been during the first winter here.

Family History Library

The **Family History Library** (35 N. West Temple St., 801/240-2331, 8am-5pm Mon., 8am-9pm Tues.-Fri., 9am-5pm Sat., closed most federal holidays, free) houses the largest collection of genealogical information in the world. Library workers have made extensive travels to many countries to microfilm documents and books. The LDS Church has gone to this effort to enable members to trace their ancestors, who can then be baptized by proxy. In this way, according to Mormon belief, the ancestors will be sealed in the family and the church for eternity. However, the spirits for whom these baptisms are performed have a choice of accepting or rejecting the baptism.

The library is open to the public. If you'd like to research your family tree, bring what information you have and get the library's booklet *A Guide to Research.* A brief slide presentation explains what types of records are kept and how to get started. Staff will answer questions. In most cases the files won't have information about living people for privacy reasons.

If you are new to genealogical investigation, you may want to start your research at the **FamilySearch Center** (15 E. South Temple St., 801/240-4085, 9am-9pm Mon.-Fri., 9am-5pm Sat., closed most federal holidays), on the main floor in the Joseph Smith Memorial Building. The center has individual computer stations with access to family history resources, and staff is available to help you free of charge.

Brigham Young Monument

This monument, standing in the middle of Main Street near North Temple Street, celebrates the first 50 years of settlement in Salt Lake City. Unveiled on July 24, 1897, it portrays Brigham Young in bronze, atop a granite pedestal with figures below representing a Native American, a fur trapper, and a pioneer

family. A plaque lists the names of the first 148 Mormon pioneers. The statue is also the originating point for the city's street-numbering system.

Joseph Smith Memorial Building

Built of white terra-cotta brick in modern Italian Renaissance style, the **Joseph Smith Memorial Building** (15 E. South Temple St., Mon.-Sat., closed Sun. except to those attending worship services) opened in 1911 as the first-class Hotel Utah, built for church and business leaders. However, in 1987 the LDS Church, which owned the hotel, converted it into an office building and a memorial to LDS founding father Joseph Smith. The opulent lobby, with its massive marble columns, chandeliers, and stained-glass ceiling, remains intact; you definitely should walk through the lobby and admire the grand architecture. The 10th floor offers observation areas, the formal **Roof Restaurant** (801/539-1911), and the less formal **Garden Restaurant** (801/539-1911).

LDS Office Building

Day-to-day administration of the massive LDS Church organization is centered in the 28-story tower of the **LDS Office Building** (50 E. North Temple St., 801/240-2190, 9am-5pm Mon.-Fri. Apr.-Sept., 9am-4:30pm Mon.-Fri. Oct.-Mar.), east of Temple Square. Such a volume of correspondence takes place that the building has its own zip code. The big attraction is a visit to the 26th-floor observation deck (free). You'll see Temple Square and the whole city spread out below like a map.

Beehive House

The former house of Brigham Young, **Beehive House** (67 E. South Temple St., 801/240-2671, tours every 10 minutes 9am-8:30pm daily, last tour begins 8:15pm, free) was built in 1854 and occupied by Young and his family until his death in 1877. The adobe and brick structure stood out as one of the most ornate houses in early Salt Lake City. Free tours lasting 30-40 minutes take visitors through the house and tell of family life within its walls. The interior has been meticulously restored with many original furnishings. A beehive symbol, representing industry, caps the house and appears in decorative motifs inside. Brigham Young had about 27 wives, but only one at a time stayed in this house; other wives and children lived next door in the Lion House. Downstairs in the main house, Young's children gathered in the sitting room for evenings of prayer, talks, and music. Upstairs, he entertained guests and dignitaries in a lavish reception room called the Long Hall.

The **Lion House** (63 E. South Temple St.), next door, was built of stuccoed adobe in 1855-1856; a stone lion guards the entrance. Brigham Young used it as a supplementary dwelling for his many wives and children. Today, the pantry and basement of the building are open to the public as the Lion House restaurant.

Eagle Gate

This modern replacement of the original 1859 gate spans State Street just north of South Temple Street. It once marked the entrance to Brigham Young's property, which included City Creek Canyon. The bronze eagle has a 20-foot wingspan and weighs two tons. The present gate, designed by Brigham Young's grandson, architect George Cannon Young, was dedicated in 1963.

DOWNTOWN SIGHTS
Abravanel Hall

One of the most striking modern buildings in Salt Lake City, **Abravanel Hall** (123 W. South Temple St., 801/355-2787) glitters with gold leaf, crystal chandeliers, and more than a mile of brass railing. Careful attention to acoustic design has paid off: The concert hall is considered one of the best in the world; the Utah Opera also performs here.

Utah Museum of Contemporary Art

A civic art gallery, the **Utah Museum of Contemporary Art** (20 S. West Temple St.,

801/328-4201, www.slartcenter.org, 11am-6pm Tues.-Thurs. and Sat., 11am-9pm Fri., suggested $5 donation) hosts a changing lineup of traveling and thematic exhibits, including displays of painting, photography, sculpture, ceramics, and conceptual art. Diverse art classes and workshops are scheduled along with films, lectures, poetry readings, concerts, and theater. A gift shop offers art books, posters, crafts, and artwork.

Salt Palace Convention Center

The enormous **Salt Palace Convention Center** (along West Temple St., between 200 South and South Temple St., 801/534-4777) is one of the largest convention centers in the West, with 515,000 square feet of exhibit space and 164,000 square feet of meeting space, including a 45,000-square-foot ballroom and 66 meeting rooms. Even in the sprawling scale of downtown Salt Lake City, this is a big building. The center houses the Salt Lake Convention and Visitors Bureau and the **Visitor Information Center** (90 S. West Temple St., 801/521-2822, www.visitsaltlake.com).

Clark Planetarium

A planetarium and science center, the **Clark Planetarium** (110 S. 400 W., 801/456-7827, www.clarkplanetarium.org, 10:30am-7pm Sun.-Wed., 10:30am-8pm Thurs-Sat, check website for hours of the Hansen Dome Theatre, most exhibits free, IMAX movies require payment), in the new Gateway shopping center, offers a 3-D IMAX theater with a five-story screen, plus popular family-oriented science and space exhibits. A highlight is the Hansen Dome Theatre, which employs state-of-the-art technology to project a star show on a 360-degree 55-foot dome. Also in the Star Theatre are *Cosmic Light Shows*, which combine computer animation, special effects, and a 12,000-watt digital surround-sound system.

The Leonardo

A contemporary museum of science and culture, **The Leonardo** (209 E. 500 S., 801/531-9800, 10am-5pm Sun.-Wed., 10am-10pm

Salt Palace Convention Center

smaller paintings and statues show all of the territorial and state governors along with prominent Utah figures of the past. The Gold Room, used for receiving dignitaries, provides a formal setting graced by chandeliers, wall tapestries, elegant furniture, and cherubs on the ceiling. Enter the chambers of the House of Representatives, Senate, and Supreme Court from the mezzanine. Photo exhibits of the state's scenic and historic spots, mining, agriculture, and beehive memorabilia line hallways on the ground floor.

Forty acres of manicured parks and monuments surround the capitol. From the steps leading to the building, you can look out over Salt Lake City and straight down State Street, which runs south about 28 miles without a curve. From near the Mormon Battalion Monument, east of the capitol, steps lead down into a small canyon and **Memory Grove,** another war memorial, and a series of streamside parks.

You're welcome to tour the capitol on your own during open hours; tour brochures are available from the visitors center just inside the east doors. Free **guided tours** (information and Wednesday evening reservations 801/538-1800) are also available, departing every hour 9am-5pm Monday-Friday, except on state holidays, with additional tours (by reservation only) at 6pm and 7pm on Wednesday evenings. Meet in front of the large map on the first floor. Visitors are welcome to dine at the circular cafeteria (7am-4pm Mon.-Fri.) behind the capitol. Annual legislative sessions begin in January and last about 45 days.

Council Hall

The venerable Council Hall lies across the street from the capitol. Dedicated in 1866, the brick building served as the city hall and a meeting place for the territorial and early state legislatures. Council Hall used to stand downtown before being moved here in 1963.

It is now the home of the **Utah Travel Council** (www.utah.com). Drop in to see the

Thurs.-Sat., general admission $9 adults, $8 seniors, students, military, and youths 12-17, $7 children 6-11, 5 and under free; tickets to special exhibitions may be extra) is housed in the former Salt Lake City Public Library. The Leo, as it's called, has permanent exhibits on science, technology, engineering, art, and math but is largely known for hosting traveling exhibits such as the Dead Sea Scrolls, Mummies of the World, and the Bodies exhibition.

CAPITOL HILL
★ State Capitol

Utah's granite **State Capitol** (300 North and State St., 801/538-3000, http://utahstatecapitol.utah.gov, 7am-8pm Mon.-Fri., 8am-6pm Sat.-Sun.) occupies a prominent spot on a hill just north of downtown. The architectural style may look familiar: The building was patterned after the national capitol. The interior, with its Ionic columns, is made of polished marble from Georgia. Murals depict early explorers and pioneers;

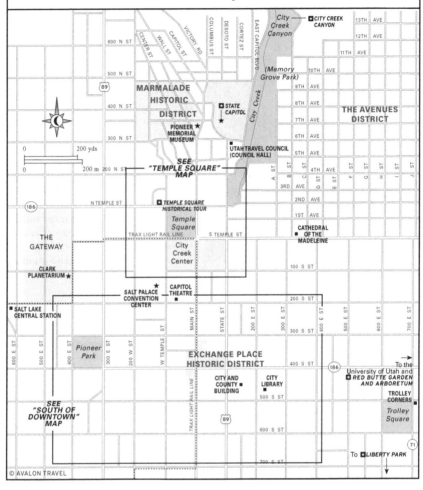

Downtown Salt Lake City

staff of the **Salt Lake City Welcome Center** (801/538-1030, 8am-5pm Mon.-Fri., 10am-5pm Sat.-Sun.) on the main floor for information on sights, services, and events in the state.

UNIVERSITY OF UTAH AND VICINITY
Gilgal Gardens

On the way to the university from downtown is one of the oddest of Salt Lake City's public parks. The **Gilgal Gardens** (749 E. 500 S., 8am-dusk daily, free) is a colossally weird sculpture garden created by an LDS bishop whose spiritual quest led him to create stone-carved monuments and engrave stones with biblical and other religious verses.

Thomas Child began Gilgal Gardens in 1945, and work on the gardens and its sculptures continued until his death in 1963. The carvings and statues reflect a curious mix of Mormon, Old Testament, and Egyptian influences: A sphinx has the face of LDS founder

University of Utah and Vicinity

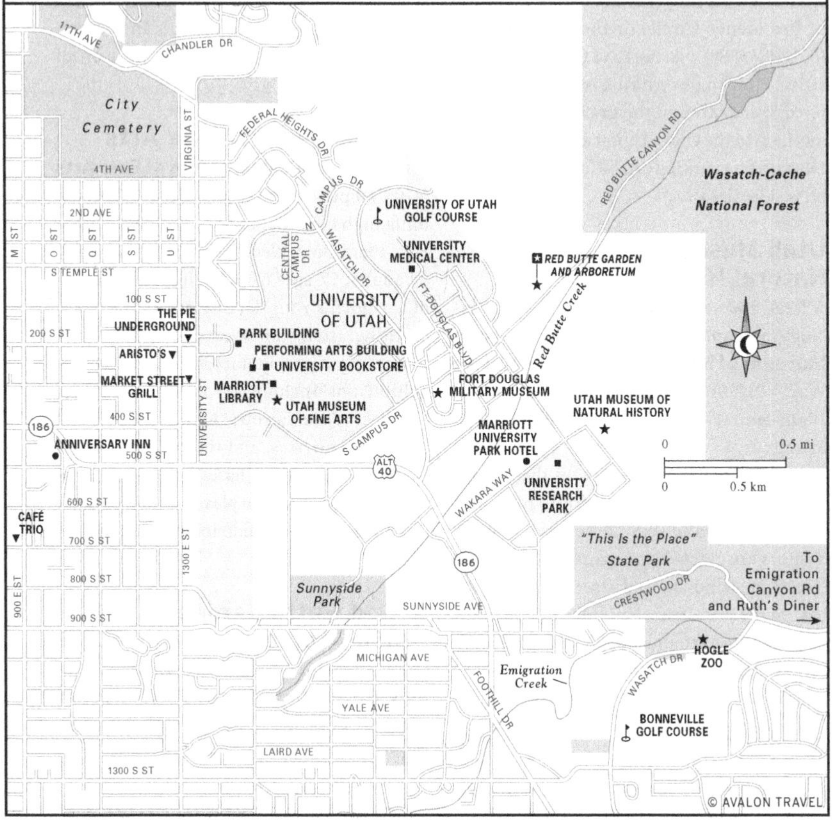

Joseph Smith, while other sculpture vignettes represent Nebuchadnezzar's dream and a monument to the masonry trade. In all, there are 13 carved stone sculptures, plus innumerable flagstones with etched quotations within a garden setting. It's all very strange and oddly moving, and if you're attracted by people's curious spiritual journeys, you should make this one of your SLC stops—there's no other garden quite like this one.

University of Utah

Mormon pioneers established a university in their short-lived town of Nauvoo, Illinois, and they brought its books with them to Utah. The University of Deseret opened in 1850, just two and a half years after the first colonists reached the Salt Lake Valley. It was renamed the **University of Utah** (201 Presidents Circle, 801/581-7200) in 1892 and now sprawls across a 1,500-acre campus.

About 28,000 students study in a wide range of fields—there are some 16 colleges and schools in all. The adjacent Research Park is a partnership of the university and private enterprise involving many students and faculty. Visitors are welcome at cultural and sporting events, libraries, the bookstore, the movie theater, and Olpin Union food services. Most recreational facilities are reserved for students. For a campus map, a list of scheduled events, and other information, drop by the **Park Building** (801/581-6515), at the top of President's Circle, or the **Olpin Union** (801/581-5888), just north of Central Campus Drive. On-campus parking is available at metered spaces around the grounds and in pay lots next to the Olpin Union and the Marriott Library; free parking can be found off campus on residential streets.

Utah Museum of Natural History

A large and varied collection of geology, biology, and anthropology exhibits, the **Utah Museum of Natural History** (301 Wakara Way, 801/581-6927, http://nhmu.utah.edu, 10am-5pm Thurs.-Tues., 10am-9pm Wed., $11 adults, $9 ages 13-24 and over age 64, $8 ages 3-12, free under age 3) tells the natural history and early Native American history of Utah in a new and very impressive museum. Visitors are greeted by expansive views from five-story windows and a series of exhibits that make great use of audiovisual technology and projected images. The exhibits touch on the state's early Native American history and feature eye-catching dioramas of various ecosystems. Young children can study insects and crawl "underground" in the Our Backyard exhibit, but easily the most impressive displays here are the skeletons of ancient creatures that once lived in Utah. In addition to a gift shop, the museum has a café open all museum hours.

Utah Museum of Fine Arts

The ambitious **Utah Museum of Fine Arts** (410 Campus Center Dr., 801/581-7332, www.umfa.utah.edu, 10am-5pm Tues. and Thurs.-Fri., 10am-8pm Wed., 11am-5pm Sat.-Sun., $9 adults, $7 ages 6-18, seniors, and non-U of U students with ID) displays a little of everything, from 5,000-year-old Egyptian art to works by contemporary artists. Permanent exhibitions include art of China, India, Southeast Asia, Europe, Africa, the pre-Columbian Americas, and the early American West. Three large galleries host visiting exhibitions; there's also a pleasant café. Limited free parking is available in university parking lot 11.

★ Red Butte Garden and Arboretum

Utah's largest botanical garden, the **Red Butte Garden and Arboretum** (300 Wakara Way, 801/581-4747, www.

Red Butte Garden is worth a visit any time of year.

"This Is the Place" State Park

Legion, the Mormon Battalion, and U.S. Army life in pioneer Utah. In late 1862, Colonel Patrick Connor marched to this site with his California-Nevada volunteers and built Camp Douglas. Officially the post defended the mail route and kept the local Native Americans in check. Connor also felt it necessary to keep an eye (and cannons) on the Mormons, whom he and other federal officials distrusted.

The museum's exhibits show the histories of Fort Douglas and other military bases in Utah. A World War I room includes photos of German POWs once interned here. Other exhibits illustrate the big military buildup during World War II, when Utah even had a naval base.

The museum building, officers' row, and some of the other structures at Fort Douglas date from the 1870s and 1880s and are built in an architectural style termed Quartermaster Victorian. Pick up a walking-tour leaflet of the fort at the museum. Turn north onto Wasatch Drive from 500 South and travel 0.5 mile to the fort.

redbuttegarden.org, irregular hours and days but generally 9am-dusk, year-round, $10 adults, $8 seniors, $6 ages 3-17, free access to hiking trails in the natural area) offers 30 acres of floral displays, ponds, waterfalls, and four miles of mountain nature trails in a 200-acre natural area. The garden visitors center features botanical gifts and books, and the Courtyard Garden is an excellent place for a family picnic.

To reach the garden from I-15, take the 600 South exit, which will take you east, then turn north and go two blocks to 400 South, and head east past where 400 South merges into 500 South. After rising up a hill, take the left onto Wakara Way and continue east to the Red Butte Garden and Arboretum exit.

Fort Douglas Military Museum

At the **Fort Douglas Military Museum** (32 Potter St., 801/581-2151, www.fortdouglas.org, noon-5pm Tues.-Sat., free, grounds dawn-dusk daily), artifacts and historical photos take visitors back to the days of the Nauvoo

"This Is the Place" State Park

It is believed that Brigham Young gazed on the Salt Lake Valley for the first time from this spot, now known as **"This Is the Place" State Park** (2601 Sunnyside Ave., 801/582-1847, www.thisistheplace.org, visitors center 9am-6pm daily, park 9am-5pm Mon.-Sat., 10am-5pm Sun., free), southeast of the University of Utah near the mouth of Emigration Canyon. He then spoke the famous words, "This is the right place. Drive on." Exactly 100 years later, on July 24, 1947, a crowd gathered to dedicate the massive *This Is the Place* monument. Twelve-foot bronze statues of Brigham Young flanked by Heber C. Kimball and Wilford Woodruff stand atop a central pylon. The park has a pleasant picnic area, and the monument honors not only the Mormon pioneers but also the Catholic missionaries from Spain, fur trappers and traders, government explorers, and California immigrants who contributed to the founding of an empire in "the top of the mountains."

A visitors center displays a mural depicting major events during the migration of the "Saints" from Nauvoo, Illinois, to their promised land. An eight-minute narration recounts the journey; foreign-language narration can also be requested.

Heritage Village (9am-5pm Mon.-Sat., 10am-5pm Sun. Memorial Day-Labor Day, check website for hours Labor Day-Memorial Day, $11 adults, $8 seniors and children 3-11 Mon.-Sat., $5 adults, $3 seniors and children 3-11 Sun.), formerly called Old Deseret, on the grounds near the monument, re-creates a Utah pioneer village. During the summer it comes alive with farming and crafts demonstrations and wagon and pony rides. In addition, three "mini trains" make loops around the park. Most of the two dozen buildings that were moved here are originals, some of the first in the valley. Some notable structures include Brigham Young's forest farmhouse, the 1847 Levi Riter cabin, and the Charles Rich house, designed in the 1850s for polygamous family living.

Hogle Zoo

Utah's state zoo, **Hogle Zoo** (2600 E. Sunnyside Ave., 801/582-1631, www.hogle-zoo.org, 9am-5pm daily Mar.-Oct., 9am-4pm daily Nov.-Feb., $14.95 adults, $12.95 ages 3-12 and over age 65), an especially popular spot with the kids, is on the eastern edge of town and across from "This Is the Place" State Park. Children like to ride the miniature train (spring-fall, $1.50) and see exhibits in the Discovery Center. Many of the large-animal enclosures have natural settings; the elephants and rhinos have newly redesigned habitat. The Rocky Shores exhibit is home to arctic North American animals such as polar bears, sea lions, grizzly bears, and bald eagles. An extensive new African savanna exhibit opened in 2014.

SOUTH OF DOWNTOWN
★ Liberty Park

The large **Liberty Park** (bounded by 900 South, 1300 South, 500 East, and 700 East), southeast of downtown, is the jewel of the city's public park system and contains abundant recreational facilities in addition to an excellent aviary, an arts center, and 80 acres of grass and shady boulevards. A fun addition to the park is a conceptual "map" of northern Utah that re-creates the rivers, lakes, and mountains as a series of fountains and wading pools.

The Children's Garden—a playground,

Liberty Park is the setting for many community festivals.

amusement park, snack bar, and large pond with rental boats (all spring-fall)—sits in the southeast corner of the park. The tennis center on the west side of the park offers 16 lighted courts and instruction; an outdoor swimming pool adjacent to the tennis center is open in summer.

Tracy Aviary

Birds have taken over the southwest corner of Liberty Park. **Tracy Aviary** (589 E. 1300 S., 801/596-8500, www.tracyaviary.org, 9am-5pm daily, $7 adults, $6 students and seniors, $5 ages 3-12) houses more than 400 individual birds of 135 species and offers shows with trained free-flying birds such as falcons. Birds on display include majestic golden and bald eagles, showy flamingos and peacocks, the hyacinthine macaw (the world's largest parrot), the golden pheasant of China, and hundreds of other feathered friends. Emus from Australia prance across fields while ducks, geese, swans, and other waterfowl keep to the ponds. You'll also get to meet Utah's only native vulture, the turkey vulture.

Bird shows can change from season to season, so call or check the website to verify what's happening. There are free **flight shows** (1pm daily summer), but check the website for lots of extra activities, especially in summer.

The Chase Mill

Just north of the aviary entrance, the Chase Mill was built by Isaac Chase in 1852 and is one of the oldest buildings in the valley. Free flour from the mill saved many families during the famine of 1856-1857. The mill is open daily as a historic monument. Formal gardens are north of the mill.

Chase's adobe brick house, built 1853-1854, farther to the north, has been restored. Go inside to see exhibits of the **Chase Home Museum of Utah Folk Art** (801/533-5760, 8am-5pm Mon.-Thurs., 8pm-6pm Fri., 10am-6pm Sat. Apr.-Oct., 8am-5pm Mon.-Fri. Nov.-Mar., free) sponsored by the Utah Arts Council. On display is contemporary Utah folk art, including quilts, rugs, woodcarvings, international art, and Native American works.

Entertainment and Events

Salt Lake City offers a wide variety of high-quality arts and cultural institutions; classical and religious music venues are particularly noteworthy. Jazz, blues, and alternative music clubs and dance bars are also numerous. In short, there's a lot more going on here than you might think.

Local publications are the best places to check for information on what's happening. The *City Weekly* is the largest and most comprehensive free newspaper, with lots of arts and entertainment coverage. The daily papers, the *Deseret News* and the *Salt Lake Tribune,* both have listings in their Friday Weekend and Sunday Art and Entertainment sections. The Salt Lake Convention and Visitors Bureau website (www.visitsaltlake.com) also has

lengthy listings of events and entertainment options.

Most of Salt Lake City's top-flight music and arts performances take place in a handful of venues, themselves world-class facilities worthy of a visit. When you know the dates of your visit, contact the Salt Lake County Center for the Arts (801/355-2787 or 888/451-2787, www.arttix.org), which handles ticketing for most of the city's arts offerings, to find out what's going on while you're here.

The city's main performance space is the **Capitol Theatre** (50 W. 200 S., 801/534-6364), a glittering vaudeville house from the turn of the 20th century that has been refurbished into an elegant concert hall. **Abravanel Hall** (123 W. South Temple St., between the Salt Palace and Temple Square,

Salt Lake City for Kids

DISCOVERY GATEWAY

None of the exhibits at **Discovery Gateway** (Gateway complex, 444 W. 100 S., 801/456-5437, www.discoverygateway.org, 10am-6pm Mon.-Thurs., 10am-8pm Fri.-Sat., noon-6pm Sun., $8.50 adults, $6 seniors, free under age 1) display Do Not Touch signs; in fact, most of the displays are hands-on. This children's favorite provides engaging interactive activities that inspire learning in children and fun for the whole family. Kids get to put on plays, host the morning TV news, make short animated films, and engage in many other activities. They can also take part in a mock Life Flight or rescue operation in an authentic life-size helicopter.

LAGOON AMUSEMENT PARK AND PIONEER VILLAGE

History, recreation, and thrilling rides come together at the attractively landscaped **Lagoon Amusement Park and Pioneer Village** (375 Lagoon Dr., Farmington, 801/451-8000 or 800/748-5246, www.lagoonpark.com), 16 miles north of Salt Lake City. Lagoon traces its own history back to 1887, when bathers came to Lake Park on the shores of Great Salt Lake, two miles west of its present location. The vast Lagoon Amusement Park area includes roller-coaster rides, a giant Ferris wheel, and other midway favorites. There are also musical performances and miniature golf. Lagoon A Beach provides thrilling waterslides and landscaped pools.

Pioneer Village brings the past to life with authentic 19th-century buildings, stagecoach and steam train rides, an Ute museum, a carriage museum, a gun collection, and many other exhibits. Wild West shoot-outs take place several times daily. Food booths are scattered throughout the park, or you can dine at the Gaslight Restaurant near the Opera House.

The complex is open 11am-10pm Sunday-Thursday, 11am-11pm Friday, and 10am-11pm Saturday June-late August or whenever the local school year begins. The complex is also open Saturday-Sunday early April-May and September-October, and there are other open days; check the website for the rather complex off-season schedule. An all-day ride pass is $48 adults, $40 over age 3 and up to 48 inches tall, and $43 for seniors. The all-day pass includes Lagoon A Beach privileges. Parking is $10. Take I-15 to the Lagoon exit and follow the signs.

WHEELER HISTORIC FARM

Kids will enjoy a visit to the **Wheeler Historic Farm** (6351 S. 900 E., 801/264-2241, www. wheelerfarm.com, dawn-dusk daily, free admission) to experience the rural life of milking cows, gathering eggs, churning butter, and feeding animals. Hayrides in warmer weather and sleigh rides in winter take visitors around the farm. Henry and Sariah Wheeler started the farm in 1886 and developed it into a prosperous dairy and ice-making operation. Tour guides take you through the Wheelers' restored Victorian house, built 1896-1898, the first in the county to have an indoor bathroom. The Rosebud Country Store sells crafts and snacks.

The Salt Lake County Recreation Department operates the farm and offers special programs for both youngsters and adults. There's no admission charged to visit the farm, but you'll pay for individual activities.

801/533-5626) has fantastic acoustics and is home to the Utah Symphony and other classical music performances. The **Rose Wagner Performing Arts Center** (138 W. 300 S., 801/323-6800) has three performance spaces and is home to several local dance and theater troupes.

In **Temple Square** (800/537-9703), the Mormon tabernacle and the Assembly Hall host various classical and religious concerts, including performances by the famed Mormon Tabernacle Choir.

NIGHTLIFE

Utah's liquor laws no longer require you to join a bar's private club just to have a drink. The best way to check out the club scene is to pick up a copy of *City Weekly*, a free and widely available news and entertainment weekly. If you're just looking for a beer and a chance to chat with the locals, try one of the brewpubs.

Bars

In the category of high-spirited, only-in-Salt-Lake fun, try out **Bar Deluxe** (666 S. State St., 801/521-5255), offering live music, karaoke, or other high jinks nightly, and **Burt's Tiki Lounge** (726 S. State St., 801/521-0572, Tues.-Sat.), with live bands and shenanigans five nights a week. Another good stop to go for drinks and good times right downtown is **Bar X** (155 E. 200 S., 801/355-2287).

If you just want to dance, SLC offers a number of options. **Area 51** (400 W. 451 S., 801/534-0819) has theme nights (80s Insanity, Alterna-Mash, and more). The vast multiple-floor **Hotel/Club Elevate** complex (155 W. 200 S., 801/478-4310) has enough dance floors and bar areas to fill an entire night's worth of fun.

Live Music

The **Tavernacle Social Club** (201 E. 300 S., 801/519-8900) is a hipper-than-thou piano bar, with an updated lounge act that features dueling pianos, sing-alongs, and karaoke Sunday-Tuesday.

To catch the flavor of local and regional bands, check out **Urban Lounge** (241 S. 500 E., 801/746-0557) or **In the Venue** (219 S. 600 W., 801/359-3219).

Touring national acts stop at **The Depot** (in the Gateway Center at 400 S. West Temple St., 801/355-5522), a nightclub in the cavernous Union Station; it's also a good spot for meeting friends when there's no live band.

Gay and Lesbian

Salt Lake City isn't known for its vibrant gay scene, but there are a growing number of gay clubs. A good place to start the evening is **Club Try-Angles** (251 W. 900 S., 801/364-3203), with a pleasant patio for drinks and sunning. **Jam** (751 N. 300 W., 801/382-8567, 8pm-2am Wed.-Sun.) is the city's gay nightlife center, with dancing, karaoke, drag shows, and theme parties.

THE ARTS
Theater

Pioneer Theatre Company (801/581-6961, www.pioneertheatre.org), one of Salt Lake City's premier theater troupes, offers a seven-show season running September-May. The company performs a mix of contemporary plays, classics, and musicals. Although the company operates from the University of Utah's **Pioneer Memorial Theatre** (300 South and University St.), it is not part of the university itself. The Pioneer Memorial Theatre is also the site of University of Utah student productions and the Young People's Theatre, which produces plays for children.

The city's cutting-edge theater group is the **Salt Lake Acting Company** (168 W. 500 N., 801/363-7522, www.saltlakeactingcompany.org). This well-established troupe doesn't shy away from controversy: Its excellent production of Tony Kushner's *Angels in America* raised eyebrows and stirred strong reactions. Besides presenting new works from around the world, the company is also committed to staging plays by local playwrights; there are performances year-round.

The **Grand Theatre** (1575 S. State St., 801/957-3459 or 801/957-3263, www.thegrand.org), on the Salt Lake City Community College campus, is home to a year-round program of theatrical performances (mostly musicals) by both student and semiprofessional troupes.

For something spoofier, the **Off Broadway Theatre** (272 S. Main St., 801/355-4628, www.theobt.com) is the place for improv competitions, Broadway comedies, and topical farces. At the **Desert Star Playhouse** (4861 S. State St., 801/266-7600, www.desertstar.biz), you'll find musical comedy revues and cabaret-style comedy skits, such as *My Big Fat Utah Wedding* or *Kicking the Hobbit: Bored of the Rings*.

Classical Music and Dance

From its modest beginnings in 1940, the **Utah Symphony** (tickets 801/533-6683, www. utahsymphony.org) has grown to be one of the best-regarded orchestras in the West. Each season, the symphony performs in the glittering Abravanel Hall (123 W. South Temple St.) in Salt Lake City and travels to Snowbird, Deer Valley, Ogden, Provo, Logan, and other cities.

The **Utah Opera Company** (tickets 801/533-6683, www.utahopera.org), founded in 1978, stages four operas during its October-May season at the **Capitol Theatre** (50 W. 200 S.).

Another center for classical music and performance is the **University of Utah** (801/581-6772, www.utah.edu/arts). The university's symphony orchestra, chamber orchestra, jazz ensembles, opera, bands, and ballet, dance, and choral groups present regular concerts and performances on and off campus; the season runs September-May.

Ballet West (801/323-6900, www.balletwest.org) began in Salt Lake City in 1963 as the Utah Civic Ballet, but as the group gained fame and began traveling widely, it chose its present name to reflect its regional status. This versatile group's repertoire includes classical and contemporary works. Most Utah performances take place September-May at either the **Capitol Theatre** (50 W. 200 S.) or the **Rose Wagner Performing Arts Center** (138 W. 300 S.).

The professional **Ririe-Woodbury Dance Company** (801/323-6801, www.ririewoodbury.com) has one of the most active dance programs in the United States. The varied repertoire includes mixed media, eye-catching choreography, and humor. The group also shares its expertise by teaching production and dance skills to students and professionals. Ririe-Woodbury Dance Company is based at the Rose Wagner Performing Arts Center, as is the **Repertory Dance Theatre** (801/534-1000, www.rdtutah.org), a professional company focusing on classical American and contemporary dance.

A new performing arts center is under construction at South Main and 200 South, due to open in 2016.

Concert Series and Music Festivals

The **Madeleine Arts and Humanities Program** is held in the historic **Cathedral of the Madeleine** (331 E. South Temple St., 801/328-8941, www.utcotm.org, all events free). This series of choral, organ, and chamber music concerts takes place on Sunday evenings throughout the spring and early summer. Lectures, theatrical performances, and dance concerts are also held.

In June, the **Gina Bachauer Piano Competitions** (801/521-9200, www. bachauer.com) take over Salt Lake City. Competitions are divided into three categories based on age, and the three competitions are part of a four-year cycle of events that occur during the month of June. Dozens of young pianists from around the world take part in a two-week-long series of performances both as solos (early in the competition) and with the Utah Symphony (only the finalists). The winners compete for recording contracts and thousands of dollars in cash. It's a good chance to enjoy the musicianship of tomorrow's rising piano stars and to savor the thrill of musical competition.

Temple Square Concert Series

The concert series at **Temple Square** (801/240-3318, 801/240-2534, or 800/537-9703, www.visittemplesquare.com) presents hundreds of performances a year for the public; all are free. The LDS Church sponsors the varied musical fare to provide a common meeting ground of great music for Mormons and non-Mormons alike. You might hear chamber music, a symphony, operatic selections, religious choral works, piano solos, organ works, a brass band, or a percussion ensemble.

The renowned 360-voice **Mormon Tabernacle Choir** sings at 9:30am Sunday morning (you must be seated by 9:15am and remain seated during the entire performance). You can also hear the choir rehearse 8pm-9:30pm Thursday evening (you can come and go during the rehearsals). The Mormon Youth Symphony rehearses in the tabernacle 8pm-9:30pm Wednesday evening, and the Youth Chorus rehearses 8pm-9:30pm Tuesday evening.

In June-August and December, rehearsals and broadcasts are held across the street in the Conference Center, which can accommodate the larger summer and Christmas season crowds. Broadcasts are also held in the Conference Center during LDS semiannual General Conferences, which take place on the first Sunday of October and April. Admission on these two Sundays is available only to Conference ticket holders. Occasionally, when the choir is on tour, a youth choir, youth symphony, or other group replaces it.

The Temple Square Concert Series presents complimentary hour-long concerts in the Assembly Hall featuring local and international artists at 7:30pm every Friday and Saturday evening. Tickets are not required, but attendees must be age eight and older. June-August, the Temple Square Concert Series presents Concerts in the Park, held in the Brigham Young Historic Park (southeast corner of State St. and 2nd Ave.). These outdoor concerts begin at 7:30pm on Tuesday and Friday evenings June-August.

Organists demonstrate the sounds and versatility of the tabernacle's famous instrument in 30-minute **organ recitals** (noon and 2pm Mon.-Sat., 2pm Sun.).

Summer Concerts and Festivals

Salt Lake City is filled with free music concerts in summer, when local parks and public spaces become makeshift concert halls. Check local media or the visitors center for details on the following ongoing concert series.

Gallivan Center Concerts and Films features free noontime concerts on weekdays in summer, plus such free events as big band dance nights and al fresco movie nights at the downtown **Gallivan Center** (Main

St. and 200 South, 801/535-6110, www.thegallivancenter.com/events.htm). The **Utah Symphony** (801/533-5626, www.utahsymphony.org) also offers an extensive summer series of concerts at Wasatch Front ski areas, a short drive from downtown Salt Lake City.

Cinema

First-run multiplexes are spread around downtown Salt Lake City; check the daily newspapers for listings. The city is lucky to have the **Salt Lake Film Society** (http://saltlakefilmsociety.org), which sponsors a "year-round film festival" with art and foreign films at the **Broadway Centre** (111 E. 300 S., 801/321-0310) and the **Tower Theatre** (876 E. 900 S., 801/328-1645).

Brewvies (677 S. 200 W., 801/355-5500) is a brewpub-cinema combo where you can buy an ale and a burger and watch a first-run or cult favorite film.

For a selection of major-release first-run movies in the downtown area, check out what's playing at the **Megaplex 12 at the Gateway** (165 S. Rio Grande St., 801/325-7500).

FESTIVALS AND EVENTS

Concerts, festivals, shows, rodeos, and other special events happen here nearly every day, and the **Salt Lake Convention and Visitors Bureau** (90 S. West Temple St., 801/521-2822, www.visitsaltlake.com) can tell you what's going on. Also check the visitors bureau's *Salt Lake Visitors Guide* for some of the best-known annual happenings.

The first weekends of April and October see the annual **General Conference of the Church of Jesus Christ of Latter-day Saints,** held at **Temple Square** (801/240-2531). The church president, believed to be a prophet of God, and other church leaders give guidance to members throughout the world; hotel rooms are in short supply at this time.

A large celebration of multiculturalism comes the third weekend of May, when the grounds of the Salt Lake City and County

Building (State St. and 400 South) erupt with the **Living Traditions Festival** (801/596-5000). Enjoy dances, food, and entertainment of the many different cultures that make up the Utah mosaic.

The **Utah Arts Festival** (801/322-2428, www.uaf.org) takes place the last weekend in June and includes lots of music, dance, readings, art demonstrations, craft sales, and food booths. The event is held at **Library Square** (200 E. 400 S.).

The summer's single largest festival is in July. The **Days of '47 Celebration** (801/247-8545) commemorates the arrival of Mormon pioneers here on July 24, 1847. The city celebrates with three parades, including the huge 24th of July Pioneer Parade (the day is a state holiday), a marathon, lots of fireworks, and the year's biggest rodeo, held at the Delta Center.

The **Greek Festival** (Hellenic Center, 300 S. 300 W., 801/328-9681) in September celebrates Greek culture with food, music, folk dancing, and tours of the historic Holy Trinity Greek Orthodox Cathedral. The festival is held the weekend after Labor Day. The **Utah State Fair** (North Temple St. and 1000 West, 801/538-8441, www.utahstatefair.com/home), held at the state fairgrounds in September, is a celebration of the state's agricultural heritage and features rodeos, livestock shows and judging, arts and crafts exhibits, musical entertainment, and a midway carnival.

Shopping

The big shopping news in Salt Lake City is City Creek Center, a huge redevelopment at the center of the city, where the former ZCMI and Crossroads Plaza shopping centers once stood.

Besides the shopping areas noted below, you'll find some massive malls in the suburbs. **Cottonwood Mall** (Highland Rd. and Murray Holiday Rd.), south of the city, and **Valley Fair Mall** (I-215 exit 18), southwest of the city, are two popular malls, each containing more than 100 stores.

Salt Lake City also boasts several unique shopping areas and unusual stores, including some excellent boutique centers and one large downtown mall. Remember that many shops are closed on Sunday.

SHOPPING MALLS
City Creek Center
The 700,000-square-foot **City Creek Center** (50 S. Main St., 801/521-2012), built in part with funding provided by the LDS Church, stands at the very center of downtown Salt Lake City. Opened in 2012, it's one of the nation's largest mixed-use downtown redevelopment projects, with over 100 stores and restaurants including Nordstrom, Macy's, and Tiffany & Co. The structure's design is notable: The indoor-outdoor space features a retractable roof, a 140-foot sky bridge over Main Street, a 1,200-foot-long re-creation of the historic City Creek, two 18-foot waterfalls, and some amazing fountains.

The Gateway
Just west of downtown, on the site of the former rail yards, **The Gateway** (bounded by 400 West, 600 West, 200 South, and North Temple St., 801/456-0000) was built in the run-up to the 2002 Winter Olympics as a destination boutique shopping mall, entertainment center, and condo development. The shops, restaurants, and entertainment venues line a winding pedestrian street that represents a developer's idea of Ye Olde Worlde. Here you'll find chain stores such as Abercrombie and Fitch, J. Crew, Barnes and Noble, and Virgin Megastore, plus the Megaplex 12 cinema (801/325-7500) and an impressive selection of restaurants and bars.

Trolley Square

Salt Lake City's most unusual shopping center came about when developers cleverly converted the city's old trolley barn. Railroad magnate E. H. Harriman built the barn in 1908 as a center for the city's extensive trolley system. The vehicles stopped rolling in 1945, but their memory lives on in **Trolley Square** (500 South and 700 East, 801/521-9877, daily). Inside you'll see several trolleys, a large stained-glass dome, salvaged sections of old mansions and churches, and many antiques. More than 100 shops and restaurants call this gigantic barn home.

Gardner Village

An attractive shopping village in West Jordan, 12 miles south of downtown Salt Lake City, **Gardner Village** (1100 W. 7800 S., 801/566-8903) offers a restaurant and crafts shops in the refurbished Gardner Mill, built in 1877. Old houses and cabins have been moved to the grounds and restored as additional shops. The village also has a small museum of historical exhibits. Take I-15 exit 301 for Midvale onto 7200 South, turn west, and follow signs to the Gardner Mill.

BOOKS

Weller Book Sellers (607 Trolley Square, 801/328-2586, 10am-9pm Mon.-Sat., noon-5pm Sun.), which has been in operation since 1925 as Sam Weller's Zion Book Store, has left its longtime downtown location and moved to the Trolley Square shopping center just east of downtown. It's still a great store, with a mix of new, used, and rare books covering many topics. The **University of Utah's bookstore** (270 S. 1500 E., 801/581-6326, 8am-5:30pm Mon.-Fri., 9am-4pm Sat.) has a varied selection on many subjects.

OUTDOOR EQUIPMENT

If you suddenly realize you need a new tent pole, some zip-off pants, or any other gear for hiking, camping, bicycling, skiing, river-running, rock climbing, or travel, swing by **REI** (3285 E. 3300 S., 801/486-2100, 10am-9pm Mon.-Fri., 9am-7pm Sat., 11am-6pm Sun.). Gear can also be rented here, and the book section is a good place to look for regional outdoor guides. Topo maps cover the most popular hiking areas of Utah.

Utah Ski and Golf (134 W. 600 S., 801/355-9088) rents golf clubs in summer and ski equipment when the snow falls. Another all-sport rental outfit is **Wasatch Touring** (702 E. 100 S., 801/359-9361).

Trolley Square shopping area is in the city's old trolley barn.

Sports and Recreation

In Salt Lake City, a glimpse at the horizon and the craggy snow-covered Wasatch Mountains tells you that outdoor recreation is very close at hand. Even on a short visit to the Salt Lake area, you'll want to get outdoors and enjoy a hike or a bike ride up a mountain canyon. You won't be alone: The city's newest immigrants, young professionals, are as attracted to the city's right-out-the-back-door access to the great outdoors as to the region's vibrant economy.

PARKS

Salt Lake City has lovely parks, many of which have facilities for recreation. The U.S. Forest Service manages **Mill Creek** and **Big and Little Cottonwood Canyons** (entrance via E. 3800 S./E. Mill Creek Rd., east of Wasatch Blvd.) as part of the Wasatch National Forest. Located just east of the city, these canyons provide easy access to hiking and biking trail systems and to popular fishing streams.

For more information, visit Uinta-Wasatch-Cache National Forest's Public Lands Information Center in the REI store (3285 E. 3300 S., 801/466-6411). For information about the city's park system, contact the Parks and Recreation office (801/972-7800, www.slcgov.com/cityparks); for county park information, call 801/468-2560 (www.recreation.slco.org).

★ City Creek Canyon

In the city itself, a pleasant and relaxing route for a stroll or a jog follows City Creek Canyon, a shady stream-filled ravine just east of the state capitol. The road that runs up the canyon extends more than five miles from its beginning at Memory Grove, just northeast of the intersection of East North Temple Street and State Street, to Rotary Park at the top of the canyon. Since pioneer days, people have obtained precious water from City Creek and enjoyed its diverse vegetation, wildlife, and

scenery. Because City Creek is still part of the city's water supply, regulations exclude dogs, horses, and overnight camping.

Hikers and joggers may travel on the road every day. In summer (Memorial Day-Sept. 30), bicyclists may enter only on odd-numbered days. Motorized vehicles are allowed on holidays and on even-numbered days during summer; a gate at the bottom controls entry. No motorized vehicles are allowed the rest of the year, but bicycles can use the road daily, weather permitting. A $3 charge applies if you drive through to the trailhead at the upper end (no reservation needed).

The entrance to City Creek Canyon is reached via Bonneville Boulevard, a one-way road. From downtown Salt Lake City, head east on North Temple Street, which becomes 2nd Avenue after crossing State Street, then turn left (north) and go 1.3 miles on B Street, which becomes Bonneville Boulevard after 11th Avenue, to City Creek Canyon Road. Returning from the canyon, you have to turn right onto Bonneville Boulevard to the state capitol. Bicyclists and joggers may approach City Creek Canyon from either direction.

Hiking

A popular hiking destination from the trailhead at road's end (elev. 6,050 feet) is **City Creek Meadows,** four miles away and 2,000 feet higher. After 1.5 miles, you'll pass Cottonwood Gulch on the left; a side trail leads up the gulch to an old mining area. After another 0.5 mile on the main trail, a spring off to the right in a small meadow is the last reliable source of drinking water. During the next mile, the trail grows steeper and winds through aspen groves and then passes two shallow ponds. The trail becomes indistinct here, but you can continue one mile northeast to the meadows (elev. 8,000 feet); a topo map and compass will help. For splendid views of the Wasatch Range, climb north 0.5 mile from the meadows up the ridge to where Davis, Salt Lake, and Morgan Counties meet. Hikers also enjoy shorter strolls from the trailhead along the gentle lower section of trail.

Picnics

The big attraction for many visitors is a stop at one of the picnic areas along the road. Picnickers can reserve sites (801/483-6705). Sites are sometimes available on a first-come, first-served basis; midweek is best. Picnic permits cost $3 and up, depending on the size of the group.

Liberty Park

There are abundant reasons to spend time at **Liberty Park** (bounded by 900 South, 1300 South, 500 East, and 700 East, 801/538-2062), southeast of downtown, including the Tracy Aviary, the children's play area, and the acres of shade and lawn. The park also affords plenty of opportunity for recreation. The tennis center on the west side offers 16 lighted courts. The outdoor swimming pool adjacent to the tennis center is open in summer. During the sweltering Salt Lake summer, the shady boulevards provide a cool environment for jogging. You'll find horseshoe pits to the north of the park's historic Chase House.

Mill Creek Canyon

Great mountain biking, plentiful picnic areas, and many hiking possibilities lie along Mill Creek, just outside Salt Lake City. You can bring your dog along too—this is one of the few canyons where pets are welcome. In fact, odd-numbered days are designated "leash-free" days in Mill Creek Canyon. Obey the posted regulations when you begin your hike. Bicycles are allowed in Mill Creek Canyon only on even-numbered days, the days when dogs must be leashed.

Hiking

Salt Lake Overlook on Desolation Trail is a good hiking destination for families. The trail climbs 1,200 vertical feet in two miles for views of the Salt Lake Valley. Begin from the lower end of Box Elder Picnic Area (elev. 5,760 feet) on the south side of the road. Energetic hikers can continue on Desolation Trail beyond the overlook to higher country near the timberline and go all the way to Desolation Lake (19 miles). The trail runs near the ridgeline separating Mill and Big Cottonwood Canyons, connecting with many trails from both canyons. Much of this high country lies in the Mount Olympus Wilderness. See the 7.5-minute topo maps for Mt. Aire and Park City West.

Alexander Basin Trail winds to a beautiful wooded glacial bowl below Gobblers Knob; the trailhead (elev. 7,080 feet) is on the south side of the road, eight miles up Mill Creek Canyon, 0.8 mile beyond Clover Springs Picnic Area. The moderately difficult trail begins by paralleling the road northwest for a few hundred feet, then turns southwest through switchbacks for one mile to the beginning of Alexander Basin (elev. 8,400 feet). The trail to Bowman and Porter Forks turns right here, but continue straight 0.5 mile for the meadows of the upper basin (elev. 9,000 feet). The limestone rock here contains many fossils, mostly shellfish. From the basin it's possible to rock-scramble to the summit of Gobblers Knob (elev. 10,246 feet). The name comes from an attempt by mine owners to raise turkeys after their ore played out; the venture ended when bobcats ate all the birds. See the 7.5-minute topo map for Mt. Aire.

Mountain Biking

Bikers should follow Alexander Basin Trail to the end of the Mill Creek Canyon road, then set out on the Big Water Trail. The Great Western Trail (a 3,000-mile ridgetop trail stretching from Canada to Mexico) intersects Big Water at 1.5 miles. Bikers can turn off Big Water Trail and follow the Great Western Trail to the ridgetop divide overlooking the Canyons Ski Resort. Here, the route turns south and follows the Wasatch Crest Trail along the ridge and around the head of the upper Mill Creek basin. To avoid conflicts with hikers, Big Water, Little Water, and the

Great Western Trail are closed to mountain bikes on odd-numbered days.

Picnics

Picnic sites are free and available on a first-come, first-served basis; most lack water. The first one, **Church Fork Picnic Area,** is three miles in at an elevation of 5,700 feet; **Big Water Picnic Area** is the last, 8.8 miles up at an elevation of 7,500 feet. A usage fee ($3 per vehicle) is charged in Mill Creek Canyon.

Red Butte Garden

The four miles of trails outside **Red Butte Garden** (300 Wakara Way, 801/581-4747, www.redbuttegarden.org, irregular hours and days, year-round, $10 adults, $8 seniors, $6 ages 3-17, free access to hiking trails in the natural area), east of the University of Utah, are a quiet place for a walk or a jog. The hiking trails wind through wildflower meadows and past old sandstone quarries. You don't need to pay the admission to the gardens to hike the trails.

Sugarhouse Park

Mormon pioneers manufactured beet sugar at **Sugarhouse Park** (1300 East and 2100 South, 801/467-1721), on the southeast edge of Salt Lake City, beginning in 1851; the venture later proved unprofitable and was abandoned. Today, expanses of rolling grassland in the 113-acre park are ideal for picnics, strolling, and jogging. The park has a playground and fields for baseball, soccer, and football. In winter, the hills provide good sledding and tubing. A lake attracts seagulls and other birds for bird-watching. Sweet scents rise from the Memorial Rose Garden in the northeast corner.

WINTER SPORTS

Skiing has always been Utah's biggest recreational draw, and as host of the 2002 Winter Olympics, the Salt Lake City area drew the attention of international skiing and winter sports lovers. Summer visitors will find lots to like after the snow melts: Most ski areas remain open for warm-weather recreation, including mountain biking, hiking, trail rides, tennis, and plain old relaxing.

Downhill Skiing

Utah's "Greatest Snow on Earth" is close at hand. Within an hour's drive from Salt Lake City you can be at one of seven downhill areas in the Wasatch Range, each with its own character and distinctive skiing terrain. The snow season runs from about mid-November to April or May. Be sure to pick up the free *Utah Ski Vacation Planner* from **Ski Utah Inc.** (150 W. 500 S., Salt Lake City, UT 84101, 801/534-1779 or 800/754-8824, snow conditions 801/521-8102, fax 801/521-3722); it's also available at most tourism offices in Utah. Alternatively, check out the website (www.skiutah.com). The planner lists most Utah resorts and has diagrams of the lifts and runs, lift-ticket rates, and detailed information on lodging.

Salt Lake City-area ski resorts are grouped quite close together. Although they are in different drainages, Solitude and Brighton ski areas in Big Cottonwood Canyon and Snowbird and Alta ski areas in Little Cottonwood Canyon all share the high country of the Wasatch Divide with Park City, Deer Valley, and the Canyons ski areas. There is no easy or quick route among the three different valleys, however, and traffic and parking can be a real hassle. Luckily, there are plenty of options for convenient public transportation from Salt Lake City to the ski areas and among the resorts themselves.

Alternatively, you can ski between the various ski areas with **Ski Utah Interconnect** (801/534-1907, www.skiutah.com/the-interconnect-tour/, $295 per day), which provides a guide service for backcountry touring among Wasatch Front ski areas. Skiers should be experienced and in good physical condition because of the high elevations (around 10,000 feet) and the need for some walking and traversing. Touring is with downhill equipment. Tours depart daily from Deer Valley Resort or Snowbird

Ski and Summer Resort and go through Park City Mountain Resort, Solitude Mountain Resort, Brighton Resort, and Alta Ski Area. The rates include the guide's services, lunch, and all lift tickets.

Transportation

Salt Lake City's public bus system, the **UTA** (801/287-4636, www.utabus.com), has regularly scheduled service to the four resorts on the west side of the Wasatch Range: Solitude, Brighton, Snowbird, and Alta. You can get on the buses downtown, where they connect with the TRAX light rail; at the University of Utah; or at the bottoms of the canyons. A couple of early-morning buses run up to the ski areas every day; return buses depart the ski areas around 5pm.

All Resort Express (435/649-3999, ext. 1, or 800/457-9457, www.allresort.com, $44 pp round-trip) offers daily skier shuttles from the airport or downtown Salt Lake City hotels to Park City, Deer Valley, Canyons, Alta, and Snowbird. Custom shuttle services are also available.

Cross-Country Skiing

During heavy snowfalls, Salt Lake City parks and streets become impromptu cross-country ski trails, and any snowed-under Forest Service road in the Wasatch Range is fair game for cross-country skiers. The Mill Creek Canyon road is a favorite. If you don't mind cutting a trail or skiing ungroomed snow, ask at ski-rental shops for hints on where the backcountry snow is good.

Otherwise, there are numerous organized cross-country ski areas in the Salt Lake City area. The Mountain Dell Golf Course in Parley's Canyon (off I-80 toward Park City) is a favorite place to make tracks. There are cross-country facilities at Alta and Solitude ski resorts as well as at the White Pine Touring Center in Park City.

GOLF AND TENNIS

Salt Lake City claims to have the highest number of golf courses per capita in the nation, with more than a dozen in the metro area. There's a course for every level of expertise, from city-owned nine-hole courses for beginners to championship-level courses like the 27-hole private **Stonebridge Golf Club** (4415 Links Dr., West Valley City, 801/957-9000, www.golfstonebridgeutah.com) and the 36-hole par 71 or 72 public **Mountain Dell Golf Course** (I-80 exit 134, 801/582-3812, www.slcgov.com), each offering challenging terrain and incredible mountain views. Other courses include **Bonneville** (954 Connor St., 801/583-9513, 18 holes, par 72), east of downtown; **University** (University of Utah campus, 100 S. 1900 E., 801/581-6511, 9 holes, par 33); **Forest Dale** (2375 S. 900 E., 801/483-5420, 9 holes, par 36), near Sugarhouse Park; **Nibley Park** (2730 S. 700 E., 801/483-5418, 9 holes, par 34); **Glendale** (1603 W. 2100 S., 801/974-2403, 18 holes, par 72); and **Rose Park** (1386 N. Redwood Rd., 801/596-5030, 18 holes, par 72), northwest of downtown.

Seventeen city parks have tennis courts; call the Salt Lake City Parks and Recreation Department (801/972-7800) for the one nearest you. **Liberty Park** (1300 S. 500 E.) has 16 courts.

ICE-SKATING AND ROLLER-SKATING

Cottonwood Heights Recreation Center (7500 S. 2700 E., 801/943-3160) offers year-round ice-skating and lessons, indoor and outdoor pools, racquetball courts, and a weight room. Roller-skate at the **Utah Fundome** (4998 S. 360 W., Murray, 801/293-0800) or at **Classic Roller Skating Centers** (9151 S. 255 W., Sandy, 801/561-1791).

ROCK CLIMBING

Rockreation (2074 E. 3900 S., 801/278-7473) offers instruction, equipment rental, and a massive rock gym with 6,700 square feet of climbing terrain. Day passes are available; there's also a weight and fitness room at the complex.

SWIMMING

Two of the best and most central outdoor public pools are at **Liberty Park** (1300 S. 700 E.) and **Fairmont Park** (2361 S. 900 E.). Serious lap swimmers should check out the **Salt Lake City Sports Complex** (near the University of Utah, 645 S. Guardsman Way, 801/583-9713); it has a 25-meter indoor pool and a lovely 50-meter outdoor pool with great views of the mountains.

For an even bigger splash, try **Raging Waters** (1200 W. 1700 S., 801/972-8300), a water-sports theme park that features water-slides and a wave pool. The children's area has waterfalls, geysers, a "dinosaur beach," and a small wave pool.

SPECTATOR SPORTS

University of Utah (1825 E. South Campus Dr., 801/581-8849) athletic teams compete in football, basketball, baseball, softball, tennis, track and field, gymnastics, swimming, golf, skiing, and other sports.

Baseball

The **Salt Lake Bees** (801/485-3800) are the AAA affiliate of baseball's Angels of Anaheim. Games are played at the impressive Franklin Quest Field April-September; it's hard to imagine a more astonishing backdrop to a game of baseball than the craggy Wasatch Front.

Basketball

Utah professional sports fans love their **Utah Jazz,** who are usually strong contenders in the NBA's Western Division. The team plays at the EnergySolutions Arena (300 West and South Temple St.). Tickets are hard to come by at the last minute, but it's worth a call to the team's box office (801/355-7328) to inquire. Otherwise, you'll need to rely on scalpers or ads in the classifieds.

Soccer

Real Salt Lake (801/727-2700, www.realsalt-lake.com) is the city's Major League Soccer team, which plays at Rio Tinto Stadium (State St. between 9000 South and 9400 South), south of Salt Lake City in the suburb of Sandy.

Ice Hockey

The **Utah Grizzlies** (3200 S. Decker Lake Dr., 801/988-8000) are Salt Lake City's International League ice-hockey team.

Racing

For roaring engines, smoking tires, and checkered flags, visit the **Bonneville Raceway Park** (6555 W. 2100 S., West Valley City, 801/250-2600) during the April-October season.

Accommodations

Salt Lake City has the best selection of accommodations in Utah. Unless your budget is very tight, you may want to avoid the cheapest motels along West Temple Street or State Street. Many of these older motor-court units have become residential lodgings, and the owners don't put much effort into upkeep. However, you should have a pleasant stay at all of the following accommodations.

There are several major lodging centers. Downtown Salt Lake City has the advantage of being close to Temple Square, EnergySolutions Arena, the Salt Palace, and most other visitor attractions. South of downtown near 600 South and West Temple Street is a clutch of hotels and motels, including several business-oriented hotels. While these lodgings are only six blocks from the center of the city at Temple Square, remember that blocks are very long in SLC (six blocks per mile). Another cluster of hotels and motels is west along North Temple Street, the primary surface street leading to the airport; these are very convenient via the TRAX light rail line between downtown Salt

Lake City and the airport. If your trip involves visiting the university, there are a couple of good lodging options near the campus.

Room rates can be rather high, although quality is good. The prices listed below are standard rack rates. You can frequently beat these prices by checking the hotel's website for specials. Also, because of hotel over-building for the 2002 Olympics—63 new hotels were built in the Salt Lake area after the city won the Olympic nod—you can often find real deals at Internet booking sites if there's not a convention in town. Prices can vary by as much as $100 per night within the same week, so the following prices are only guidelines.

If you have trouble locating a room, consider using the city's free reservation service (800/847-5810, www.visitsaltlake.com).

TEMPLE SQUARE AND DOWNTOWN
$50-100

You can find several good moderately priced motels near Temple Square. The **Howard Johnson Express Inn** (121 N. 300 W., 801/521-3450 or 800/541-7639, www.hojo.com, $59-100) is an older but well-maintained motor-court motel with an outdoor pool, complimentary continental breakfast, and an airport shuttle.

Just east of Temple Square is the pleasant, well-maintained **Carlton Hotel** (140 E. South Temple St., 801/355-3418 or 800/633-3500, www.carltonhotel-slc.com, $84-129). The Carlton is an older hotel in a great location, and it offers a full breakfast and an in-room fridge and microwave; there are also five suites.

Overlooking Temple Square is the **Salt Lake Plaza Hotel** (122 W. South Temple St., 801/521-0130 or 800/366-3684, http://plaza-hotel.com, $89-100), which offers a pool and an on-site restaurant in addition to its great location.

$100-150

The first of SLC's historic older hotels to be refurbished into a natty, upscale lodging was the ★ **Peery Hotel** (110 W. 300 S., 801/521-4300 or 800/331-0073, www.peeryhotel.com, $129-149). Its 1910 vintage style is preserved in the comfortable lobby, while the guest rooms are completely updated, nicely furnished, and quite spacious. There are two restaurants on the premises, as well as an exercise room.

$150-200

Some of Salt Lake's grandest heritage homes sit on Capitol Hill, just below the state capitol. Surely one of the most eye-catching is the red sandstone mansion now called the **Inn on the Hill** (225 N. State St., 801/328-1466, www.innonthehillslc.com, $150-239). Built in 1906 by a local captain of industry, the inn has 13 guest rooms decorated with period detail, but all with modern amenities like private baths. Practically every room has broad views over Salt Lake City. Full gourmet breakfasts are included.

One block west of the temple is the **Radisson Salt Lake City Hotel Downtown** (215 W. South Temple St., 801/531-7500 or 888/201-1718, www.radisson.com, $174-235). At this modern 15-story hotel, you'll find a pool, a restaurant, and conference, business, and exercise facilities.

One of SLC's most popular convention hotels, the **Hilton Salt Lake City Center** (255 S. West Temple St., 801/328-2000 or 800/445-8667, www1.hilton.com, $174-208) is a huge complex with an indoor pool, two fine-dining restaurants, a bar, fitness facilities, and valet laundry. When there's no convention in town, it's also a supremely comfortable (and often surprisingly affordable) spot for travelers.

Over $200

The **Salt Lake City Marriott Downtown** (75 S. West Temple St., 801/531-0800 or 800/228-9290, www.marriott.com, $239-269) is directly across from the Salt Palace Convention Center. At this high-quality hotel, there's an indoor-outdoor pool, a sauna, a fitness center, a good restaurant, and a lounge. Weekend rates are often deeply discounted.

The ★ **Hotel Monaco** (15 W. 200 S., 801/595-0000 or 877/294-9710, www.monaco-saltlakecity.com, $209-309) occupies a grandly renovated historic office building in a very convenient spot in the middle of downtown; on the main floor is **Bambara,** one of the most sophisticated restaurants in Utah. Guest rooms are sumptuously furnished with real élan: This is no anonymous business hotel in beige and mauve. Expect wild colors and contrasting fabrics, lots of flowers, and excellent service. Facilities include an on-site fitness center, meeting rooms, and concierge and valet services. Pets are welcome, and if you forgot your own pet, the hotel will deliver a companion goldfish to your room. If you want to splurge on a hotel in Salt Lake, make it this one.

The ★ **Salt Lake City Marriott City Center** (220 S. State St., 801/961-8700, www.marriott.com, $209-249) sits above Gallivan Plaza, an urban park and festival space. A luxury-level business hotel, the Marriott has an indoor pool, a recreation area, and a fine-dining restaurant.

SOUTH OF DOWNTOWN

Just south of the religious sites and convention areas downtown is a large complex of hotels and motels, mostly representatives of large chains, with rooms in almost every traveler's price range. These lodgings aren't entirely convenient for travelers on foot, but if you have a car or intend to ride buses or TRAX (unfortunately, the free public transit zone doesn't extend this far south, but the zone is just a short walk from these hotels), these are some of the newest and nicest places to stay in the city.

$50-100

Motel 6 Downtown (176 W. 600 S., 801/531-1252 or 800/466-8356, $61-65) is a standard motel, but it does have a pool. Pets are allowed at the **Rodeway Inn Salt Lake City** (616 S. 200 W., 801/534-0808 or 877/424-6423, www.rodewayinn.com, $59-69). The

Metropolitan Inn (524 S. West Temple St., 801/531-7100 or 800/578-7878, www.metropolitaninn.com, $69-129) offers nicely maintained guest rooms, all with coffeemakers and access to a heated pool and a hot tub. Pets are accepted.

The **Royal Garden Inn** (154 W. 600 S., 801/521-2930 or 800/521-9997, www.royalgardeninnsaltlake.com, $50-57) offers a pool, a fitness room, a restaurant, guest laundry, and a free airport shuttle.

$100-150

If you're looking for comfortable rooms without breaking the bank, the ★ **Little America Hotel and Towers** (500 S. Main St., 801/363-6781 or 800/304-8970, http://saltlake.littleamerica.com, $109-209) is a great place to stay. This large lodging complex, with nearly 850 guest rooms, offers three types of room: Courtside rooms and garden suites are scattered around the hotel's nicely manicured grounds, with most guest rooms overlooking a pool or fountain. Tower suites are executive-level suites in a 17-story block offering some of SLC's best views. All guests share the hotel's elegant public areas, two pools, and a fitness room. The restaurant is better than average, and there is free airport transfer.

Another of the nicer-for-the-money hotels in this part of Salt Lake City is the **Crystal Inn** (230 W. 500 S., 801/328-4466 or 800/366-4466, www.crystalinnsaltlake.com, $100-219). Guest rooms here are very large and nicely furnished; all come with fridges and microwaves. There's a free hot breakfast buffet for all guests. For recreation, there's an indoor pool, an exercise room, a sauna, and a hot tub.

Red Lion Hotel Salt Lake Downtown (161 W. 600 S., 801/521-7373 or 800/325-4000, http://saltlakedowntown.redlion.com, $119-159) has a pool, a spa, exercise facilities, room service, guest laundry, and free airport transfers.

$150-200

One of the best situated of all the south downtown motels is **Courtyard by Marriott**

South of Downtown Salt Lake City

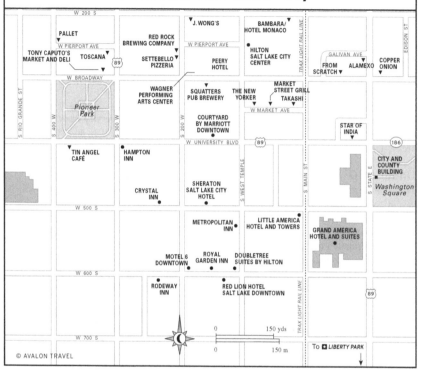

Downtown (130 W. 400 S., 801/531-6000, www.marriott.com, $169-199). It's very centrally located to all the restaurants and happenings in the city's fast-changing warehouse-loft district. There's a pool, a hot tub, a fitness facility, and an airport shuttle.

Hampton Inn (425 S. 300 W., 801/741-1110 or 800/426-7866, http://hamptoninn.hilton.com, $154-204) offers complimentary breakfast, an indoor pool, a hot tub, and a business center.

If you're in Salt Lake for an extended time or are traveling with a family, consider the **DoubleTree Suites by Hilton** (110 W. 600 S., 801/359-7800 or 800/362-2779, http://doubletree3.hilton.com, $150-199). All suites have efficiency kitchens with a coffeemaker, a fridge, and a microwave along with separate living and sleeping areas; there are two

two-bedroom units. Facilities include a pool, a sauna, an exercise area, a restaurant, and a lounge.

Sheraton Salt Lake City Hotel (150 W. 500 S., 801/532-3344 or 800/421-7602, www.sheratonsaltlakecityhotel.com, $157-278) is one of the city's best addresses for high-quality comfort and service. The lobby areas are very pleasant, and facilities include a great pool, an exercise room, and a spa. The rooftop restaurant and lounge are also notable.

Over $200

The behemoth ★ **Grand America Hotel and Suites** (555 S. Main St., 801/258-6000 or 800/621-4505, www.grandamerica.com, $279-309) is a full Salt Lake City square block (remember, that's 10 acres), and its 24 stories contain 775 guest rooms, more than half of them suites. Guest rooms have luxury-level amenities; expect all the perks and niceties that modern hotels can offer, delivered in an over-the-top package that borders on the indulgences of Las Vegas hotels.

EAST OF DOWNTOWN

There aren't many lodging choices in this part of the city, but this is a pleasant residential area without the distinct urban jolt of much of the rest of central Salt Lake City. This is also where most of the city's bed-and-breakfasts are located.

Under $50

The Avenues (107 F St. at 2nd Ave., 1 mile east of Temple Square, 801/363-3855, www.saltlakehostel.com, $23-57) offers dorm rooms with use of a kitchen, a TV room, and laundry. Information-packed bulletin boards list city sights and goings-on, and you'll meet travelers from all over the world. Beds are available in the dorm (sheets included) or in private rooms, only half of which have private baths. Reservations (with first night's deposit) are advised in the busy summer travel and winter ski seasons. From downtown, head east on South Temple Street to F Street, then turn north and go two blocks.

$100-150

The **Armstrong Mansion** (667 E. 100 S., 801/531-1333 or 800/708-1333, www.armstrongmansion.com, $139-229) is a Queen Anne mansion converted into a comfortable B&B. Each of the 13 guest rooms has a private bath and is decorated with full Victorian flair.

$150-200

The **Anniversary Inn** (460 S. 1000 E., 801/363-4900 or 800/324-4152, www.anniversaryinn.com, $199-299) caters to couples and newlyweds interested in a romantic getaway. All 32 guest rooms are imaginatively decorated according to a theme: Beds may be in a covered wagon or a vintage rail car, and baths may be in a "sea cave." Chances are good that your guest room will have its own

private waterfall. You get to pick your suite from choices that include The Lighthouse, The Opera House, South Pacific, and Venice. These guest rooms aren't just filled with kitsch; they are luxury-class accommodations with big-screen TVs, hot tubs, stereos, and private baths. Rates vary widely by room. There's also a second Anniversary Inn (678 E. South Temple St.).

Right in the University of Utah's Research Park, the **Marriott University Park Hotel and Suites** (480 Wakara Way, 801/581-1000 or 800/637-4390, www.marriott.com, $179-204) is one of the city's best-kept secrets for luxurious lodgings in a lovely setting. You can't miss with the views: All guest rooms either overlook the city or look onto the soaring peaks of the Wasatch Range, directly behind the hotel. Guest rooms are very nicely appointed—the suites are some of the best in the city. All guest rooms have minibars, fridges, and coffeemakers; there's a pool and exercise room, and bicycles are available for rent.

WEST OF DOWNTOWN

Nearly all of the following hotels offer transfers to the Salt Lake City Airport. Those with the lowest-numbered addresses on West North Temple Street are closest to downtown; these hotels are about one mile from Temple Square and downtown, and they are inexpensive options if you're looking for a centrally located place to stay.

Under $50

Gateway Motel (819 W. North Temple St., 801/533-0603 or 877/388-8311, $45-65) is a basic budget hotel on the road to the airport, but it's still quite close to downtown.

$50-100

Of the many older motor-court motels along North Temple Street, perhaps the best maintained is the **Overniter Motor Inn** (1500 W. North Temple St., 801/533-8300 or 800/914-8301, $75-99), with an outdoor pool and clean guest rooms.

Moderately priced guest rooms are

available at the **Motel 6 Airport** (1990 W. North Temple St., 801/364-1053, www.motel6. com, $55-59), where there's a pool.

Although it's on the road to the airport, the **Econo Lodge** (715 W. North Temple St., 801/363-0062 or 877/233-2666, www. econolodge.com, $52-56) is also convenient to downtown, as it's just west of the I-15 overpass. The motel offers a courtesy car to the airport and has a pool and guest laundry.

Practically next door to the airport terminal is the **Ramada Salt Lake City** (5575 W. Amelia Earhart Dr., 801/537-7020 or 800/272-6232, www.ramada.com, $69-109), with a pool and a spa.

$150-200

The **Salt Lake Inn Airport** (1659 W. North Temple St., 801/533-9000, http://saltlakeinn. com, $139-159) offers nicely furnished guest rooms, a restaurant, a bar, a pool, and a spa.

The **Radisson Hotel Salt Lake City Airport** (2177 W. North Temple St., 801/364-5800 or 800/333-3333, www.radisson.com, $162-177) is a very attractive lodge-like building with nicely furnished guest rooms. Guests receive a complimentary continental breakfast and a newspaper, and in the evenings there's a manager's reception with free beverages. Facilities include a pool, a spa, and a fitness room. Suites come with a loft bedroom area.

At the **DoubleTree by Hilton SLC Airport** (5151 Wiley Post Way, 801/539-1515 or 800/999-3736, www1.hilton.com, $149-193), guest rooms are very spacious and nicely furnished, and facilities include two pools, a putting green, a sports court, an exercise room, and a spa. The hotel even has its own lake.

CAMPGROUNDS

Of the several commercial campgrounds around the periphery of Salt Lake City,

Camp VIP/Salt Lake City KOA (1350 W. North Temple St., 801/328-0224, www.koa. com, year-round) is the most convenient, located between downtown and the airport. It offers sites for tents (from $27) and RVs (from $47) with showers, a swimming pool, a game room, a playground, a store, and laundry. From I-15 northbound, take exit 311 for I-80; go west 1.3 miles on I-80, exit north for 0.5 mile on Redwood Road (Hwy. 68), then turn right and continue another 0.5 mile on North Temple Street. From I-15 southbound, take exit 313 and go south 1.5 miles on 900 West, then turn right and drive less than one mile on North Temple Street. From I-80, either take the North Temple exit or the one for Redwood Road (Hwy. 68).

There are two good U.S. Forest Service campgrounds in Big Cottonwood Canyon, about 15 miles southeast of downtown Salt Lake City, and another two in Little Cottonwood Canyon, about 19 miles southeast of town. All have drinking water, and all prohibit pets because of local watershed regulations; rates range $19-22, and some can be reserved (877/444-6777, www.recreation.gov, $10 reservation fee).

In Big Cottonwood Canyon, **Spruces Campground** (9.1 miles up the canyon, elev. 7,400 feet) is open early June-mid-October. The season at **Redman Campground** (elev. 8,300 feet, first-come, first-served) is mid-June-early October. It's between Solitude and Brighton, 14 miles up Big Cottonwood Canyon.

Little Cottonwood Canyon's **Tanners Flat Campground** (4.3 miles up the canyon, elev. 7,200 feet, first-come, first-served) is open mid-May-mid-October. **Albion Basin Campground** (elev. 9,500 feet, first-come, first-served) is high in the mountains a few miles past Alta Ski Area and is open early July-late September; go 11 miles up the canyon (the last 2.5 miles are gravel).

Food

Travelers will be pleased with the quality of food in Salt Lake City. If you've been traveling around the more remote areas of the state, the abundance of restaurants serving international cuisine will be a real treat. The city has become a hotbed of local and seasonal cooking, and many fine dining restaurants boast adventurous young chefs cooking with locavore directives.

Despite Mormon nondrinking culture, brewpubs caught on in Salt Lake City and are often the most convenient places to enjoy good food and drink. Note that by law all draft beer in Utah is 3.2 percent alcohol. Beer with higher alcohol content is considered hard alcohol and is sold only by the bottle. However, these bottles are now available at brewpubs, so if you'd rather have high-octane beer (outside Utah, known as regular beer), just order bottled beer.

The free *Salt Lake Visitors Guide* lists dining establishments. Dinner reservations are advisable at more expensive restaurants. Also note that most restaurants are closed on Sunday; if you're going to be in Salt Lake over the weekend, ascertain that your hotel has a restaurant, or you may be wandering the streets looking for an eating establishment that's open.

TEMPLE SQUARE AND DOWNTOWN
American
Lamb's (169 S. Main St., 801/364-7166, www.lambsgrill.com, 7am-9pm Mon.-Fri., 8am-9pm Sat., $15-20) claims to be Utah's oldest restaurant; it started in Logan in 1919 and moved to Salt Lake City in 1939. You can still enjoy the classic 1930s diner atmosphere as well as the tasty food. The menu offers seafood, steak, chops, chicken, and sandwiches; Lamb's is an especially good place for breakfast.

For moderately priced food and history of a different sort, try **The Lion House** (63 E. South Temple St., 801/539-3257, 11am-8pm Mon.-Sat., $8-18). Built in 1856, this was one of Brigham Young's homes, where his 27 wives and 56 children spent most of their time. High-quality cafeteria-style meals are available for lunch and dinner in the basement dining room, formerly the household pantry.

Some of the best views in the city are from the top of the 10-story Joseph Smith Memorial Building (15 E. South Temple St., www.templesquarehospitality.com), the former Hotel Utah, where you'll find two excellent restaurants. The **Garden Restaurant** (801/539-1911, 11am-9pm Mon.-Thurs., 11am-10pm Fri.-Sat., $12-18) offers unparalleled views onto downtown Salt Lake City. What's more, the restaurant is reasonably priced, offering sandwiches and salads for lunch and steaks, seafood, and continental dishes at dinner. With even better views onto Temple Square, the **Roof Restaurant** (801/539-1911, 5pm-9pm Mon.-Thurs., 5pm-10pm Fri.-Sat., $40 adults, $18 ages 11-17, $9 ages 4-6) offers an upscale buffet with prime rib, salmon, ham, shrimp, salads, desserts, and all the trimmings. Reservations are recommended; no alcohol is served at either restaurant.

If fast food is more your style, then at least try the local purveyor: **Crown Burgers** (downtown at 377 E. 200 S., 801/532-1155; 118 N. 300 W., 10am-10:30pm Mon.-Sat., $5), with many outlets throughout the Salt Lake area, is the local favorite for char-grilled burgers and good fries. For that special Utah touch, ask for "fry sauce" with your french fries—it's a local condiment that's remarkably like Thousand Island dressing without relish.

Asian
Salt Lake City has a number of excellent Asian restaurants. For the best and freshest sushi, go to **Takashi** (18 W. Market St., 801/519-9595, 11:30am-2pm and 5:30pm-10pm Mon.-Thurs.,

The Lion House restaurant was once Brigham Young's home.

11:30am-2pm and 5:30pm-11pm Fri., 5pm-11pm Sat., $6-16), though the non-seafood dishes are also excellent (try the Asian ribs).

Naked Fish Bistro (7 W. 100 S., 801/595-8888, 11:30am-2pm and 5-10pm Mon.-Sat., 5-10pm Sun., $8-39), in fact goes quite a ways beyond just sushi (though it's excellent here). Naked Fish is equally renowned for grilled yushiyaki skewers, house-made ramen, wagyu steaks, and fusion dishes such as vanilla-honey teriyaki.

For the city's top Chinese food, go to **J. Wong's Asian Bistro** (163 W. 200 S., 801/350-0888, www.jwongutah.com, 11am-3pm and 5pm-10pm Mon.-Sat., 4pm-9pm Sun., $9-26). You'll find an upscale dining room, beautifully prepared regional Chinese food—plus a few Thai dishes tucked in at the back of the menu.

Breakfast
If your idea of breakfast is excellent pastries and baked goods, head straight to **Eva's Bakery** (155 S. Main St., 801/355-3942, http://evasbakeryslc.com, 7am-6pm Mon., 7am-9pm Tues.-Sat.) for marvelous pastries, breads, soups, and sandwiches.

French
★ **Martine Cafe** (22 E. 100 S., 801/363-9328, http://martinecafe.com, 11:30am-2pm and 5pm-10pm Mon.-Fri., 5pm-10pm Sat.) offers delicious food in an atmospheric but informal atmosphere. The antique high-ceilinged dining room is coolly elegant, and the cooking and presentation spans French, Spanish, and North African cuisines. You have a choice of ordering tapas style ($8-15) or à la carte ($18-32), featuring delicacies such as a grilled pork chop with tart cherry jus and sweet potato-goat cheese gratin.

Italian and Mediterranean
A swank spot to enjoy delicious, well-priced Italian food and pizza is **Vinto** (418 E. 200 S., 801/539-9999, www.vinto.com, 11am-10pm Mon.-Thurs., 11am-11pm Fri.-Sat., 4pm-9pm Sun., $6-13), a bustling spot that's perfect when you're looking for good food without the fine-dining formality.

Caffé Molise (55 W. 100 S., 801/364-8833, www.caffemolise.com, 11:30am-9pm Mon.-Thurs., 11:30am-10pm Fri.-Sat., 10am-9pm Sun., $15-28), offers a bistro atmosphere and tasty mid-priced Italian specialties, including pasta, grilled chicken, and beef dishes.

Mexican and Southwestern
Right downtown, **Blue Iguana** (165 S. West Temple St., 801/533-8900, www.blueiguanarestaurant.net, 11:30am-9pm Mon.-Thurs., 11:30am-10pm Fri., noon-10pm Sat., 4pm-9pm Sun., $6-15) offers high-quality Mexican cooking in a lively basement dining room. In addition to standard tacos and burritos, you'll find seven different moles.

At **Alamexo** (268 S. State St., 801/779-4747, 11:30am-2pm and 5pm-10pm Mon.-Fri., 5pm-10pm Sat., 5pm-9pm Sun., $18-27), traditional Mexican cooking gets reinvigorated with the freshest of ingredients and unusual juxtapositions of flavors. In this airy, brightly painted dining room, you'll find fried halibut tacos with mango and cilantro mojo, and slow-cooked salmon fillet with crispy bananas, pineapple pico de gallo, and chili-fruit mole.

Middle Eastern and Indian

Convenient to downtown, **Cedars of Lebanon** (152 E. 200 S., 801/364-4096, www.cedarsoflebanonrestaurant.com, 11:30am-3pm Mon., 11:30am-3pm and 5pm-10pm Tues.-Fri., 5pm-11pm Sat., $7-18) has exotic Mediterranean flavors from Lebanon, Morocco, Armenia, Greece, and Israel, along with many vegetarian items. Belly dancers enliven the scene on Friday-Saturday evenings.

Tandoori and northern Indian cooking are the specialty at the **Star of India** (55 E. 400 S., 801/363-7555, www.starofindiaonline.com, 11:30am-10pm Mon.-Thurs., 11:30am-10:30pm Fri.-Sat., 3pm-9:30pm Sun., $13), a favorite for tandoor-roasted meats and full-flavored curries. The lunch buffet ($11) is very popular; ask about the Bollywood movie nights.

Pizza

Convenient to downtown, and offering highly regarded pies, ★ **Settebello Pizzeria** (260 S. 200 W., 801/322-3556, http://settebello.net, 11am-10pm Mon.-Thurs., 11am-11pm Fri.-Sat., noon-9pm Sun., $3-5 per slice) makes Neapolitan-style pizza that many consider the best in Utah—or for many states around.

Tucked in the Gallivan Center complex at the heart of downtown, **From Scratch** (62 E. Gallivan Ave., 801/538-5090, www.from-scratchslc.com, 11:30am-3pm Mon., 11:30am-3pm and 5pm-9:30pm Tues-Fri., 11:30am-3pm and 5pm-10:30pm Fri., 5pm-10:30pm Sat., 12-inch pizzas $13-16) takes its name seriously. The restaurant mills its own flour from local wheat and hand-makes pretty much everything else that is on the menu or goes into the food from scratch. The pizzas are baked in a wood-fired oven but at lower temperatures than typical, resulting in a crisp but chewy slice. The menu offers a few non-pizza items, including a burger, salads, braised short ribs, and pasta Alfredo with pesto.

Steak and Seafood

For the best fish and seafood in SLC, go to the **Market Street Grill** (48 Market St., 801/322-4668, www.gastronomyinc.com, 6:30am-2pm and 5pm-9pm Mon.-Thurs., 6:30am-2pm and 5pm-9:30pm Fri., 8am-2pm and 4pm-9:30pm Sat., 9am-3pm and 4pm-9pm Sun., $14-33), featuring fresh seafood, steak, prime rib, chops, chicken, and pasta. Adjacent is an oyster bar. Three-course early-bird specials ($20) are available before 7pm and all evening Sunday-Monday. Market Street Grill is also a very popular spot for a stylish breakfast.

The New Yorker (60 W. Market St., 801/363-0166, www.gastronomyinc.com, 11:30am-2pm and 5:30pm-9:30pm Mon.-Fri., 5:30pm-10pm Sat., $22-38) is yet another fine dining house in a historic storefront. Here the emphasis is on seafood and excellently prepared certified Angus beef and fresh American lamb. If you're not up to a full meal, there's also a café (4pm-9:30pm Mon.-Thurs., 4:30pm-11pm Fri., 5:30pm-11pm Sat.). Or just go to the oyster bar and fill up on bivalves. The atmosphere is lively; the spot is in Salt Lake's financial district, so expect an audience of stockbrokers and businesspeople.

Other steak house choices include **Spencer's** (in the downtown Hilton, 255 S. West Temple St., 801/238-4748, www.spencersforsteaksandchops.com, 11:30am-10pm Mon.-Thurs., 11:30am-11pm Fri., 5pm-10pm Sat.-Sun., $23-42), which has a big reputation as the city's best high-rolling steak house.

Brewpubs

The state's oldest brewpub is ★ **Squatters Pub Brewery** (147 W. Broadway, 801/363-2739, www.squatters.com, 11am-midnight Mon.-Thurs., 11am-1am Fri., 10:30am-1am Sat., 10:30am-midnight Sun., $7-18). In addition to fine beers and ales, the pub, part of Salt Lake Brewing Company, serves sandwiches, burgers, and other light entrées in a handsome old warehouse. In summer, there's seating on the back deck.

Very popular and kind of a scene, the **Red Rock Brewing Company** (254 S. 200 W., 801/521-7446, www.redrockbrewing.com, 11am-11pm Sun.-Thurs., 11am-midnight Fri.-Sat., $8-27) offers steaks, pasta, salads, and sandwiches, including an excellent variation on the hamburger, baked in a wood-fired oven inside a bread pocket. There's often a wait to get in the door, but the food and brews are worth it.

In addition to proper brewpubs (with beer made on premises), there are also taphouses, and downtown the best is the **Beerhive** (128 S. Main St., 801/364-4268, noon-2am daily). This handsome old storefront offers over two dozen regional microbrews on draft and over 200 in bottles. You'll be able to taste beers from all around the state in one sitting. The Beerhive is within walking distance of most downtown hotels (cocktails available too). Food is from the Italian restaurant next door—and very good.

Fine Dining

★ **The Copper Onion** (111 E. Broadway, 801/355-3282, http://thecopperonion.com, 11:30am-3pm and 5pm-10pm Mon.-Thurs., 11:30am-3pm and 5pm-11pm Fri., 10:30am-3pm and 5pm-11pm Sat., 10:30am-3pm and 5pm-10pm Sun., $12-29) always gets a mention when people talk about the best restaurant in Salt Lake City. Emphasizing full-flavored New American cooking, the Copper Onion offers a choice of small and large plates, with such delights as mussels with creamy black pepper sauce and griddled pork chop with fresh polenta, capers, and piquillo peppers. For the quality, the prices are very reasonable.

★ **Bambara** (202 S. Main St., 801/363-5454, http://bambara-slc.com, 7am-10am, 11am-2pm, and 5:30pm-10pm Mon.-Thurs., 7am-10am, 11am-2pm, and 5:30pm-10:30pm Fri., 8am-11am and 5:30pm-10:30pm Sat., 8am-noon and 5:30pm-9pm Sun., $20-28), in the Hotel Monaco, is another exciting fixture in the Salt Lake dining scene. The menu emphasizes the freshest and most flavorful local meat and produce, with preparations in a wide-awake New American style that's equal parts tradition and innovation. This is easily one of the most beautiful dining rooms in the city.

Delis and Groceries

Siegfried's Delicatessen (20 W. 200 S., 801/355-3891, 9am-6pm Mon.-Fri., 9am-5pm Sat.) has a great selection of charcuterie, cold cuts, breads, pastries, and cheeses.

SOUTH OF DOWNTOWN
American

An excellent option for barbecue and soul food is **Sugarhouse Barbecue Co.** (880 E. 2100 S., 801/463-4800, www.sugarhousebbq.com, 11:30am-9pm Mon.-Thurs., 11:30am-10pm Fri.-Sat., noon-8pm Sun., $9-15), with Memphis-style slow-smoked ribs and Carolina pulled pork.

Asian

Salt Lake City has more Asian restaurants than you might expect. **Thai Siam** (1435 S. State St., 801/474-3322, http://thaisiam.net, 11am-9:30pm Mon.-Thurs., 11am-10pm Fri., noon-10pm Sat., 3pm-9pm Sun., $10-17) serves top-notch Thai food in an attractive storefront just south of downtown.

Breakfast

A pleasant place for a traditional breakfast is the **Park Cafe** (604 E. 1300 S., 801/487-1670, http://theparkcafeslc.com, 7am-3pm daily). The Park is directly across from Liberty Park, which makes a great before- or after-breakfast destination.

In the same neighborhood, **Pig and a Jelly Jar** (401 E. 900 S., 385/202-7366, www.pigandajellyjar.com, 7:30am-3:30pm Mon.-Wed., 7:30am-9pm Thurs.-Sun., $8-11) takes the house-made charcuterie craze to the breakfast table. Everything here is made from scratch in-house, including all the pork sausages, bacon, ham, and other porky bits. At lunch and dinner, you'll find soups, salads, and sandwiches.

If you're looking for breakfast with a view, head to the lodges and resorts up nearby Wasatch Front canyons. The **Silver Fork Lodge** (11 miles up Big Cottonwood Canyon, 435/649-9551, www.silverforklodge.com, 8am-9pm daily, $7-14) is a favorite destination for a scenic brunch, perhaps followed by a hike.

French

For excellent French cuisine, drive a few miles south of downtown to the ★ **Paris Bistro** (1500 S. 1500 E., 801/486-5585, www.theparis.net, 6pm-9:30pm Mon.-Thurs., 5pm-10pm Fri.-Sat., 5pm-9:30pm Sun., $15-35), a lovely dining room in gold and burgundy that serves up classics such as duck confit, steak au poivre, and mussels *moulinière*, plus pasta and wood-fired pizza.

For classic French cuisine when budget is no issue, **La Caille Restaurant** (9565 Wasatch Blvd., near Little Cottonwood Canyon, 801/942-1751, www.lacaille.com, 4pm-9pm Tues.-Sat., 10am-9pm Sun., $28-56) offers superb pastry, crepes, seafood, and meat dishes in an 18th-century rural French atmosphere. Vineyards, gardens, ponds, and manicured lawns surround the re-created French château—it's hard to believe it's in Utah. Antique furnishings grace the dining rooms and halls. Dress is semiformal, and reservations are advised. The Sunday brunch ($26-34) is where to head if you feel like putting on the ritz.

Italian and Mediterranean

Many people feel that ★ **Fresco Italian Cafe** (1513 S. 1500 E., 801/486-1300, http://frescoitaliancafe.com, 5pm-9:30pm Sun.-Thurs., 5pm-10pm Fri.-Sat. May-Oct., 5pm-9pm Sun.-Thurs., 5pm-9:30pm Fri.-Sat. Nov.-Apr., $18-27) is SLC's finest Italian eatery, if not the city's best restaurant overall. The pleasant setting features an intimate dining room entered through a garden, and the property is on a quiet street a few miles south of the city

center. The main courses are full-flavored yet subtle: House-made ravioli are stuffed with sweet potatoes and chestnuts, then topped with shaved Brussels sprouts, black currants, and ricotta, while Roman-spiced roast chicken comes with roast squash manicotti.

Middle Eastern and Indian

For updated Middle Eastern cooking, try the very popular ★ **Mazza** (912 E. 900 S., 801/521-4572, www.mazzacafe.com, 11am-3pm and 5pm-10pm Mon.-Sat., $16-22), a bit of a drive from downtown but with an excellent Lebanese menu that goes far beyond the usual kababs. There's another branch a few blocks southeast (1515 S. 1500 E., 801/484-9259).

Vegetarian

Even a meat-loving place like SLC offers a selection of dining options for vegetarians. **Sage's Café** (234 W. 900 S., 801/322-3790, www.sagescafe.com, 11:30am-10pm Mon.-Fri., 10am-10pm Sat.-Sun., $12-15) serves satisfying organic vegetarian cuisine, while the wine list emphasizes organic wines.

Brewpubs

Epic Brewing has been brewing great beers in Salt Lake City since 2008, but until recently they didn't have a brewpub in which to enjoy their beers with food. Though a ways from downtown in the Sugarhouse district, **The Annex by Epic Brewing** (1048 E. 2100 S., 801/742-5490, http://theannexbyepicbrewing.com, 11am-10pm Sun.-Thurs., 11am-11pm Fri.-Sat.) makes a special point of pairing the food on their menu with their beers. The result is way better than average pub grub: Expect dishes such as beer-poached salmon salad with eggs, asparagus, potatoes, olives, and capers, or grilled trout with cannellini bean ragout and lemon-butter sauce.

Even farther from downtown is **Bohemian Brewery** (94 E. 7200 S., Midvale, 14 miles south of central SLC, 801/566-5474, www.bohemianbrewery.com, 11am-11pm Mon.-Fri., 10am-11pm Sat., 10am-10pm Sun.). This excellent brewery features Czech-style lagers, and is worth the drive if you like Central European food and brews.

Fine Dining

A log cabin in the woods might seem like a perfect Utah destination, and at historic **Log Haven** (6451 E. Millcreek Canyon Rd., 801/272-8255, www.log-haven.com, 5:30pm-11pm daily, $20-40), that cabin also serves remarkably good food. Built in the 1920s, the restaurant is splendidly rustic yet upscale, with ample outdoor seating in good weather. Though probably best thought of as a steak house, the menu offers a wide selection of New American dishes, including game, fresh seafood, and pasta. Log Haven is four miles east of Salt Lake City in Mill Creek Canyon.

EAST OF DOWNTOWN
American

Despite Mormon restrictions on caffeine, several fine coffeehouses exist in Salt Lake City. Look no farther than **Salt Lake Roasting Co.** (320 E. 400 S., 801/363-7572, www.roasting.com, 6:45am-10:30pm Mon.-Wed., 6:45am-11pm Thurs.-Sat.), which offers a wide selection of coffees, freshly baked European-style pastries, a vaguely alternative atmosphere, and a pleasant outdoor patio in good weather. You'll find a second location at Library Square (210 E. 400 S., 9am-8pm Mon.-Thurs., 9am-6pm Fri.-Sat., 1pm-5pm Sun.).

Asian

Ichiban Sushi and Japanese Cuisine (336 S. 400 E., 801/532-7522, http://watkinsrg.com, 5pm-10pm Sun.-Thurs., 5pm-11pm Fri.-Sat., $10-19) is a transplant from Park City, where it had a huge reputation as a superlative sushi house. Its reputation has only grown since its move to Salt Lake, where it's currently housed in a converted Lutheran church.

Breakfast

For one of Salt Lake's favorite breakfasts, drive (or ride your bike) a couple of miles east of the city to **Ruth's Diner** (4160 Emigration Canyon, 801/582-5807, www.ruthsdiner.com, 8am-10pm daily summer, 8am-9pm Sun.-Thurs., 8am-10pm Fri.-Sat. winter, $8-15). The restaurant's namesake was a cabaret singer in the 1920s who opened her own restaurant in 1930. Ruth's has been in continuous operation ever since (the ads used to read "70 years in business... boy am I tired!"). Ruth's is full of atmosphere and overlooks a rushing stream. It's a great place to go for an old-fashioned breakfast or a hearty lunch. Live music is featured at Sunday brunch.

Greek

The city's best Greek food by far is served at ★ **Aristo's** (224 S. 1300 E., 801/581-0888, www.aristosslc.com, 11am-10pm Mon.-Sat., 4pm-9pm Sun., meze $5-11, main courses $17-30), a swanky dining room up by the university. The flavors and quality are outstanding, and while the main courses are not cheap (but the lamb chops are worth it), it's easy to put together a meal of small plates, "street eats," and meze dishes.

Indian

Saffron Valley East India Café (26 E St., 801/203-3325, 11am-3pm and 5pm-10pm Tues.-Sat., 11am-3pm and 5pm-9pm Sun., $12-16) offers an especially large selection of street-food starters, dosas, salads, and other small plates, including unusual dishes such as Bombay (vegetarian) sloppy joes and crispy chicken poppers, in addition to more classic dishes from India and southeast Asia. The food here is sophisticated and unusual, far removed from the usual gloppy stew that passes for Indian food.

Italian and Mediterranean

The owners of top-ranked Fresco Italian Cafe also run **Café Trio** (680 S. 900 E., 801/533-8746, www.triodining.com, 11am-9:30pm Mon.-Thurs., 11am-10pm Fri., 10am-10pm Sat., 10am-9pm Sun. May.-Sept., $12-25), serving a somewhat more casual version of the same lovingly prepared food, set in a hip dining room between downtown and the university.

Stoneground (249 E. 400 S., 801/364-1368, www.stonegroundslc.com, 11am-11pm Mon.-Sat., 5pm-9pm Sun.) has at least two personalities—it's both a hipster hangout with pool tables and a reasonably priced Italian restaurant and pizzeria. The atmosphere is industrial, but windows look out onto a gorgeous view of the Wasatch Front. Pizzas are excellent ($11-18), and pasta dishes and main courses are flavorful and full of character ($9-21).

Pizza

The Pie Underground (1320 E. 200 S., 801/582-5700, www.thepie.com, 11am-1am Mon.-Thurs., 11am-3am Fri.-Sat., noon-11pm Sun, slices $3-5), downstairs from the University Pharmacy, offers New York-style hand-thrown pizza.

Vegetarian

★ **Oasis Café** (151 S. 500 E., 801/322-0404, www.oasiscafeslc.com, 7am-9pm Mon.-Thurs., 7am-10pm Fri., 8am-10pm Sat., 8am-9pm Sun., $13-21) serves an ambitious all-organic menu that borrows tastes and preparations from around the world; while most dishes are vegetarian, fresh fish and some organic meats are also served.

Brewpubs

Desert Edge Brewery (700 E. 500 S., 801/521-8917, www.desertedgebrewery.com, 11am-midnight Mon.-Wed., 11am-1am Thurs.-Fri., 11:30am-1am Sat., noon-10pm Sun., $9-11), in Trolley Square, is also known simply as "The Pub." The inexpensive menu offers sandwiches, pasta, Mexican dishes, and salads all day; some of the ales are cask-conditioned. The atmosphere is retro industrial chic, and there's a second-floor outdoor veranda.

The **Avenues Proper Restaurant and Publick House** (376 8th Ave., www.avenuesproper.com, 11am-3pm and 5pm-10pm Tues.-Sat., 10:30am-2:30pm and 5pm-9pm

Sun., with "bites" and drinks till midnight Fri.-Sat., $13-26) is Utah's smallest craft brewery, and from its location in the Avenues offers some of the best pub dining in the state. The food aspires to Food Network quality, with such dishes as duck fat popcorn with fennel pollen, rye pappardelle with wild mushrooms and kale, and beer-braised short ribs with whole-grain mustard spatzle.

Fine Dining

A top spot for locavore cuisine is ★ **Pago** (878 S. 900 E., 801/532-0777, http://pago-slc.com, 11am-3pm and 5pm-10pm Mon.-Fri., 10am-2:30pm and 5pm-10pm Sat.-Sun., $18-32), where the best of local produce, mushrooms, fish, and meat are cooked with Mediterranean flair; try the roast chicken with harissa and chickpeas.

A restaurant with lots of swagger, **The Wild Grape New West Bistro** (481 E. South Temple St., 801/746-5565, www.wildgrapebistro.com, 8am-9:30pm Tues.-Thurs., 8am-10:30pm Fri., 3pm-10:30pm Sat., 3pm-9:30pm Sun., $18-28) is a fashionable but casual restaurant that celebrates the flavors of the mountain West, with quite a bit of European verve and technique tossed in to keep things interesting. The steaks, chops, and seafood are excellent, but it's hard to ignore more inventive dishes like gnocchi with braised beef, snap peas, and wild mushrooms, all topped with truffle oil. The wine list is also excellent.

WEST OF DOWNTOWN
Asian

At the **Happy Sumo** (153 S. Rio Grande St., 801/456-7866, www.happysumosushi.com, 11:30am-9:30pm Mon.-Thurs., 11:30am-10:30pm Fri.-Sat., noon-9pm Sun., $9-17), traditional sushi mixes with eclectic pan-Asian dishes in a lively upscale setting. The outdoor patio features live music some evenings.

Italian and Mediterranean

Not far from downtown, ★ **Toscana** (307 W. Pierpoint Ave., next to Tony Caputo's Market, 801/328-3463, http://toscanaslc.

com, 5:30pm-9:30pm Mon.-Thurs., 5:30pm-10pm Fri.-Sat., $15-43) offers high-quality grilled meats, salads, and pasta in a coolly elegant dining room. Reservations are a must, as Cucina Toscana is frequently jammed—for the best service, try to avoid peak dining hours.

Even though **Tin Angel Café** (365 W. 400 S., 801/328-4155, www.thetinangel.com, 11am-3pm and 5pm-9pm Mon.-Thurs., 11am-3pm and 5pm-10pm Fri.-Sat., $5-24) offers small plates and tapas, the excellent preparations are largely Italian. In addition to a selection of tempting salads and pasta, bravura main courses include chicken confit with fennel/apple pilaf, and prosciutto-wrapped beef tenderloin with mashed horseradish cauliflower.

Mexican and Southwestern

★ **Red Iguana** (736 W. North Temple St., 801/322-1489, http://rediguana.com, 11am-10pm Mon.-Thurs., 11am-11pm Fri., 10am-11pm Sat., 10am-9pm Sun., $6-11) is one of the city's favorite Mexican restaurants; it offers excellent south-of-the-border cooking with a specialty in Mayan and regional foods. Best of all, flavors are crisp, fresh, and earthy. The Red Iguana is very popular, so arrive early—especially at lunch—to avoid the lines. There's also a second location (866 W. South Temple St., 801/214-6050), with the same hours, and a branch in the new City Creek Center mall food court (28 S. State St., 801/214-6350, 7:30am-9pm Mon.-Fri., 10am-10pm Sat.).

★ **Frida Bistro** (545 W. 700 S., 801/983-6692, http://fridabistro.com, 11:30am-3pm and 5pm-9pm Mon.-Thurs., 11:30am-3pm and 5pm-10pm Fri., 11am-3pm and 5pm-10pm Sat., $15-28) takes the basic elements of hearty, flavorful Mexican cooking and elevates it to the level of sophisticated French cuisine. Dishes such as grilled duck breast quesadillas with goat cheese and three chili-mango marmalade, or bacon-wrapped chicken breast stuffed with cotija cheese and avocado-citrus-yellow pepper sauce are elegant and sophisticated without losing their earthy vitality. The specialty margaritas (fresh raspberry with rosemary, smoked pineapple with jalapeño, and more) provide a vivid start to the meal. This is not your typical Mexican restaurant!

Fine Dining

The joke is that ★ **Pallet** (237 S. 400 W., 801/935-4431, http://eatpallet.com, 5pm-9:30pm Mon.-Sat., $21-29) is right out of Portlandia. But who cares—the locally-sourced food is both delicious and ingenious. In this handsome refitted industrial space, expect to find such dishes as roasted pork belly with Brussels sprouts, apples, yams, and honey ginger sauce, and grilled lamb chops with pineapple and spicy harissa glaze.

Delis and Markets

A good place to stop for provisions is ★ **Tony Caputo's Market and Deli** (314 W. 300 S., 801/531-8669, http://caputosdeli.com, 9am-7pm Mon., 9am-9pm Tues.-Sat., 10am-5pm Sun.), with great sandwiches, Italian-style sausage and cheese, loads of olives and other Mediterranean temptations, and a park nearby where you can have an impromptu picnic. Next door, **Carlucci's Bakery** (314 W. 300 S., 801/366-4484, www.carluccisbakery.com, 7am-7pm Mon.-Fri., 8am-5pm Sat.) offers European-style breads and pastries.

In summer, the **Salt Lake Farmers Market** (300 S. 300 W., 8am-1pm Sat. June-Oct.) takes over Pioneer Park. The market offers a wide variety of international fare and to-go eating options, along with a selection of fresh fruits, vegetables, and baked goods.

Information and Services

Salt Lake City's visitors centers are well stocked with information and enthusiastic volunteers. Couple that with excellent public transportation, and you'll find the city and surrounding areas easy to negotiate despite the intimidating sprawl.

INFORMATION
Tourism Offices

Volunteers at the **Salt Lake Convention and Visitors Bureau** (downtown in the Salt Palace, 90 S. West Temple St., Salt Lake City, UT 84101, 801/534-4900 or 800/541-4955, www.visitsaltlake.com, 9am-5pm daily) will tell you about the sights, facilities, and goings-on in town. The office also has many helpful magazines and brochures.

The **Utah Travel Council** (300 N. State St., 801/538-1030, www.utah.com, 8am-5pm Mon.-Fri., 10am-5pm Sat.-Sun.) publishes a well-illustrated *Utah Travel Guide,* travel maps, and other helpful publications. The staff at the Travel Council information desk provides advice and literature about Utah's national parks and monuments, national forests, Bureau of Land Management areas, and state parks as well as general travel in the state.

U.S. Forest Service

Although visiting the U.S. Forest Service headquarters or a ranger station is always an option, travelers may find it easier to go to **REI** (3285 E. 3300 S., 801/486-2100), where the Forest Service maintains the **Public Lands Information Center** (801/466-6411, 10:30am-5:30pm Mon.-Fri., 9am-1pm Sat.). The staff is often more oriented to serving outdoor recreationalists than is staff at ranger stations. A full selection of maps, books, and printed material is available.

The **Uinta-Wasatch-Cache National Forest** supervisor's office (857 W. South Jordan Pkwy., South Jordan, UT, 84109,

801/999-2103, www.fs.usda.gov/uwcnf, 8am-4:30pm Mon.-Fri.) has general information and forest maps for all the national forests in Utah, and some forest and wilderness maps of Nevada, Idaho, and Wyoming.

Libraries

The large **City Library** (210 E. 400 S., 801/524-8200, www.slcpl.lib.ut.us, 9am-9pm Mon.-Thurs., 9am-6pm Fri.-Sat.) contains a wealth of reading material, a children's library, recordings, and DVDs. The architecture of the library building is striking and effective—full of natural light, it's a great place to read and then glance up at the mountains.

The **Marriott Library** (University of Utah, 801/581-6085 or 801/581-8558, 7am-10pm Mon.-Thurs., 7am-5pm Fri., 9am-5pm Sat., shorter hours in summer and school breaks) ranks as one of the leading research libraries in the region. The large map collection has topo maps of all 50 states as well as maps and atlases of distant lands. Hikers can photocopy maps of areas they plan to visit. The public is welcome to use materials inside the library; purchase a Library Permit Card to borrow materials.

Media

The *Salt Lake Tribune* morning daily reflects the city's non-LDS viewpoints. The LDS-owned daily *Deseret News* comes out in the afternoon and offers a conservative viewpoint and greater coverage of LDS Church news. The free *City Weekly* describes the latest on art, entertainment, events, and social spots and covers local politics and issues.

Salt Lake City has good public radio stations. KUER (90.1 FM) offers a varied musical mix along with National Public Radio (NPR) news. KCPW, at both 88.3 and 105.1 FM, offers more NPR news and programming as well as foreign news programs. KRCL (91 FM) is a community radio station with progressive news and locally produced programming.

Useful Numbers

- **Highway emergency assistance:** 801/576-8606, or *71 from cell phones
- **Police** (Salt Lake City): 801/799-3000
- **Road conditions:** 801/964-6000
- **Salt Lake Convention and Visitors Bureau** (local travel information): 801/521-2822 or 800/541-4955
- **Sheriff** (Salt Lake County): 801/535-5441
- **Utah Division of Wildlife Resources:** 801/538-4700
- **Utah Recreation and Ski Report:** 801/521-8102
- **Utah State Parks:** 801/538-7220
- **Utah Transit Authority** (UTA): 801/287-4636
- **Utah Travel Council** (statewide travel information): 801/538-1030

SERVICES

There is a main **post office** (230 W. 200 S., 801/974-2200) downtown. The University of Utah has a post office in the bookstore.

Salt Lake City is a major regional banking center, and you'll have no trouble with most common financial transactions. ATMs are everywhere and make obtaining money easy. If you are depending on foreign currency, consider changing enough for your trip around Utah while you're in Salt Lake City. Exchanging currency is much more difficult in smaller rural towns.

Minor medical emergencies can be treated by **InstaCare Clinics** (2000 S. 900 E., 801/464-7777, 9am-9pm daily). Hospitals with 24-hour emergency care include **Salt Lake Regional Medical Center** (1050 E. South Temple St., 801/350-4111), **LDS Hospital** (8th Ave. and C St., 801/350-4111), **St. Mark's Hospital** (1200 E. 3900 S., 801/268-7111), and **University Hospital** (50 N. Medical Dr./1900 East, 801/581-2121). For a physician referral, contact one of the hospitals or the Utah State Medical Association (801/355-7477).

For a 24-hour pharmacy, try **Rite Aid** (5540 S. 900 E., 801/262-2981). If you're looking for a drugstore, check the phone book for **Smith's Pharmacy;** there are more than 25 in the Salt Lake metro area.

The **American Automobile Association** (AAA) has offices at 560 East 500 South (801/541-9902).

Transportation

AIR

Salt Lake City International Airport (SLC, 776 N. Terminal Dr., 801/575-2400, www.slcairport.com) is conveniently located seven miles west of downtown; take North Temple or I-80 to reach it. Most major U.S. carriers fly into Salt Lake City, and it is the western hub for Delta Air Lines, the region's air transportation leader.

Delta Connections (800/325-8224, www.skywest.com) is Delta's commuter partner and flies from SLC to Vernal, Moab, Cedar City, and St. George in Utah and to smaller cities in adjacent states.

The airport has three terminals; in each you'll find a ground-transportation information desk, food service, motel-hotel courtesy phones, and a ski-rental shop. Auto rentals (Hertz, Avis, National, Budget, and Dollar) are in the parking structure immediately across from the terminals. Just follow the signs.

Staff at the ground-transportation information desks will know the bus schedules into town and can advise on limousine services direct to Park City, Sundance, Provo, Ogden, Brigham City, Logan, and other communities. By far the easiest way to get from the airport to downtown is via the new TRAX rail line, which runs between the SLC airport and the Salt Lake Central Station. The train stop is located at the south end of Terminal 1. Trains run every 15 minutes on weekdays, every 20 minutes on weekends; hours are 6am-11pm Mon.-Sat., 9:45am-10pm Sun. One-way fare is $2.50.

TRAIN

Amtrak (340 S. 600 W., information and reservations 800/872-7245, www.amtrak.com) trains stop at the Salt Lake Central Station (300 S. 600 W.), which also serves as a terminus for local buses, light rail, and commuter trains. The only Amtrak train that currently passes through the city is the *California Zephyr,* which runs west to Reno and Oakland and east to Denver and Chicago once daily in each direction. Call for fares, as Amtrak prices tickets as airlines do, with advance-booking discounts, special seasonal prices, and other special rates available. Amtrak office hours, timed to meet the trains, are irregular, so call first.

LONG-DISTANCE BUS

Salt Lake City is at a crossroads of several major interstate highways and has good **Greyhound** bus service (300 S. 600 W., 801/355-9579 or 800/231-2222, www.greyhound.com). Generally speaking, buses go north and south along I-15 and east and west along I-80. In summer, one bus daily leaves from Salt Lake City for Yellowstone National Park.

LOCAL BUS AND LIGHT RAIL

Utah Transit Authority (UTA, 801/287-4636, www.rideuta.com, 6am-7pm Mon.-Sat.) provides inexpensive bus and light rail train service in town and to the airport, the University of Utah, and surrounding communities. Buses go as far north as Ogden, as far south as Provo and Springville, and as far west as Tooele. TRAX light rail trains connect the EnergySolutions Arena, the University of Utah, downtown Salt Lake City, the airport, and the southern suburbs. No charge is made for travel downtown within the "Free-Fare Square" area, generally bounded by North Temple Street, 500 South, 200 East, and 400 West; on TRAX, service is fare-free to Salt Lake Central Station at 600 West.

The new TRAX line that connects Salt Lake City International Airport with Salt Lake Central Station means that you can board a light rail train at the airport and ride public transport downtown—or with a bit of patience, to your Wasatch Front ski area.

During the winter ski season, skiers can hop on the Ski Bus Service to Solitude, Brighton, Snowbird, and Alta ski areas from downtown, the University of Utah, and other locations. A bus route map and individual schedules are available on the website and at the ground transportation information desk at the airport, at the Salt Lake Convention and Visitors Bureau downtown, and at Temple Square visitors centers. Free transfers are provided on request when the fare is paid. On Sunday, only the airport, Ogden, Provo, and a few other destinations are served. UTA shuts down on holidays. Fares are $2.50 for two hours of travel on both TRAX and the buses; a day pass is $6.25.

CAR RENTAL

All the major companies and many local outfits are eager to rent you a set of wheels. In winter you can find "skier-ized" vehicles with snow tires and ski racks ready to head for the slopes. Many agencies have an office or delivery service at the airport: **Avis Rent A Car** (Salt Lake City International Airport, 801/575-2847 or 800/331-1212, www.avis. com), **Budget Rent A Car** (641 N. 3800 W., 801/575-2586 or 800/527-0700, www.budget.com), **Dollar Rent-A-Car** (601 N. 3800 W. and Salt Lake City International Airport, 801/575-2580 or 800/421-9849, www.dollar.com), **Enterprise Rent-A-Car** (151 E. 5600 S., 801/266-3777 or 801/534-1888, www.enterprise.com), **Hertz** (Salt Lake City International Airport, 801/575-2683 or 800/654-3131, www.hertz.com), **National Car Rental** (Salt Lake City International Airport, 801/575-2277 or 800/227-7368, www. nationalcar.com), and **Payless Car Rental** (1974 W. North Temple St., 801/596-2596 or 800/327-3631, www.paylesscar.com).

TAXI

City Cab (801/363-8400), **Ute Cab** (801/359-7788), and **Yellow Cab** (801/521-2100) have 24-hour service.

Vicinity of Salt Lake City

Travelers may think that northern Utah is dominated by the sprawling suburbs of the Wasatch Front. However, there is plenty to see and do in the state's chunky panhandle. Great Salt Lake, one of Utah's signature features, is a remnant of a network of ice-age lakes that once covered the West. It's not exactly easy to visit the lake itself—and at certain times of the year, not exactly pleasant—but this one-of-a-kind destination does merit a detour to scenic Antelope Island, where bison and bighorn sheep graze alongside with the island's namesake pronghorn, or a visit to Great Salt Lake State Park to explore the southern shores by kayak.

The region has a rich railroad history. Ogden was born of the railroads, and the city's historic downtown is dominated by Union Station, now home to multiple museums.

The first transcontinental railway joined the Atlantic and Pacific coasts near here in 1869, at Promontory Summit. This windswept pass is preserved as the Golden Spike National Historic Site, with a visitors center and exhibits to beguile the student of history and the rails.

Logan is one of Utah's most pleasant towns, home to Utah State University and a profusion of summer festivals, including the Utah Opera Festival. The town's alpine setting and surrounding dairy farms make the deserts and saline lakes of Utah seem far away.

The mountains of the Wasatch Range east of both Logan and Ogden are filled with great recreational opportunities. Ogden Canyon, just east of town, is the site of good hiking trails and the road to some of the state's best skiing at Snowbasin. Logan

52

Vicinity of Salt Lake City

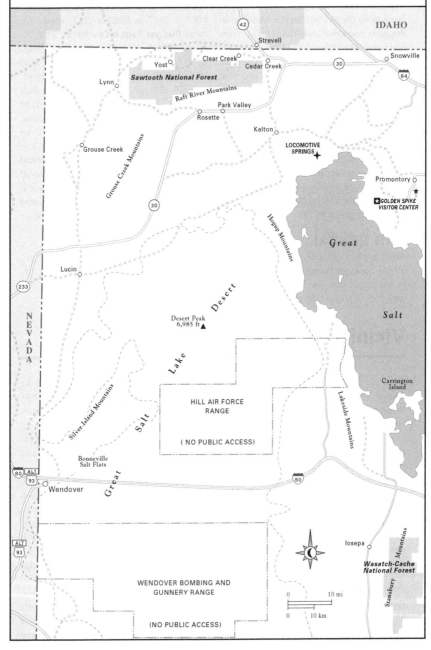

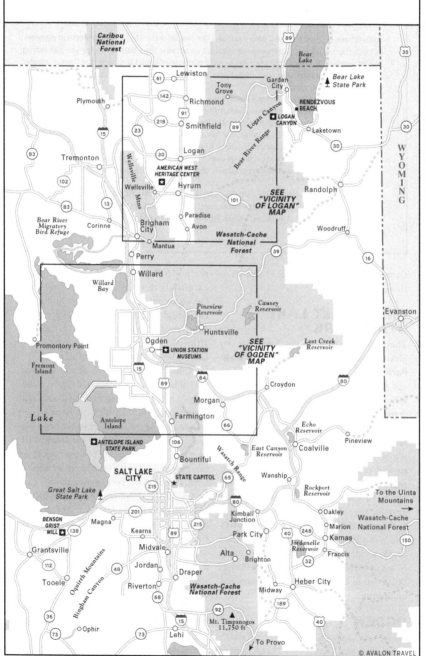

© AVALON TRAVEL

The Ghost of Saltair

Bathers have enjoyed hopping into Great Salt Lake ever since the 1847 arrival of Mormon pioneers. Extreme buoyancy in the dense water makes it impossible for a bather to sink—no swimming ability needed! But if you put your head underwater, you'll quickly realize that the salty water causes great irritation to the eyes, throat, and nose. Also note that during summer algae blooms, and the odor of the water can irritate the nose.

Beginning in the 1880s, several resorts popped up along the lake's east and south shores. Besides bathing, guests could enjoy lake cruises, dances, concerts, bowling, arcade games, and roller-coaster rides. Saltair Resort represented the grandest of the old resorts. Completed in 1893, the Moorish structure rose five stories and contained a huge dance floor where as many as 1,000 couples could enjoy the orchestra's rhythms. A rail line from Salt Lake City ran out on a 4,000-foot pier to the resort, which stood on pilings over the water. After 1930, low water levels, the Great Depression, fires, and fewer visitors gradually brought an end to Saltair. Its buildings burned for the second time in 1970.

In the 1980s, a developer built a smaller replica of the **Saltair Resort** (13 miles west of Salt Lake City, near I-80 exit 104, www.thesaltair.com) on Great Salt Lake's southern shore. The building is now mostly used as a concert venue. From the Saltair parking, visitors can cross the beach for a swim in the lake.

Canyon includes trails to lakes and wildflower meadows.

GREAT SALT LAKE STATE PARK

The lake is popular for sailing, kayaking, and pleasure boating, and **Great Salt Lake State Park** (14 miles west of Salt Lake City, take I-80 exit 104, 801/250-1898, sunrise-sunset, $3 per vehicle), with paved launches, is the primary marina along the southern shores. In addition, there's a visitors center and gift shop, a picnic area, and restrooms. Adjacent to the marina is a beach, and when the lake waters are high enough, this is a good spot to go swimming or wading. Because of the salty residue that the water can leave on your skin, you'll also be glad that the park offers freshwater showers.

Gonzo Boat Rentals and Tours (801/698-6288, www.gonzofun.com) offers kayak, paddleboard, and pedal boat rentals from the marina, mostly on weekends, though call ahead to arrange customized tours and excursions.

OGDEN

Located at the northern edge of the Wasatch Front urban area, Ogden, off I-15 and 35 miles north of Salt Lake City, remains very much its own city even as it is engulfed by suburbs. Ogden was one of the West's most important rail hubs at the beginning of the 20th century, and in the downtown area vestiges of the city's affluence remain in the grand architecture and the impressive Union Pacific Depot.

Ogden is named for Peter Skene Ogden of the Hudson's Bay Company. He explored and trapped in the upper reaches of the Ogden and Weber Valleys in 1828-1829, but he never descended to the site of the city that bears his name. In 1846, Miles Goodyear established an out-of-the-way trading post and stockade here, one of the first permanent settlements in Utah, and named it Fort Buenaventura.

Arrival of the transcontinental railroad in 1869 changed Ogden forever. Although the railroad's Golden Spike had been driven at Promontory Summit, 55 miles to the northwest, Ogden earned the title "Junction City" as lines branched from it through Utah and into surrounding states. New industries and an expanding non-Mormon population transformed the sleepy farm town into a bustling city. Today, Ogden, with a population of 83,000, serves as a major administrative, manufacturing, and livestock center for the

(801/528-5348, www.iflyutah.com), a vertical wind tunnel that re-creates the experience of free-fall skydiving. (If skydiving lessons are going on, it's fun just to stop in to watch.) Also at the Junction is a Megaplex 13 movie theater and a number of restaurants, mostly chains.

★ Union Station Museums

Travelers thronged into the cavernous **Union Station Building** (2501 Wall Ave., www. theunionstation.org) during the grand old days of railroading. Completed in 1924, it saw more than 120 trains daily during the peak World War II years. When passenger trains stopped serving Ogden in 1977, the station was leased to the city of Ogden. Today, the depot is mostly known for its fine museums and the **Forest Service Information Center** (801/625-5306, 8am-4:30pm Mon.-Fri.), which provides recreation information for public lands in the Wasatch Range.

Union Station's museums and art gallery are well worth a visit. A single ticket allows admission to all exhibitions (10am-5pm Mon.-Sat., $5 adults, $4 ages 13-17 and over age 61, $3 ages 3-12).

The **Browning-Kimball Classic Car Museum** displays a glittering collection of about a dozen antique autos, ranging from a one-cylinder 1901 Oldsmobile to a 16-cylinder 1930 Cadillac sports sedan.

The **Utah State Railroad Museum** comprises two rail exhibits. In the **Wattis Dumke Model Railroad** collection, highly detailed dioramas illustrate railroad scenes and construction feats. Eight HO-scale model trains roll through the Ogden rail yard, wind through a model of the Sierra and Humboldt Palisades, cross Great Salt Lake on the Lucin Cutoff, and descend Weber Canyon. Exhibits and photos show railroading history and great trains, such as the "Big Boys," which weighed more than one million pounds and pulled heavy freights up the mountain ranges. A documentary film about the first transcontinental railroad is shown on request. Outside, just south of the station, at the **Eccles Railroad Center,** you can visit giant diesel locomotives and some cabooses.

Great Salt Lake State Park

intermountain West; it's also home to a large Air Force base.

Ogden is worth exploring for its museums, historic sites, and access to scenic spots in the Wasatch Range, which looms precipitously just behind the city. From here it's quick to get out into the hinterlands of northern Utah. Ogden Canyon, beginning on the east edge of town and leading into the Wasatch, leads up to lakes, campgrounds, hiking trails, and three downhill ski areas. Several 2002 Winter Olympic events took place in the Ogden area, including the downhill and super-G ski races and the men's and women's curling competition.

Sights

The Junction, a downtown entertainment, retail, and residential complex, fills the area around 23rd and Kiesel Streets. The complex is anchored by the Salomon Center, a sports, recreation, and fitness center complete with Gold's Gym, a wave pool for surfing practice, a climbing wall, and **iFLY Indoor Skydiving**

Browning Firearms Museum (upstairs) contains the gun shop and many examples of firearms invented by the Browning family. John M. Browning (1855-1926), a genius in his field, held 75 major gun patents. He developed the world's first successful automatic firearms, which used gases from the bullet to expel the old shell, load a new one, and cock the mechanism. The skillfully done exhibitions display both military and civilian handguns, automatic weapons, rifles, and shotguns.

The **Utah Cowboy and Western Heritage Museum** commemorates Utah's frontier past, honoring the cowboy and the other men and women who settled Utah—and those who continue to champion the Western way of life.

Myra Powell Gallery displays paintings, sculpture, and photography in a former pigeon roost. Exhibitions rotate monthly.

The station also houses the Union Grill Restaurant, a model train store, and a gift shop.

Historic 25th Street

When Ogden was the railroad's main transport hub, 25th was the city's main street. Running like a wide boulevard between Washington Boulevard and the palatial Union Pacific Depot, the street boasted the city's first grocery and hardware stores, blacksmith shops, livery stables, hotels, and restaurants, many of them run by immigrants attracted by the railroads. Most of the buildings were built for posterity in redbrick and handsome vernacular styles.

After the city's residents came to rely less on the railway and more on the motor car, the city's orientation changed, and this historic precinct fell into disrepair. Artists and small cafés have since colonized the lovely historic commercial buildings. The street now serves as a combination gallery and restaurant row while still functioning as the city's bowery. It's a pleasant place for a stroll, and many of the shops and cafés are worth a detour. Pick up a brochure detailing histories of many of these buildings from the tourism office on Washington Boulevard.

On summer Saturdays, the **25th Street Farmers and Art Market** (25th St. and Grant Ave.) takes over Ogden Municipal Park. Also in the park is the **Ogden Amphitheater,** which hosts free events all summer, including movies and classical music concerts on Monday nights.

Peery's Egyptian Theater

You can't miss the unusual facade of the venerable **Peery's Egyptian Theater** (2415 Washington Blvd., 801/689-8700 or 866/472-4627, www.peerysegyptiantheater. com). Looking suspiciously like an Egyptian sun temple, this old-time movie palace and vaudeville theater was built in 1924 in the "atmospheric" style during the fit of Egyptomania that followed the discovery of King Tut's tomb. After falling into disrepair for many years, the old theater was completely refurbished; it now serves as Ogden's performing arts center. The interior of the hall is equally astonishing, with a sun that moves across the ceiling, floating clouds, and glittering stars. With columns, hieroglyphs, and mummies everywhere, the theater looks like the set for *Aida*. The Egyptian keeps very busy with a series of top-notch musical performances and regional theater productions.

Adjacent to the Egyptian Theater is the **David Eccles Conference Center** (801/689-8600), a handsome building designed to harmonize architecturally with the theater. Together the conference center and the theater form the core of Ogden's convention facility.

Ogden Temple and Tabernacle

The **Ogden LDS Temple** (350 22nd St.), once a modern structure much like the Provo Temple, began a huge reconstruction in 2011 that is expected to last through 2014, resulting in a much grander and more classical granite-clad building. When the temple reopens, the **Daughters of Utah Pioneers Museum** (closed during temple construction)

Ogden

To Brigham City (Golden Spike Fruitway)

2ND ST
MONROE
HARRISON BLVD
7TH ST
9TH ST
BLVD
203
89
39

OGDEN NATURE CENTER
12TH ST

To I-15 and Best Western
High Country Inn

CANYON RD
CANYON RD
16TH ST
CANYON
CANYON RD
39

ECCLES
DINOSAUR PARK
AND MUSEUM ★

To Ogden
Valley Ski
Resorts

Ogden River

LORIN FARR
COMMUNITY
POOL

PARK BLVD
VALLEY DR

EL MONTE
GOLF
COURSE

TIMBER-
MINE

To
Comfort Suites
104

20TH ST
21ST
21ST ST
WILSON LN
EXCHANGE RD

PRAIRIE
SCHOONER

ST
ST
22ND
TABERNACLE SQUARE ★

MONROE BLVD

ST
ST
23RD ST
POLK
TAYLOR
FILLMORE

THE JUNCTION/
SALOMON CENTER ■
SONORA GRILL ▼

HILTON GARDEN
INN ●

UNION
GRILL

24TH
25TH
SEE
DETAIL
89

WEBER COUNTY
MAIN LIBRARY ■

ST
203

UNION STATION ★
MUSEUMS

Fort
Buenaventura ▲
State Park

26TH
POST OFFICE ■

OGDEN RANGER DISTRICT ■
ECCLES ★
COMMUNITY ART
CENTER

ST

27TH

MARSHALL WHITE
CENTER POOL ■

28TH ST
WASHINGTON
MADISON
QUINCY

15
River

29TH ST
30TH ST
31ST ST
32ND ST

POLK
LAUREL ST

MOUNT OGDEN PARK
AND GOLF COURSE

79

OGDEN
MUNICIPAL
AIRPORT
✈

Weber

DAYS INN ●
OGDEN

WALL
LINCOLN
GRANT
ADAMS
JEFFERSON
JACKSON
VAN BUREN
HARRISON
TYLER
TAYLOR

36TH ST

89
26

To I-84

WEBER STATE
UNIVERSITY ■
(ENTRANCE AND
INFORMATION
BOOTH)

SKYLINE DR

WEBER
STATE
UNIVERSITY

To Hill
Aerospace
Museum

COUNTRY HILLS
203

DEE EVENT CENTER/
ICE SHEET ■

46TH ST

© AVALON TRAVEL

Detail inset:

24TH ST
LINCOLN
GRANT
KIESEL
WASHINGTON

THE SUMMIT ▼

HAMPTON INN
AND SUITES OGDEN ●

TONA,
SUSHI
BAR
AND
GRILL ▼

PEERY'S
EGYPTIAN THEATER ★

LA FERROVIA
RISTORANTE ▼

ZENGER'S DELI/ ▼
GREAT HARVEST
BAKERY

VISITOR CENTER ●

BISTRO
258 ▼

HEARTH ▼
Ogden
Municipal
Park

BEN LOMOND ●
SUITES/
MACCOLL'S

25TH ST

GROUNDS
FOR
COFFEE ▼

ROOSTER'S
25TH STREET
BREWING COMPANY ▼

Scale:
0 — 0.5 mi
0 — 0.5 km

will be just west of the temple on the corner of Lincoln Street and 21st Avenue. On Tabernacle Square, the white-steepled **Ogden Tabernacle** (2133 Washington Blvd., 9am-5pm Mon.-Sat. in summer), completed in 1956, sits just to the north. Visitors are welcome inside the tabernacle.

Fort Buenaventura State Park

Miles Goodyear built the original **Fort Buenaventura** (office 2450 S. A Ave., 801/399-8099, www.co.weber.ut.us, 9am-dusk daily spring-fall, $2 with tour, $1 without) in 1846 to serve as a trading post and way station for travelers crossing the remote Great Basin region. Now a replica of the tiny fort provides a link with Utah's mountain-man past. The location, dimensions, and materials used for the stockade and three cabins inside closely follow the originals. Special programs are scheduled throughout the year, including a mountain-man rendezvous on Labor Day weekend and a pioneer skill show held on July 24. The 32-acre park has a campground and a pond popular for canoeing in summer (rentals are available). From downtown Ogden, take 24th Street west across the rail yard and the Weber River, turn left onto A Avenue, and follow the signs.

Eccles Community Art Center

A series of monthly changing exhibitions at the **Eccles Community Art Center** (2580 Jefferson Ave., 801/392-6935, www.ogden-4arts.org, 9am-5pm Mon.-Fri., 9am-3pm Sat., free), in a historic mansion, displays the best of regional paintings, sculpture, photography, and mixed media. The ornate mansion, once owned by the philanthropic Eccles family, whose name is attached to many arts centers in northern Utah, is an attraction in itself. Turrets, cut glass, and carved woodwork decorate the brick and sandstone structure, built in 1893 in a Richardsonian-Romanesque style. The carriage house in back contains a sales gallery, and the grounds are used as a sculpture garden.

Ogden Nature Center

The **Ogden Nature Center** (966 W. 12th St., 801/621-7595, www.ogdennaturecenter. org, 9am-5pm Mon.-Fri., 9am-4pm Sat., $4 ages 13-65, $3 over age 65, $2 ages 2-12) is a 127-acre wildlife sanctuary on the outskirts of Ogden. It's a popular spot for school field trips, and it's also fun to just visit on your own. Hiking trails lead through woods, wetlands, and open fields. Deer, porcupines, muskrat,

Ogden's historic Union Station is home to several museums.

Peery's Egyptian Theater

rabbits, snakes, and about 130 species of birds have been spotted here. The new visitors center offers classes, workshops, displays, picnic facilities, and activities year-round. To get here, follow West 12th Street northwest from downtown.

Eccles Dinosaur Park and Museum

Paths at the leafy **Eccles Dinosaur Park** (1544 E. Park Blvd., 801/393-3466, www. dinosaurpark.org, 10am-8pm Mon.-Sat., 10am-6pm Sun. Labor Day-Memorial Day, 10am-6pm daily Memorial Day-Labor Day, $7 adults, $6 seniors and students, $5 ages 2-12) lead to over 100 realistic life-size replicas of dinosaurs, complete with robotics, making this a favorite with children. Exhibitions are based on the most up-to-date studies of paleontologists, and the replicas were created by the same folks who build "dino-stars" for Hollywood films. A large museum includes an area to watch technicians work on recently excavated dinosaur bones.

Hill Aerospace Museum

Construction of Hill Field began in 1940, just in time to serve the aircraft maintenance and storage needs of the military during the hectic World War II years. The decades since have seen a parade of nearly every type of bomber, fighter, helicopter, trainer, and missile belonging to the U.S. Air Force. At **Hill Aerospace Museum** (7961 Wardleigh Rd., 801/777-6868, www.hill.af.mil, 9am-4:30pm daily, donation), about 50 of these can be seen close-up in outdoor and indoor exhibits. To get here, take I-15 exit 341 for Roy, five miles south of Ogden, and follow the signs east.

Weber State University

Weber State University (3848 Harrison Blvd., 801/626-6000, www.weber.edu), pronounced WEE-bur, is southeast of downtown on a bench of prehistoric Lake Bonneville; the Wasatch Range rises steeply behind. Visitors are welcome on campus for the **Museum of Natural Science** (1551 Edvalson St., 801/626-6653, 8am-5pm Mon.-Fri., free), **Shaw Art Gallery** (Kimball Visual Arts building, 801/626-7689, 11am-5pm Mon.-Fri., noon-5pm Sat.), Olympic ice-skating rink, library, student union and bookstore, and cultural and sporting events. **Wilderness Recreation Center** (4022 Taylor Ave., 801/626-6373, www.weber.edu, 11am-6pm Mon.-Sat.), next to the Swenson Gym, rents kayaks, rafts, skis, camping gear, and other sports equipment; although it's geared toward students, the center also rents to visitors and people from the local community.

Recreation
Hiking

Hikers, trail runners, and winter snowshoers have easy access to trails in and around Ogden. Right in town, the 9.6-mile **Ogden River Parkway** links a number of the city's major parks and attractions along the Ogden River, including Eccles Dinosaur Park and the Utah State University Botanical Gardens. The easternmost end trail is at the mouth of Ogden Canyon, near Rainbow Gardens (1851

Valley Dr.), which is a busy gift shop, and its western terminus is at Fort Buenaventura, just west of 24th Street. Join the trail at 18th Street and Washington Boulevard, at 1700 Monroe Boulevard, or at the east end of Park Boulevard.

Several trails into the Wasatch Range start on the east side of town. Good resources for trail information include the **Forest Service Information Center** in Odgen's Union Station (801/625-5306) and **Weber Pathways** (www.weberpathways.org), a nonprofit trail advocacy group whose excellent printed trail map is widely available around town, including at the visitors center.

The **Bonneville Shoreline Trail** follows the eastern bench of ancient Lake Bonneville along the western edge of the Wasatch Range. This relatively new trail is still being developed, and it may someday run along the entire Wasatch Front. For now, the stretch near Ogden can be accessed by five trailheads (from north to south): Rainbow Gardens, where Valley Drive intersects Highway 39; 22nd Street; 29th Street; 36th Street; and 46th Street. The trail is right on the urban interface, and it is popular with mountain bikers as well as hikers and trail runners. Also right at the eastern edge of town, **Indian Trail,** which follows an old Shoshoni route 4.3 miles into Ogden Canyon, can be accessed from the 22nd Street trailhead at the western edge of the canyon; follow it to its terminus at the Cold Water Canyon trailhead in Ogden Canyon. There's also a spur trail off Indian Trail leading to a nice viewpoint; about 0.5 mile up the trail, take a sharp right turn, and head 1.4 miles uphill to Hidden Valley.

At the eastern edge of the canyon, just across from the Pineview Dam, the easy **Wheeler Creek Trail** is also popular with mountain bikers. Head 1.8 miles up the canyon to emerge at the Art Nord trailhead; it's also possible to fashion loop hikes from this trail.

Ogden's 9,712-foot **Ben Lomond Peak** was supposedly the inspiration for the Paramount Pictures logo. The 7.6-mile **Ben Lomond Trail** starts from North Fork Park in Liberty. To get here from Ogden, head up Ogden Canyon, go left over the Pineview Reservoir Dam, and keep left. At the four-way stop in Eden, go left on Highway 162 and travel north until you must stop at the three-way stop in Liberty at Liberty Park. Go left (west) at the three-way stop for one block, then go right (north) on 3300 East and follow it 1.5 miles; veer left at the Y intersection and travel one mile to the park and trailhead sign. For an early start, plan to camp at the trailhead.

Golf

The Ogden area has a number of golf courses, with some of the lowest greens fees you'll find anywhere (all prices are for 18 holes unless noted). Try any of these courses: **Ben Lomond** (1800 N. U.S. 89, 801/782-7754, $26); the municipal courses **El Monte** (1300 Valley Dr., at the mouth of Ogden Canyon, 801/629-0694, nine holes $13) and **Mount Ogden** (1787 Constitution Way, 801/629-0699, $26); **Nordic Valley** (3550 Nordic Valley Way, Eden, 801/745-0306, nine holes $15), 15 miles east of Ogden; **Valley View** (2501 E. Gentile St., Layton, 801/546-1630, $28); **The Barn Golf Club** (305 W. Pleasant View Dr., North Ogden, 801/782-7320, $26); and **Wolf Creek** (3900 N. Wolf Creek Dr., Eden, 801/745-3365, $45), 15 miles east of Ogden.

Skiing

You'll find good **downhill skiing** in the Wasatch Range 15-19 miles east of Ogden at Snowbasin, Powder Mountain, and Nordic Valley. **Cross-country skiers** can use the easy set tracks at Mount Ogden Golf Course (1787 Constitution Way) or head into the mountains for more challenging terrain. One place that's groomed for classic and skate skiing is the trail system at North Fork Park, at the base of Ben Lomond Peak in Liberty.

Swimming

Swim year-round at **Marshall White Center Pool** (222 28th St., 801/629-8346) or at the **Weber State University gym**

(3848 Harrison Blvd., 801/626-6466), on the south end of campus. The outdoor **Lorin Farr Community Pool** (1691 Gramercy Ave., 801/629-8291) is open in summer.

Accommodations
$50-100

The huge ★ **Ben Lomond Suites** (2510 Washington Blvd., 866/627-1900, www.benlomondsuites.com, $84-170), a downtown landmark, was built in 1927 in Italian Renaissance Revival style. The lobby is pretty spectacular, and the rooms are spacious, though a bit frumpily decorated. All of the guest rooms are suites, with sitting rooms and bedrooms; there are also short-stay condo units on the upper floors with full kitchens. Pets are allowed in some guest rooms.

A few blocks south of downtown is **Days Inn Ogden** (3306 Washington Blvd., 801/399-5671, www.daysinn.com, $70-80), with reasonably spacious guest rooms, an indoor pool, a spa, and a fitness room. **Sleep Inn** (1155 S. 1700 W., 801/731-6500, www.sleepinn.com, $70-80), just west of I-15 exit 344, is a good bet if you don't mind staying out by the freeway.

At I-15 exit 347 is the **Best Western High Country Inn** (1335 W. 12th St., 801/394-9474 or 800/594-8979, www.bestwestern.com, $90-126), with a pool, a spa, and a fitness room. Pets are accommodated, and there's a good restaurant in the motel.

$100-150

The ★ **Hampton Inn and Suites Ogden** (2401 Washington Blvd., 866/394-9400, http://hamptoninnogden.com, $169-206) is a grand art deco souvenir of the early 20th century. In addition to comfortable guest rooms and a gracious formal lobby, guests are offered exercise facilities, a business center, and a fine-dining restaurant. The Hampton Inn was completely renovated and refurbished for the Olympics, and it's a charming place to stay, with frequent rate specials on the hotel's website.

At I-15 exit 347, the pet-friendly **Comfort Suites of Ogden** (2250 S. 1200 W., 801/621-2545, www.comfortsuites.com, $100-184) has an indoor pool and a fitness center; all guest rooms have efficiency kitchens and coffeemakers, and rates include continental breakfast. Ogden's newest hotel is the ★ **Hilton Garden Inn** (2271 S. Washington Blvd., 801/399-2000, http://hiltongardeninn3.hilton.com, $107-179), a striking-looking hotel right next to the Salomon Center with amenities such as HD TVs, a business center, an indoor

The Ben Lomond Suites hotel has a grand lobby and spacious rooms.

pool, and a fitness room. Although breakfast is not included in the basic rates (it's available for about $10 extra per couple), there's a good restaurant in the hotel.

Near the city center is **Summit Hotel** (247 24th St., 801/627-1190 or 888/825-3163, www. marriott.com, $119-179), with an indoor pool, a hot tub, guest laundry, and a business center; there's a lounge and a good restaurant on the premises.

For a unique lodging experience in a pretty setting, consider the ★ **Alaskan Inn** (435 Ogden Canyon, 801/621-8600, www. alaskaninn.com, $125-179), six miles east of Ogden. A 26-unit log lodge and cabin complex, the Alaskan Inn sits along the banks of a mountain stream. Lodging is either in suites in the central lodge building or in individual log cabins. The rustic decor includes hand-hewn pine furniture, brass lamps, and Western art. Breakfast is included in the rates.

Campgrounds

Camp in town at historic **Fort Buenaventura** (office 2450 S. A Ave., 801/399-8099, Apr.-Oct., tents or RVs without hookups $18, RVs with hookups $23); it's a pleasant riverside spot, with canoes available for rent. Near I-15, **Century Mobile Home and RV Park** (1399 W. 21st St. S., 801/731-3800, year-round, RVs $38) is suitable for RVs, although it caters largely to long-term renters; take I-15 exit 346, then head one block west on Wilson Lane.

Food

Quite a number of good restaurants line 25th Street, the somewhat gentrified Main Street of turn-of-the-20th-century Ogden. In addition to the dining options noted below, there are bakery cafés, a Greek restaurant, sushi joints, taverns with burgers, and home-style Mexican food. If you've got time, just saunter along 25th Street, and you'll be sure to find someplace to suit your fancy.

Breakfast and Light Meals

If your idea of breakfast is strong coffee, fresh pastries, and the option of an omelet, plan on

Lots of restaurants, from old-fashioned taverns to fine dining, line 25th Street.

frequenting ★ **Grounds for Coffee** (111 25th St., 801/392-7370, www.groundsforcoffee.com, 7am-8pm Mon.-Sat., 8am-5pm Sun., $5), the city's best coffee shop; there's often entertainment in the evening. The coffee shop is in a beautifully preserved 19th-century storefront along historic 25th Street.

The combined **Zenger's Deli-Great Harvest Bakery** (272 25th St., 801/334-9494, www.ogdenbread.com, 7am-6pm daily, $4-9) serves up hearty baked goods and sandwiches made on tasty whole-grain breads.

Casual Dining

One of the liveliest places along 25th Street is ★ **Roosters Brewing Company** (253 25th St., 801/627-6171, http://roostersbrewingco.com, 11am-10pm Mon.-Thurs., 11am-11pm Fri.-Sat., 10am-9pm Sun., $8-16), a brewpub with good food (burgers, pizza, ribs, fresh fish, steak, and sandwiches) and good microbrews. It's a popular weekend brunch spot, and in summer there's a pleasant shady deck.

The Irish pub atmosphere of **MacCool's**

(2510 Washington Blvd., 801/675-5920, www. maccoolsrestaurant.com, 11am-10pm Mon.-Sat., 11am-9pm Sun., $10-18) brings a lively crowd to the ground floor of the Ben Lomond Hotel. Dine on traditional Irish dishes such as corned beef and cabbage, Sheppard's Pie, or Guinness stew, or opt for a burger or a sandwich.

If you're looking for good modern, American-style food—grilled fish, gourmet sandwiches, and salads—head to the historic Union Pacific Station and try the **Union Grill** (2501 Wall Ave., 801/621-2830, www.union-grillogden.com, 11am-10pm Mon.-Thurs., 11am-10:30pm Fri.-Sat., $8-19).

La Ferrovia Ristorante (234 25th St., 801/394-8628, http://laferrovia.com, 11am-8:30pm Tues.-Thurs., 11am-9:30pm Fri.-Sat., $10-19) offers an inexpensive selection of pasta, pizza, and calzones. It's a good place to bring kids, but it's also possible to get a glass of wine or a beer with your meal.

Find good upscale, non-chain Mexican food, including several varieties of seviche, at ★ **Sonora Grill** (2310 S. Kiesel Ave., 801/393-1999, www.thesonoragrill.com, 11am-10pm Mon.-Thurs., 11am-11pm Fri.-Sat., 11am-9pm Sun., $10-23), just across from the Salomon Center.

The sushi is fresh and quite lovely at **Tona Sushi Bar and Grill** (210 25th St., 801/622-8662, http://tonarestaurant.com, 11:30am-2:30pm and 5pm-9:30pm Tues.-Thurs., 11:30am-2:30pm and 5pm-10pm Fri.-Sat., $11-20), with a wide range of Japanese dishes besides the sushi and sashimi; on a chilly after-skiing evening, a bowl of Japanese beef stew might be just the thing.

Head to South Ogden for some of the region's best Italian food as well as a market and deli at **Zucca Trattoria** (1479 E. 5600 S., South Ogden, 801/475-7077, www.myzucca. com, market and deli 11am-7pm Mon.-Thurs., 11am-8pm Fri.-Sat., restaurant 11am-9pm Mon.-Thurs., 11am-10pm Fri.-Sat., $11-25). The pizza is very good, and the deli is well stocked with Italian and southern European specialties; meats and cheeses are provided by Tony Caputo's, which is Salt Lake City's leading deli.

Fine Dining

Bistro 258 (258 25th St., 801/394-1595, www. bistro258.net, 11am-9pm Mon.-Thurs., 11am-10pm Fri.-Sat., $14-27) has good food in an atmosphere that's not too stuffy. The dishes have both European and Asian influences, although there's also a good selection of Utah beef. Stop in for a rice-bowl lunch ($7-10); at dinner, the rich New York steak is worth clogging a minor artery for.

Hearth on 25th (195 25th St., 801/399-0088, www.hearth25.com, 2pm-9pm Mon.-Thurs., 2pm-10pm Fri.-Sat., $12-44) is a stylish restaurant that takes the concept of "hearth" seriously. Most of the menu features live fire cooking, courtesy of a Tuscan wood-fired oven, and made-from-scratch breads, pasta, and desserts. Expect unusual, inventive dishes such as Thai curry pizza, crab ravioli with lemon pork belly cream sauce, and dried-mushroom-crusted elk sirloin. And talk about unusual—this is probably the only restaurant in Utah where you can order a yak steak.

Dine in a covered wagon at **Prairie Schooner** (445 Park Blvd., 801/392-2712, http://prairieschoonerrestaurant.com, 11am-9:30pm Mon.-Thurs., 11am-10pm Fri., 3pm-10pm Sat., 3pm-8pm Sun., $12-59). The menu includes everything from burgers to big surf-and-turf combos, with a focus on really good steaks.

Information and Services

The very helpful **Ogden Convention and Visitors Bureau Information Center** (2438 Washington Blvd., 866/867-8824, www.visitogden.com, 9am-5pm Mon.-Fri.) can tell you about the sights, facilities, and goings-on for Ogden and surrounding communities, including Davis, Morgan, and Box Elder Counties.

Visit the **U.S. Forest Service Information Center** (2501 Wall Ave., 801/625-5306, 8am-4:30pm Mon.-Sat. summer, 8am-4:30pm Mon.-Fri. fall-spring) at Union Station, or the U.S. Forest Service **Ogden Ranger District Office** (507 25th St., 801/625-5306, 8am-4:30pm Mon.-Fri.) to find out about local road conditions, camping, hiking, horseback riding, ski touring, snow-shoeing, and snowmobiling.

Hospital care and physician referrals are provided by **McKay-Dee Hospital Center** (4401 Harrison Blvd., 801/387-2800) and **Ogden Regional Medical Center** (5475 S. 500 E., 801/479-2111). There is a **post office** (2641 Washington Blvd., 801/627-4184) downtown.

Getting There

Utah Transit Authority (UTA, 2393 Wall Ave., 877/621-4636, www.rideuta.com, 7am-6pm Mon.-Fri.) buses serve many areas of Ogden and head south to Salt Lake City and Provo; buses operate Monday-Saturday and offer some late-night runs. The UTA's Front Runner commuter train also travels between Salt Lake City and Ogden. **Greyhound** (801/394-5573, www.greyhound.com) pro-vides long-distance service from the bus ter-minal (2393 Wall Ave.).

Air travelers use the **Salt Lake City International Airport** (SLC, 776 N. Terminal Dr., 801/575-2400, www.slcairport.

com), just 35 miles away. **Wasatch Crest Shuttle** (801/466-3122, www.wcshuttle.com) provides service between the airport and Ogden.

Yellow Cab (801/394-9411) provides 24-hour taxi service.

WEST OF OGDEN
★ Antelope Island State Park

Just a short distance offshore in the Great Salt Lake, **Antelope Island** (office 4528 W. 1700 S., Syracuse, 801/773-2941, http://stateparks.utah.gov, $9 per car, $3 bicycles and pedes-trians) seems a world away, and since it's ac-cessed from its north end, it is closer by road to Ogden than SLC. Its rocky slopes, roll-ing grasslands, marshes, sand dunes, and lake views instill a sense of remoteness and rugged beauty. An extension of the Oquirrh Mountains, Antelope Island is the largest of the lake's 10 islands. It measures 15 miles long and 5 miles wide; Frary Peak (elev. 6,596 feet) rises in the center.

The entire island is a state park, accessible via a seven-mile paved causeway. Antelope Island is a great place for mountain bik-ing; park trails are open to hiking, bicy-cling, and horseback riding, allowing access to much of the island; there's also a marina

A causeway leads to Antelope Island, the largest island in the Great Salt Lake.

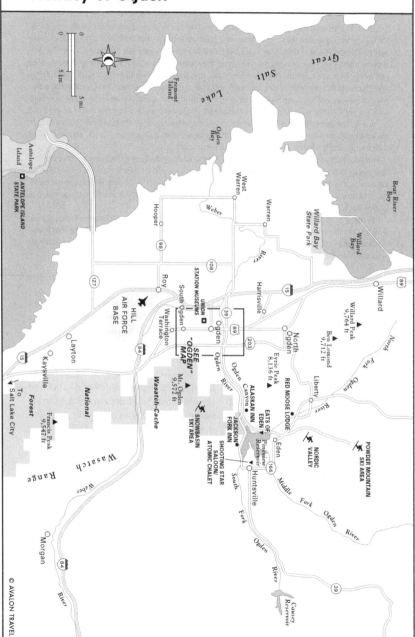

Vicinity of Ogden

Great Salt Lake

Salt Lake

Bear River Bay

Fremont Island

Ogden Bay

Antelope Island

ANTELOPE ISLAND STATE PARK

West Warren

Weber

Warren

Willard Bay State Park

Willard Bay

Hooper

98

108

Weber River

Harrisville

15

89

Willard

127

Roy

South Ogden

UNION STATION MUSEUMS

39

Ogden

89

203

North Ogden

Willard Peak 9,764 ft

Ben Lomond 9,712 ft

HILL AIR FORCE BASE

Washington Terrace

84

"SEE OGDEN" MAP

Ogden River

Eyrie Peak 8,136 ft

RED MOOSE LODGE

North Fork

Ogden

Liberty

Layton

15

Kaysville

Mt. Ogden 9,572 ft

SNOWBASIN SKI AREA

ALASKAN INN

EATS OF EDEN

JACKSON FORK INN

Pineview Reservoir

Eden

166

NORDIC VALLEY

POWDER MOUNTAIN SKI AREA

National Forest

Francis Peak 9,547 ft

Wasatch-Cache

SHOOTING STAR SALOON/ ATOMIC CHALET

Huntsville

South Fork Ogden River

Middle Fork Ogden River

To Salt Lake City

Wasatch Range

Weber River

Morgan

84

River

39

Causey Reservoir

© AVALON TRAVEL

Great Salt Lake

Since its discovery by fur trappers in the 1820s, this lake has both mystified and entranced visitors. Early explorers guessed that it must be connected to the ocean, not realizing that they had come across a body of water far saltier. Only the Dead Sea has a higher salt content. When Mormon pioneers first tried evaporating the lake water, they found the residue bitter tasting: The resulting salt is only 84 percent sodium chloride (table salt), and the remaining 16 percent is a mix of sulfates and chlorides of magnesium, calcium, and potassium. The lake's northern arm, isolated by a railroad causeway, contains the highest mineral concentrations—about twice those of the southern arm. Bacteria and algae grow in such numbers that they sometimes tint the water orange-red or blue-green. A tiny brine shrimp (Artemia salina) and two species of brine fly (Ephydra sp.) are about all that can live in the lake. The lake attracts more than 257 species of birds, depending on the season, and is a major stop for millions of migratory birds.

The lake is always changing—rising with spring snowmelt, then falling due to evaporation that peaks in late summer and autumn. Long-term changes have affected the lake too: Climate variations and diversion of river water for irrigation have caused a 21-foot difference between record low and high levels, and the lake's size has varied dramatically, from 900 square miles at the lowest water level to 2,500 square miles at the highest.

For many who just want to see and perhaps swim in the lake, the easiest access is along I-80, which skirts the southern shores of the lake and offers the **Great Salt Lake State Park** and the **Saltair** event space; at Antelope Island State Park, near Ogden in northern Utah, a causeway links the island to the mainland.

for sailboats and kayaks and a historic ranch house. The visitors center offers exhibits on the island's natural and human history. Rates for **campsites** (reservations 800/322-3770, http://utahstateparks.reserveamerica.com, $13) include the park's day-use fee. Showers and restrooms are available in the swimming area in the northwest corner of the island. Take I-15 exit 332, near Layton, and then drive nine miles west to the start of the causeway and the entrance booth.

Archaeologists have found prehistoric sites showing that Native Americans came here long ago, perhaps on a land bridge during times of low water levels. In 1843, explorers John Frémont and Kit Carson rode their horses across a sandbar to the island and named it after the antelope (pronghorn) herds that the party hunted for food. The Fielding Garr Ranch, on the southeast side of the island, was established in 1848 and operated until it became part of the park in 1981.

Antelope Island is now home to more than 600 bison as well as deer, bighorn sheep, pronghorn, and other wildlife. The best place

to see bison is usually along the road on the east side of the island near the ranch. The yearly bison roundup (late Oct.) is a big event for both cowboys and visitors: The bison are driven to corrals on the north end of the island and given veterinary checkups. Thanks largely to its population of brine flies and shrimp, Great Salt Lake attracts a wide variety of birds and is an important migratory stop. Antelope Island is a good place to look for eared grebes, avocets, black-necked stilts, willets, sanderlings, long-billed curlews, burrowing owls, chukars, and all sorts of raptors. The same insect life that attracts birds can attack visitors, especially during May-June; come prepared to do battle with no-see-ums.

EAST OF OGDEN
Ogden Canyon

Cliffs rise thousands of feet above narrow Ogden Canyon, just barely allowing Highway 39 and the Ogden River to squeeze through. In autumn, the fiery reds of maples and the golden hues of oaks add color to this scenic drive deep within the Wasatch Range. Ogden

Canyon begins on the eastern edge of Ogden and emerges about six miles later, at Pineview Reservoir in the broad Ogden Valley.

This fertile agricultural basin is a crossroads for recreationalists. In winter, skiers turn south from the reservoir to Snowbasin Ski Area and north to Nordic Valley and Powder Mountain ski areas. Summer visitors have a choice of staying at swimming beaches and campgrounds on the shore of Pineview Reservoir or heading to canyons and mountain peaks in the Wasatch Range.

Pineview Reservoir

This many-armed lake on the Ogden River provides excellent boating, fishing, waterskiing, and swimming (elev. 4,900 feet). For day-tripping, **the Bluffs** offers sandy beaches and shaded picnic areas at Cemetery Point on the lake's east side (day-use only, $13). A marina with boat ramp, docks, and a snack bar is nearby; follow Highway 39 to the Huntsville turnoff (10.5 miles east of Ogden), then turn west and go two miles. **Middle Inlet** (day-use $12) is another beach area, 1.5 miles north of Huntsville, on the lake's western shore, with a boat ramp, a small store, a dock, slips, fuel, and storage. **North Arm Wildlife Viewing Trail** makes a 0.4-mile loop at the north end of the reservoir, where the North Fork of the Ogden River joins the reservoir; the trail, built especially for wildlife viewing, is off Highway 162. The **Anderson Cove campground** (reservations 877/444-6777, www.recreation.gov, May-late Sept., $22), on the south shore, is the reservoir's main camping spot; it's only 10 miles east of Ogden.

Accommodations

A fun place to stay is the ★ **Atomic Chalet** (5917 E. 100 S., Huntsville, 801/745-0538, www.atomicchalet.com, summer $100, ski season $130), a B&B right on Pineview Reservoir near Snowbasin. It's a lodge-like building with a casual and relaxed vibe, and it's a favorite of skiers in winter, when a two-night minimum stay is required. All three guest rooms have private baths, fridges, TVs, and DVD players.

At the **Jackson Fork Inn** (7345 E. 900 S., Huntsville, 801/745-0051 or 800/609-9466, www.jacksonforkinn.com, $90-170), at milepost 18 on Highway 39, loft bedrooms are up a spiral staircase from a living area or second bedroom; this inn, which started out as a barn, also has a popular restaurant.

On the northern arm of Pineview Reservoir is a charming log B&B, the **Snowberry Inn** (1315 N. Hwy. 158, Eden, 801/745-2634, www.snowberryinn.com, $99-139). The inn overlooks the reservoir and provides access for water sports and swimming, while Ogden-area ski resorts are only 15 minutes away. All eight guest rooms come with private baths; guests share a hot tub, a billiard table, and a TV room.

A number of condo developments have sprung up in the Ogden Valley to serve the needs of skiers at the local ski areas. For a selection of condo options, check out the listings at www.lakesideresortproperties.com.

Campgrounds

A couple of campgrounds are on the south shore of Pineview Reservoir: **Anderson Cove** (801/625-5306, www.recreation.gov, May-late Sept., $22 plus $9 reservation fee) and **Jefferson Hunt** (801/625-5306, June-Sept., $18, no reservations). Both are quite close to the highway.

The **Maples Campground** (801/625-5306, June-Sept., no drinking water, free) is nestled among maples and aspens at 6,200 feet elevation in the mountains near Snowbasin Ski Area. Drive to the ski area's lower parking lot (marked "Lower Shop"), and then turn west and go 1.5 miles on a gravel road.

Travel Highway 39 east from Huntsville to find eight U.S. Forest Service campgrounds ($18) within 10 miles. Most of these campgrounds have water. **Perception Park** (reservations 877/444-6777, www.recreation.gov), 7.5 miles east of Huntsville, was specially built to accommodate people with disabilities. Some sites can be reserved.

The **Weber County Memorial Park** (801/399-8491, first-come, first-served, $18) is one mile down the paved road to Causey Reservoir, a narrow crescent-shaped lake in the upper South Fork of the Ogden River. A paved road in the park crosses the river to individual sites; three group sites can be reserved. Water is available late May-late September. The turnoff for Causey Reservoir is on Highway 39 one mile east of Willows Campground. **Monte Cristo Campground** (Highway 39, between mileposts 48 and 49, 40 miles east of Ogden, 21 miles west of Woodruff, July-Nov., $18) sits at 8,400 feet elevation in mountain forests of spruce, fir, and aspen.

Food

Some of the Ogden area's favorite places to eat are nestled in the bucolic Ogden Valley, just minutes from downtown Ogden. The little town of Huntsville offers a couple of places to eat and Utah's oldest bar—the ★ **Shooting Star Saloon** (7345 E. 200 S., 801/745-2002, noon-9pm Mon.-Sat., 2pm-8pm Sun., sandwiches $6-10), in business since 1879. This is a favorite place to come for burgers; the signature model combines a burger and a hot dog. There's interesting graffiti in the restrooms, and the bar boasts the stuffed head of an enormous St. Bernard dog that is rumored to be the subject of Jack London's *Call of the Wild*.

Downtown Huntsville is also home to the ★ **Huntsville Barbecue Company** (235 S. 7400 E., 801/745-2745, www.texaspridebarbecue.com, 11am-8pm Tues.-Sat., $6-13), serving slow-cooked Texas-style beef brisket, pulled pork, ribs, smoked chicken, and sausage as well as a full range of side dishes, including a tasty broccoli slaw.

A fun place to eat near Eden is **Eats of Eden** (2529 N. Hwy. 162, 801/745-8618, www.eatsofedenutah.com, 11:30am-9pm Tues.-Sat., $8-11), which serves good sandwiches on homemade bread; the pizza hits the spot after a day of skiing.

An old general store houses **Carlos and**

Utah's oldest bar is still a good place for burgers.

Harley's Fresh-Mex Cantina (5510 E. 2200 N., Eden, 801/745-8226, www.carlosandharleys.com, 11am-9pm daily, $8-22); during the summer, you can eat your Tex-Mex food outdoors.

Harley and Buck's (3900 N. Wolf Creek Dr., Eden, 801/745-2060, http://harleyandbucks.com, 5pm-9pm Tues.-Sun., $9-26) is an attractive restaurant on the road to Powder Mountain, with dinners ranging from burgers to pasta to steaks and seafood—basically it is well-prepared, slightly upscale American comfort food.

Getting There

Ogden Canyon begins on the eastern edge of Ogden and extends six miles to Pineview Reservoir in the broad Ogden Valley. Reach the canyon from Ogden by heading east on 12th Street (take I-15 exit 347).

SKI AREAS

Some of the best downhill skiing slopes in Utah are found in the vicinity of Ogden.

Snowbasin

Snowbasin (3925 E. Snowbasin Rd., Huntsville, 801/620-1000 or 888/437-5488, snow report 801/620-1100, www.snowbasin. com) was gussied up substantially for the 2002 Winter Olympics when it hosted the men's and women's downhill, super-G, and combined competitions. Snowbasin, which is owned by Sun Valley, is now one of Utah's largest ski areas, with an excellent lift system, great panoramic views, and few crowds. Although it gets a bit less snow than the Cottonwood resorts, Snowbasin is well equipped with snow-making machines.

Terrain and Lifts

With more than 3,200 acres of terrain and relatively few other skiers and snowboarders, there's almost always room to roam here. The area is well covered with speedy lifts, meaning that you can spend more time skiing and less time standing in line or sitting on pokey chairlifts. Four triple chairlifts, two quads, two gondolas, and a short 15-person tram serve 113 runs, of which 20 percent are rated beginner, 50 percent intermediate, and 30 percent expert; snowboarding is allowed. The longest run is three miles and drops 2,400 feet in elevation.

With 40 percent of trails marked with black diamonds, Snowbasin is clearly an expert skier's dream. The north side of the mountain (the John Paul area) has incredible expert terrain—long and *steep*. However, John Paul is sometimes closed for races. There are also extra-black chutes off the top of the Strawberry Express gondola. Several terrain parks include lots of rails, a large pipe, and many other features. But intermediate skiers can also have a good, non-terrifying time here. The Strawberry area in particular is full of nicely groomed, long blue cruisers. Beginners will find limited territory but a couple of nice long runs.

Ski season at Snowbasin normally runs Thanksgiving-mid-April. Adult lift tickets are $73 full-day, $60 half-day (sold starting at 12:15pm); youth rates are $44 full-day, $35 half-day; ages 65-74 pay $60 full-day, $44 half-day, and people over age 75 pay $22 full-day, $17 half-day.

Near parking area 2, find a 26-kilometer **Nordic area** groomed for classic and skate cross-country skiing (free) and a lift-assisted **tubing hill** (1 ride $5, all day $30).

Snowbasin offers a ski school, a ski shop, rentals, and three day lodges. Of particular note is the outdoor ice rink at Needles Lodge (801/620-1021), at the top of the Needles gondola.

Summer Activities

The lifts at Snowbasin remain open in summer for hikers ($16) and bikers ($25), making it easy to reach the high country. In addition, Snowbasin sponsors a series of Sunday afternoon concerts at Earl's Lodge (801/621-1000), located at the base of the ski runs. Hikers can pull off the ski area access road to hike the **Green Pond Trail,** which heads a relatively gentle 2.5 miles up to a picnic area and the pond.

Nordic Valley

Nordic Valley (Eden, 801/745-3511, www. nordicvalley.com), formerly called Wolf Mountain, is the closest to Ogden and is especially popular with families. It's an unintimidating place to learn to ski. Two double chairlifts and a magic carpet serve 19 runs and a terrain park. About 35 percent of the territory is beginner-level, 45 percent intermediate, and 20 percent expert. Elevation drop is 1,000 feet. You can ski at night too—all runs are under lights Monday-Saturday. The season runs daily early December-late March. Adult lift tickets cost $45 full-day, $23 half-day, and $20 at night; children's rates are $19 full-day, $14 half-day, and $18 at night. Prices bump up a couple of dollars on holidays. The resort has a ski school, a ski shop, and a day lodge. It's 15 miles northeast of Ogden; go through Ogden Canyon, turn left at Pineview Dam, and follow the signs.

Powder Mountain

If you've ever wanted to take up snow-kiting,

Powder Mountain (Hwy. 158, 8000 N. 5100 E., Eden, snow report 801/745-3771, office 801/745-3772, www.powdermountain.com) is the place to do it: Here you'll find lessons ($75), kites, and harnesses.

But, of course, Powder Mountain, a family-owned resort, is mostly about skiing and boarding. One double chairlift, a triple, and two quads (one fixed and the other detachable) reach two different peaks and serve more than 135 runs (25 percent beginner, 40 percent intermediate, and 35 percent expert). Three surface tows supplement the chairlifts for beginners; for expert skiers, there is a huge skiable area that's not lift-served (snowcats are often used to access more remote areas). High elevations of 6,895-8,900 feet catch plentiful powder snow. You can ski at night from the Sundown lift until 9pm. Powder Mountain's season lasts mid-November-mid-April. Adult lift tickets cost $69 full-day, $59 half-day, and $24 for night skiing; ages 7-12 are $37 full- or half-day, $19 night; ages 62-69 pay $52 full-day, $47 half-day, $19 night; seniors ages 70-79 pay $35 for any lift ticket. Facilities include a ski school, ski shops, rentals, and three day lodges. Powder Mountain is 19 miles northeast of Ogden; drive through Ogden Canyon, turn left at Pineview Dam, and follow the signs. In summer, mountain bikers are free to use the trails, but there is no lift-assisted hiking or biking.

Accommodations and Food

Powder Mountain is the only one of these Ogden-area ski resorts with slope-side lodging; the **Columbine Inn** (801/745-1414, www.columbineinnutah.com) has simple hotel-style guest rooms ($80-180) as well as condos, suites, and cabins with full kitchens and fireplaces ($1500-540). Rates are much lower in summer.

Most skiers and boarders drive up from Salt Lake City or Ogden; the Ogden Valley lodgings are also quite handy, with a number of B&Bs and condos catering to skiers.

Dining options are pretty limited: You can eat at casual or fancy places at Snowbasin such as **Earl's Lodge** (801/621-1000), the mountaintop **Needles Lodge** (801/620-1021, 9am-4pm Sun.-Fri., 9am-8pm Sat. in ski season, $6-20), or at **John Paul Lodge** (801/620-1021, 9am-3pm daily in ski season). Lunch will set you back $10-15 at any of these places.

GOLDEN SPIKE NATIONAL HISTORIC SITE

At 12:47pm on May 10, 1869, rails from the East Coast and the West Coast met for the first time. People across the country closely followed telegraph reports as dignitaries and railroad officials made their speeches and drove the last spikes, then everyone broke out in wild celebration. The joining of rails at this 4,905-foot-high windswept pass in Utah's Promontory Mountains marked a new chapter in the growth of the United States. A transcontinental railroad at last linked both sides of the nation.

History

The Central Pacific and Union Pacific Railroads, eager for land grants and bonuses, had both been laying track at a furious pace and grading the lines far ahead. So great was the momentum that the grader crews didn't stop when they met but laid parallel grades for 250 miles across Utah. Finally, Congress decided to join the rails at Promontory Summit and stop the wasteful duplication of effort. A ragged town of tents, boxcars, and hastily built wooden shacks sprang up along a single muddy street. Outlaws and crooked gambling houses earned Promontory Summit an awful reputation as a real hell-on-wheels town. The party ended six months later when the railroads moved the terminal operations to Ogden. Soon only a depot, roundhouse, helper engines, and other rail facilities remained. The Lucin Cutoff across Great Salt Lake bypassed the long, twisting grades of Promontory Summit in 1904 and dramatically reduced traffic along the old route. The final blow came in 1942, when the rails were torn up for scrap to feed wartime industries.

Golden Spike National Historic Site

★ Golden Spike Visitor Center

The Golden Spike National Historic Site, authorized by Congress in 1965, re-creates this momentous episode of railroad history. The **Golden Spike Visitor Center** (32 miles west of Brigham City, 435/471-2209, www.nps.gov/gosp, 9am-5pm daily except Thanksgiving, Christmas, and New Year's Day, vehicles $7 summer, $5 winter, cyclists $4 summer, $3 winter) offers exhibits and programs that illustrate the difficulties of building the railroad and portrays the officials and workers who made it possible. A short slide show introduces Promontory Summit's history. A 20-minute program, *The Golden Spike,* presents a more detailed account of building the transcontinental railroad. Rangers give talks several times a day in summer. An exhibit room has changing displays on railroading, and historical markers behind the visitors center indicate the spot where the last spike was driven.

The two locomotives that met here in 1869,

Central Pacific's *Jupiter* and Union Pacific's *119,* succumbed to scrap yards around the turn of the 20th century. However, they have been born again in authentic replicas. Every day in summer, the trains steam along a short section of track from the engine house to the historic spot. These runs include arrivals of the *Jupiter* and *119* at 10am and 10:30am, steam demonstrations of both locomotives at 1pm, and departures of the *119* and the *Jupiter* at 4pm and 4:30pm. You can't ride on the engines; they're here mostly for photo ops. During the winter, the locomotives are stored in the engine house; tours are usually available at 10am, 11:30am, 1pm, 2:30pm, and 3:30pm daily from early October until the trains come outside again at the beginning of May.

The annual **Last Spike Ceremony** (May 10) reenacts the original celebration with great fanfare. The **Railroaders Festival** in August has special exhibits, a spike-driving contest, reenactments, handcar races, and entertainment. A sales counter offers a good selection of books on railroading, Utah history, and natural history as well as postcards and souvenirs.

From I-15 exit 368 for Brigham City, head west on Highway 13 and Highway 83 and follow the signs for 29 miles. If you're coming from the north, it's about 29 miles from I-84's exit 40; follow signs to Highway 83 and the Golden Spike.

ATK

Many buildings of this giant aerospace corporation lie scattered across the countryside about six miles northeast of the historic site. You can't tour the facility, but you can see a display of missiles, rocket engines, and a space-shuttle booster casing in front of the administrative offices. Turn north and go two miles on Highway 83 at the junction with the Golden Spike National Historic Site road, eight miles east of the visitors center.

LOGAN

Without question one of the most appealing towns in Utah, Logan (pop. 48,000;

The Golden Spike Ceremony

In grade school, many of us learned that when the Union Pacific and Central Pacific Railroads met, a solid gold ceremonial stake was driven to mark the spot. One yearns to go to Promontory and pry out that golden spike. But the real story tells us the event was marked with no fewer than two golden spikes, both from California; a silver spike contributed by the state of Nevada; and an iron spike with its body plated in silver and its cap plated in gold, courtesy of the state of Arizona.

A polished myrtle-wood tie was placed at the site to receive the spikes, protecting the precious metals from the damage of driving them into the earth. At the ceremony, Central Pacific president Leland Stanford (founder of Stanford University) took the first swing at the final spike and missed it entirely—but did hit the tie. Union Pacific vice president and general manager Thomas C. Durant next tried his hand and missed not only the spike but the rail and the tie as well. A bystander was finally summoned from the crowd to tap the stake home.

Shortly after the formal ceremony concluded, the valuable spikes and tie were removed and standard fittings were substituted to link the nation by rail.

surrounding area pop. just over 125,000) is surrounded by the lush dairy and farmlands of the Cache Valley and by the lofty peaks of the Bear River Range. Of all the mountain communities in the American West that advertise their Swiss or Bavarian aspirations, Logan comes closest to actually looking alpine.

The town itself is built on stair-like terraces that mark the ancient shorelines of Lake Bonneville. Logan is also one of the state's festival centers, enlivened by theater, music, and performance series in summer. As everywhere in Utah, the outdoors is never far away: The mountains provide abundant year-round recreation, including scenic drives, boating on nearby Bear Lake, camping, fishing, hiking, and skiing. Logan also makes a good base camp if you are visiting more remote destinations, such as the Golden Spike National Historic Site or Bear Lake.

Sights

Logan has a lovely little downtown, filled with handsome architecture, lined with trees, and flanked by parks. A walk along Main Street is a pleasant diversion, but it's even more fun to walk through the old neighborhoods around downtown. Head west on Center Street for some of the grander historic homes; a good brochure from the **Cache Valley Visitors**

Bureau (199 N. Main St., 435/755-1890, www.tourcachevalley.com, 8am-5pm Mon.-Fri., 10am-2pm Sat. June-Aug., 8am-5pm Mon.-Fri. Sept.-May) details the history of many of these houses.

Mormon Temple, Tabernacle, and History Museum

The distinctive castellated **Mormon Temple** (175 N. 300 E.) rises from a prominent hill just east of downtown. After Brigham Young chose this location in 1877, church members labored for seven years to complete the temple. Architect Truman O. Angell, designer of the Salt Lake temple, oversaw construction. Timber and blocks of limestone came from nearby Logan Canyon. Only Mormons engaged in sacred work may enter the temple, but visitors are welcome on the grounds to view the exterior.

The tabernacle is also a fine example of early Mormon architecture. Construction of the stone structure began in 1865, but other priorities—building the temple and ward meetinghouses—delayed dedication until 1891. The public may enter the tabernacle, which is downtown at Main and Center Streets.

At the **Cache Museum** (160 N. Main St., 435/752-5139, 10am-4pm Tues.-Fri. June-Labor Day, free), exhibits show how Logan's

Logan

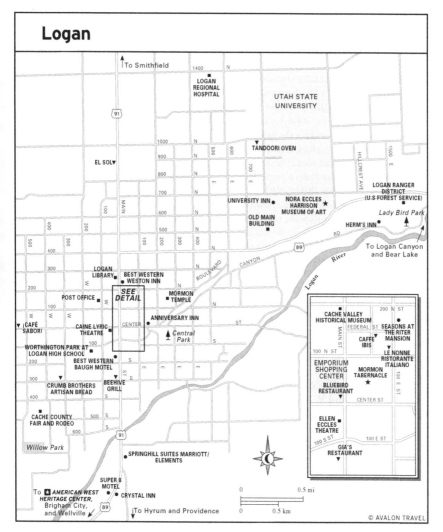

early settlers lived. You'll see their tools, household furnishings, clothing, art, and photographs. It is also the chamber of commerce office.

Willow Park Zoo

The small **Willow Park Zoo** (419 W. 700 S., 435/716-9265, www.loganutah.org, 10am-6pm daily spring-fall, $2.50 adults, $1.50 ages 3-11) displays exotic birds such as an Andean condor, a golden pheasant, a mitered conure,

and more familiar golden and bald eagles, peacocks, swans, and ducks. In fact, Willow Park has one of the greatest waterfowl collections in the region, showcasing more than 100 species. You'll also see lemurs, red foxes, coyotes, elk, deer, bobcats, and more. The setting offers walkways beside shady willow trees, and children can feed the ducks, geese, and trout. Additionally, Willow Park offers picnic areas and a playground among its large, shady trees.

★ American West Heritage Center

The **American West Heritage Center** (4025 S. U.S. 89/91, Wellsville, 435/245-6050, www. awhc.org, 11am-4pm Tues.-Sat. June-Aug., check website for complex fall and winter season openings, $5 adults, $4 students and over age 54, $3 ages 3-11, higher prices for some seasonal events), six miles southwest of Logan, is an institution that combines the function of a visitors center with a look into the history and culture of the Old West. The center is quite ambitious, and it includes a permanent living-history installation that highlights the lives and lifestyles of the Native Americans of the Cache Valley, the fur-trapping mountain men who arrived in the 1820s, and the pioneer Mormon farmers who settled here starting in the 1860s. Check the calendar for events such as mountain-man rallies, cowboy poetry recitations, art shows, harvest fairs, pioneer cooking contests, and so on. Also on the premises is the **Northern Utah Welcome Center** (9am-5pm Tues.-Fri., 10am-5pm Sat. June-Aug., hours vary Sept.-May), which provides visitor information, an introduction to local history, and a gift shop.

Logan is situated in a verdant valley that is filled with dairy farms.

Adjacent to the center and incorporated into it is the **Ronald V. Jensen Living Historical Farm,** an outdoor museum that re-creates life on a Cache Valley family farm in 1917. Workers dress in period clothing to plow soil, thresh grain, milk cows, shear sheep, and butcher hogs. Buildings here include an 1875 farmhouse, a summer kitchen, a root cellar, a smokehouse, a blacksmith shop, a horse barn, a sheep shed, and a privy or two. Special demonstrations take place all through the year, usually on Saturday. In fall, the cornfield is converted into a maze.

Utah State University

In 1888 a federal land-grant program opened the way for the territorial legislature to establish the Agricultural College of Utah. The school grew to become Utah State University (USU, www.usu.edu) in 1957 and now has eight colleges, 45 departments, and a graduate school. USU's "Aggies" number more than 25,000, led by 2,500 faculty and staff. The university has continued its original purpose of agricultural research while diversifying into atmospheric and space sciences, ecology, creative arts, social sciences, and other fields.

Attractions on campus include the **Nora Eccles Harrison Museum of Art** (650 N. 1100 E., 435/797-0163, http://artmuseum. usu.edu, 10am-5pm Tues.-Sat., free), one of the largest permanent collections of art in Utah; the student center; and several libraries. **Old Main Building,** with its landmark bell tower, was begun one year after the college was founded and has housed nearly every office and department in the school at one time or another. The oak-shaded campus is northeast of downtown on a bench left by a northern arm of prehistoric Lake Bonneville.

The USU dairy department is justifiably proud of its milk, cheese, and ice cream. Get a double scoop at **Aggie Ice Cream** (750 N. 1200 E., 435/797-2112, https://aggieicecream. usu.edu, 9am-10pm Mon.-Fri., 10am-10pm

Logan's tabernacle

opera and its hearty success. Michael Ballam, a Logan-area native and professional opera singer, decided in 1993 to start an opera company in Utah; at the same time, Logan's old movie palace and vaudeville hall, the Capitol Theatre, was remodeled and transformed into a world-class performing arts center. Renamed the Ellen Eccles Theatre, the theater has excellent acoustics and an intimate yet formal atmosphere that perfectly suited Ballam's operatic vision. Utah Festival Opera currently stages four operas and a number of music performances during its month-long season.

Old Lyric Repertory Company

The **Old Lyric** (28 W. Center St., 435/797-8022) provides a summer season of musicals, comedies, and dramas in the historic **Caine Lyric Theatre** in downtown Logan. Visiting equity actors lead the shows produced by Utah State University's drama department. Other Logan-area summer stock theaters also present light comedies and musicals.

Recreation

Parks, Swimming, and Tennis

Willow Park (450 W. 700 S.) is a good place for a picnic and has the added attractions of a small zoo, a playground, volleyball courts, and a softball field. **Bicentennial Park** (100 S. Main St.) offers picnic spots downtown. The outdoor **Logan Aquatic Center** (451 S. 500 W., 435/716-9266, June-Labor Day) has a 50-meter lap pool, a diving pool, and a kids pool with two waterslides. The **Sports Academy** (1655 N. 200 E., 435/753-7500) has indoor and outdoor pools and all the features of a good gym. The **Community Recreation Center** (195 S. 100 W., 435/750-9877) features tennis and handball-racquetball courts, basketball, volleyball, a weight room, an indoor track, table tennis, a sauna, and a whirlpool. **Tennis courts** are also available at **Mount Logan Middle School** (875 N. 200 E.), Central Park (85 S. 300 E.), and Worthington Park at Logan High School (162 W. 100 S.).

Sat. May-Sept., 9am-9pm Mon.-Fri., 10am-9pm Sat. Oct.-Apr.).

Entertainment and Events

One of the best reasons to visit Logan is to catch the community's high-quality arts and music festivals. People from all over Utah and the intermountain West come to Logan to take in an opera, a chamber music concert, or an evening of theater in this scenic alpine valley. The **Cache Valley Tourism Council** (199 N. Main St., 435/755-1890, www.tourcache-valley.com) can fill you in on what's happening in the area.

Utah Festival Opera Company

The professional **Utah Festival Opera Company** (59 S. 100 W., 435/750-0300 or 800/262-0074, www.ufoc.org) takes over the beautifully restored **Ellen Eccles Theatre** (43 S. Main St.) mid-July-mid-August. The fact that a small Utah agricultural college town has its own prominent opera company is slightly unusual. Two factors account for the

Golf

The cool and verdant Cache Valley is especially suited to golf, and there are some dandy courses in the Logan area. Play at the 18-hole municipal **Logan River Golf Course** (550 W. 1000 S., 435/750-0123, $28); the 18-hole **Birch Creek Golf Course** (600 E. Center St., Smithfield, 435/563-6825, $26-28), seven miles north; or the small but pretty nine-hole **Sherwood Hills** (Sardine Canyon, U.S. 89/91, 435/245-6055, $15 for nine holes), 13 miles southwest, which is part of the Sardine Canyon conference center, hotel, and spa (435/245-6424). Facilities here include swimming pools, horseback riding, cross-country ski trails, racquetball, and tennis.

Winter Sports

Ice-skating is popular in winter at **Central Park** (85 S. 300 E.). The **Beaver Creek Lodge** (Hwy. 39, 435/946-4485 or 800/946-4485, http://beavercreeklodge.com), 28 miles east of Logan on Highway 39, offers snowmobile rentals plus cross-country ski trails in winter. Just next door is the **Beaver Mountain Ski Area** (Garden City, 435/946-3610 or 435/753-0921, www.skithebeav.com, 9am-4pm daily early Dec.-late Mar., $45 adults, $35 over age 64 and under age

12), a family-owned downhill area served by four lifts.

Accommodations
$50-100

Logan's motels are generally well maintained and moderately priced. For a basic, inexpensive guest room at a busy road junction south of downtown, try the **Super 8 Motel** (865 S. U.S. 89/91, 435/753-8883, $54-66). Right downtown, the ★ **Best Western Baugh Motel** (153 S. Main St., 435/752-5220, www.bestwesternbaugh.com, $89-119) offers large guest rooms, an outdoor swimming pool, and an exercise room.

Head uphill from downtown for a guest room at the ★ **University Inn** (4300 Old Main Hill, 435/797-0017 or 800/231-5634, http://uicc.usu.edu, $74-114), a modern, mirrored-glass building on the USU campus. Although it's a ways from downtown, it's convenient to university-area restaurants and the Aggie Ice Cream Shop—in fact, guest rooms come with vouchers for free ice cream and a chance to work off some of the butterfat at the university's rec center.

The recently remodeled **Crystal Inn** (853 S. Main St., 435/752-0707 or 800/280-0707, www.crystalinnlogan.com, $83-173) has an

the Ellen Eccles Theatre, home to the Utah Festival Opera Company

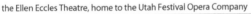

indoor pool, a fitness room, a hot tub, and nicely furnished guest rooms with efficiency kitchens. In addition to the more common complimentary breakfast, the Crystal Inn offers a free light dinner. The inn's shuttle van can take you from the busy south end of Main Street to the opera or to events at the university.

Over $100

The ★ **Best Western Weston Inn** (250 N. Main St., 435/752-5700 or 800/280-0707, www.westoninn.com, $109-145) has a great location in the center of downtown as well as an indoor pool, a hot tub, and complimentary breakfast; it accepts some pets.

The **Springhill Suites Marriott** (635 S. Riverwoods Pkwy., 435/750-5180, www.marriott.com, $129-154) is the most upscale hotel in town, with modern decor, a pool and a fitness center, and complimentary breakfast. Although its address is confusing, it's basically on South Main Street, right next to the equally upscale Elements restaurant.

Like most **Holiday Inn Express** (2235 N. Main St., 435/752-3444 or 877/859-5095, www.hiexpress.com, $131-145) properties, the one at the north end of Logan is fairly new and quite comfortable, providing the chain's reliably nice beds and linens and an indoor pool.

One of the more unusual places to stay in Logan is **Anniversary Inn** (169 E. Center St., 435/752-3443, www.anniversaryinn.com, $199-299), a complex of heritage homes with more than 30 themed guest rooms, including the "Bikers Roadhouse." The decor is fun, but it can be a bit over-the-top. All guest rooms have big-screen TVs and private baths with jetted tubs; breakfast is delivered to your room. Children are not permitted, and reservations are required.

Just a block off Main Street in a pretty neighborhood, **Seasons at the Riter Mansion** (168 N. 100 E., 435/752-7727 or 800/478-7459, www.theritermansion.com, $99-169) is a B&B that's a popular spot for weddings (don't plan to stay here on a June weekend). Unlike many B&Bs, families with kids are welcome; of the six guest rooms, one is a family suite, and another is geared toward business travelers.

Campgrounds

U.S. Forest Service campgrounds, six miles east of town on U.S. 89 in Logan Canyon, are the best bets for tent campers. At Hyrum State Park, the **Lake View Campground** (Hwy. 165, 435/245-6866, reservations 800/322-3770, http://stateparks.utah.gov, $16) is about seven miles south of town. **Traveland RV Park** (2020 S. U.S. 89/91, 435/787-2020, www.travelandrvpark.net, year-round, $38) has a few tent sites ($20) but is best for large RVs.

Food

If you're looking for a really good cup of coffee, a pastry, or perhaps a salad for lunch, head to pleasantly alternative **Caffe Ibis** (52 Federal Ave., 435/753-4777, www.caffeibis.com, 6am-7pm Mon.-Sat., 8am-6pm Sun., $2-10). Another great spot for pastries and sandwiches is ★ **Crumb Brothers Artisan Bread** (291 S. 300 W., 435/792-6063, http://crumbbrothers.com, 7am-3pm Mon.-Fri., 8am-3pm Sun., $2-9), in a pretty setting near many of Logan's historic homes.

If you're headed up Logan Canyon, take a little detour onto the old highway to find hip **Herm's Inn** (1420 E. Canyon Rd., 435/792-4321, http://hermsinn.com, 7am-2pm daily, $5-12), housed in a historic brick building; it has a great full breakfast. Lunch features classic sandwiches (tuna melt, club) and salads (cobb).

It pays to venture to the university area to find **Tandoori Oven** (720 E. 1000 N., 435/750-6836, www.tandoorivenlogan.com, 11am-10pm Mon.-Sat., $9-16), part of a minimart. The Indian food is delicious, and the restaurant gets crowded at dinnertime.

Head to the old train depot at the west end of Center Street, where **¡Cafe Sabor!** (600 W. Center St., 435/752-8088, www.cafesabor.com, 11am-10pm Mon.-Thurs., 11am-11pm Fri.-Sat., $9-14) offers tasty Mexican and Southwest-inspired fare, including a few pasta dishes. The tortillas and salsas are all made fresh on the premises. There's outdoor dining on the shaded passenger platforms.

For something uniquely Loganesque, try the **Bluebird Restaurant** (19 N. Main St., 435/752-3155, 11am-9:30pm Mon.-Thurs., 11am-10pm Fri.-Sat., $5-12), a beautifully maintained soda fountain, chocolatier, and restaurant that appears unchanged since the 1930s. Except for the candy, the food is secondary to the atmosphere.

Another only-in-Utah place is the **Beehive Grill** (255 S. Main St., 435/753-2600, www.thebeehivegrill.com, 11:30am-10pm Sun.-Thurs., 11:30am-11pm Fri.-Sat., $7-17), a root beer brewpub. It's owned by the same people that brew beer at Moab Brewery, and it also serves the alcoholic stuff as well as better-than-average pub food, including vegan and gluten-free options.

Also a Logan tradition, **Gia's Restaurant** (119 S. Main St., 435/752-8384, www.giasrestaurant.com, 4pm-10pm Mon.-Sat., 9:30am-9pm Sun., $9-16) has an atmospheric dining room and is a good bet for a traditional Italian meal.

High-quality northern Italian cooking is served up in a charming atmosphere, with live jazz on weekend nights, at ★ Le

Nonne Ristorante Italiano (129 N. 100 E., 435/752-9577, www.lenonne.com, 5:30pm-9:30pm Mon.-Thurs., 11:30am-2pm and 5:30pm-9:30pm Fri.-Sat., $10-23). The chef-owner hails from Tuscany, and the cuisine reflects cooking learned from his *nonne* (grandmothers).

Jack's Wood Fired Oven (256 N. Main St., 435/754-7523, www.jackswoodfiredoven.blogspot.com, 11:30am-9pm Mon.-Thurs, 11:30am-10pm Fri.-Sat., $4-15) turns out tasty thin-crust pizza, easily the best in town.

One of the most stylish restaurants around these parts is **Elements** (640 S. 35 E., 435/750-5170, www.theelementsrestaurant.com, 11am-9pm Mon.-Thurs., 11am-10pm Fri.-Sat., $12-28), which serves well-prepared updated American cuisine from its location next to the Marriott Springhill Suites. Even the cheapest menu item, a burger with onion marmalade, buttermilk blue cheese, and applewood bacon, is quite good. Higher up the food chain, check out the Frenched pork chop served with molasses mustard glaze with bourbon apple butter. If the weather is nice, ask to be seated outside.

Information and Services

The **Cache Valley Visitors Bureau** (199 N.

¡Café Sabor! is in Logan's old railway depot.

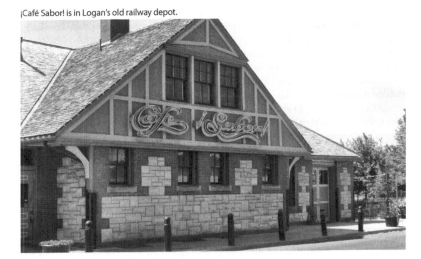

Main St., 435/755-1890, www.tourcachevalley.com, 8am-5pm Mon.-Fri.) is housed in a beautiful old courthouse downtown and has information for Cache and Rich Counties, including Logan and Bear Lake. To learn more about local history and architecture, ask for *Logan's Historic Main Street,* a brochure outlining a self-guided 45-minute walking tour. For recreation information and maps of the surrounding mountain country, visit the **Logan Ranger District Office** (1500 E. U.S. 89, 435/755-3620, 8am-4:30pm Mon.-Fri. fall-spring, 8am-5pm Mon.-Fri. summer), at the entrance to Logan Canyon.

Logan Regional Hospital (1400 N. 500 E., 435/716-1000) provides 24-hour emergency care. There is a **post office** (151 N. 100 W., 435/752-7246).

Getting There

Salt Lake Express (800/356-9796, www.saltlakeexpress.com) buses stop at several Logan hotels and make 12 trips a day to Salt Lake City; the fare is about $30. Free **city buses** (435/752-2877, www.cvtdbus.org) run throughout town. Pick up schedules and a map at the visitors bureau (199 N. Main St.).

VICINITY OF LOGAN
Crystal Hot Springs

Southwest of Logan, and just east of I-15, **Crystal Hot Springs** (8215 N. Hwy. 38, Honeyville, 435/279-8104, www.crystalhotsprings.net, 10am-10pm Mon.-Sat., 10am-8pm Sun. Memorial Day-Labor Day, noon-9pm Mon.-Thurs., noon-10pm Fri., 10am-10pm Sat., 11am-7pm Sun. Labor Day-Memorial Day, $6 adults, $4.50 seniors and ages 3-12) is fed by natural hot and cold springs. The little resort has a large swimming pool, a hot soaking pool, a waterslide, and campsites (tents $15, hookups $25). During the summer, the large pool is closed on Thursday for cleaning; during the winter, it is only open Friday night and Saturday-Sunday.

Hardware Ranch and Blacksmith Fork Canyon

The **Utah Division of Wildlife Resources** (435/753-6206, http://wildlife.utah.gov/hardwareranch) operates this ranch in the middle of the northern Wasatch Range to provide winter feed for herds of elk. In winter, concessionaires offer sleigh rides ($5 adults, $3 ages 4-8) for a closer look at the elk, and wagon rides if there's not enough snow. A **visitors center** (noon-5pm Mon. and Fri., 10am-5pm Sat.-Sun. mid-Dec.-Feb.), with displays, is also open in winter. During the spring calving season, you might see newborn baby elk. You're not likely to see elk here in the summer months, but the drive in is still pretty. Call before heading out; the ranch has some seasonal closures.

Logan Canyon

From its mouth on the east edge of Logan, Logan Canyon, with its steep limestone cliffs, winds more than 20 miles into the Bear River Range, a northern extension of the Wasatch Mountains. Paved U.S. 89 follows the canyon and is a designated scenic byway. If you're looking for a day trip out of Logan, just head up the canyon; you'll pass lots of picnic areas, campgrounds, fishing spots, and hiking trails where you can easily spend a few blissful hours.

Steep slopes on the west rise to rolling plateau country across the top of the range, and moderate slopes descend to Bear Lake on the east. The route climbs to an elevation of 7,800 feet at Bear Lake Summit, which offers a good view of the lofty Uintas of northeastern Utah. In autumn, maples of the lower canyon turn a brilliant crimson while aspens in the higher country are transformed to gold. Roadside geological signs explain features in Logan Canyon. Picnicking is free at picnic areas, but you have to pay to picnic at some campgrounds.

A mile-by-mile guide to the canyon is available from the **Cache Valley Visitors Bureau** (199 N. Main St., 435/755-1890, www.

Vicinity of Logan

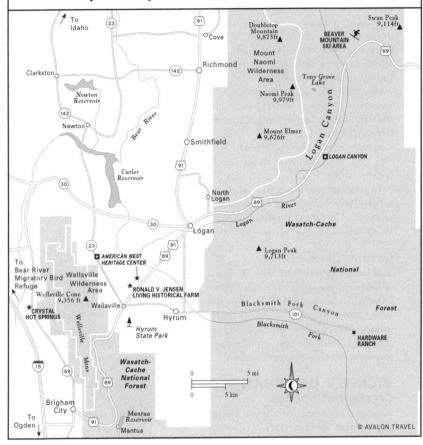

To Idaho

23

Cove

91

Clarkston

142

Richmond

Newton
Reservoir

142

Newton

Bear River

Smithfield

91

Cutler
Reservoir

30

North
Logan

89

River

30

Logan

Logan

Wasatch-Cache

23

91

89

AMERICAN WEST
HERITAGE CENTER

To
Bear River
Migratory Bird
Refuge

Wellsville
Wilderness
Area

Logan Peak
9,713ft

National

Wellsville Cone
9,356 ft

RONALD V. JENSEN
LIVING HISTORICAL FARM

Wellsville

Blacksmith Fork Canyon

Forest

CRYSTAL
HOT SPRINGS

Hyrum

101

Wellsville
Mtns

Hyrum
State Park

Blacksmith Fork

HARDWARE
RANCH

15

69

Wasatch-
Cache
National
Forest

89

0   5 mi

0   5 km

Brigham
City

Mantua
Reservoir

To
Ogden

91

Mantua

© AVALON TRAVEL

Doubletop
Mountain
9,873ft

Swan Peak
9,114ft

BEAVER
MOUNTAIN
SKI AREA

89

Mount
Naomi
Wilderness
Area

Tony Grove
Lake

Naomi Peak
9,979ft

Logan Canyon

Mount Elmer
9,676ft

LOGAN CANYON

tourcachevalley.com, 8am-5pm Mon.-Fri.) in Logan.

Hiking

A number of easy to moderate hikes make Logan Canyon a lovely and convenient destination for a little exercise and an eyeful of nature. Four miles up the canyon, **Riverside Nature Trail** winds along the Logan River between Spring Hollow and Guinavah Campgrounds, a 1.5-mile (one-way) stroll with good bird-watching opportunities. From Guinavah, you can loop back to Spring Hollow via the **Crimson Trail;** this more strenuous trail takes you up the limestone cliffs and down in another two miles. It takes its name from the autumn colors visible along the way. Five miles up is the **Wind Cave trailhead.** Wind Cave, with eroded caverns and arches, is one mile and a 1,100-foot climb from the trailhead.

Jardine Juniper Trail begins at Wood Camp Campground, 10 miles up the canyon. The trail climbs 1,900 vertical feet in 4.4 miles to Old Jardine, a venerable Rocky Mountain juniper tree. Still alive after 1,500 years, it measures about 27 feet in circumference and 45 feet high. A mile farther up the canyon is

Logan Cave, a 2,000-foot-long cavern where a gate protects the endangered Townsend's big-eared bats that nest and hibernate here.

Forest Road 174 takes off to the north about 20 miles from Logan and provides access to **Tony Grove Lake,** an exceptionally pretty high mountain lake (elev. 8,050 feet) with a nature trail, a campground, and trails into the Mount Naomi Wilderness. The eight-mile round-trip hike to Naomi Peak is known for its wildflower displays.

At **Bear Lake Summit,** 30 miles from Logan, the **Limber Pine Nature Trail** originates at the parking area on the right and terminates at a massive limber pine 25 feet in circumference and 44 feet high. At one time this tree was thought to be the world's oldest and largest limber pine, but a forestry professor at USU discovered that it is really five trees grown together and "only" about 560 years old. The easy, self-guided walk takes about an hour; Bear Lake can be seen to the east.

Skiing

Beaver Mountain Ski Area (Garden City, snow and road conditions 435/753-4822, office, ski school, and lift tickets 435/753-0921, www.skithebeav.com, 9am-4pm daily early Dec.-late Mar., $48 adults, $38 over age 65 and under age 11) operates four chairlifts serving 47 runs, the longest of which is 2.25 miles and drops 1,600 vertical feet. A cafeteria, ski shop, rentals, and lessons are available at the day lodge. Half-day passes are available for about $10 less. Go northeast 28 miles on U.S. 89, then north 1.5 miles on Highway 243.

Accommodations

A handsome timber and stone lodge, **Beaver Creek Lodge** (435/753-1707 or 800/946-4485, www.beavercreeklodge.com, $129-149) not only offers guest rooms but also has horseback trail rides, snowmobile rentals, and cross-country ski trails in winter. The layout and modest size of the lodge make it a good place for group get-togethers. The lodge is about 28 miles northeast on U.S. 89, just past the turnoff for Beaver Mountain Ski Area.

Campgrounds

There are 10 Forest Service campgrounds along U.S. 89 in Logan Canyon, so finding a place to pitch a tent is usually pretty easy. In the following listings, the higher prices denote double-size campsites. The closest ones to Logan are **Bridger** (no reservations, mid-May-early Sept., $13-26) and **Spring Hollow** (877/444-6777, www.recreation. gov, mid-May-mid-Oct., $15-30, $9 reservation fee) Campgrounds, three and four miles from town, respectively. **Wood Camp Campground** (U.S. 89, 435/755-3620, no reservations, mid-May-mid-Oct., $13) is 10 miles up Logan Canyon. **Tony Grove Campground** (877/444-6777, www.recreation.gov, mid-June-Sept., $15-30, $9 reservation fee) is 19 miles east of Logan at 8,100 feet elevation. Expect cool temps and possibly snow in summer. The 7,000-foot-high **Sunrise Campground** (877/444-6777, www. recreation.gov, late May-Sept., $15-30, $9 reservation fee), about 30 miles from Logan, has good views of Bear Lake.

TOOELE AND VICINITY

To sound like a native, pronounce the town's name "too-WILL-uh." The origin of the word is uncertain, but it may honor the Goshute chief Tuilla. The sprawling town (pop. 30,000) lies 34 miles west of Salt Lake City between the western foothills of the Oquirrh (OH-ker) Mountains and the Great Salt Lake. Mormon pioneers settled here in 1849 to farm and raise livestock, but today the major industries are the nearby Tooele Army Depot, the Dugway Proving Ground, and mining. In recent years, Tooele has become a bedroom community for Salt Lake City workers. Visitors wanting to know more about the region's history will enjoy the area's several museums.

Sights
Tooele Valley Railroad Museum

A steam locomotive and a collection of old railroad cars surround Tooele's original train station (1909), now the **Tooele Valley Railroad Museum** (35 N. Broadway,

435/882-2836, 1pm-4pm Tues.-Sat. Memorial Day-late Sept., donation). Step inside to see the restored station office and old photos showing railroad workers, steam engines, and trestle construction. Mining photos and artifacts illustrate life and work in the early days at Ophir, Mercur, Bauer, and other once-booming communities now faded to ghosts. Two railroad cars, once part of an Air Force mobile ballistic missile train, contain medical equipment and antique furniture. Outside, kids can ride the scale railway on some Saturdays, check out a caboose, or explore a replica of a mine.

Daughters of Utah Pioneers Museum

Meet Tooele's pioneers through hundreds of framed pictures and see their clothing and other possessions at the downtown **Pioneers Museum** (39 E. Vine St., 10am-4pm Fri.-Sat. May-Sept., free). The small stone building dates from 1867 and once served as a courthouse for Tooele County. The little log cabin next door, built in 1856, was one of the town's first residences.

★ Benson Grist Mill

Pioneers constructed the **Benson Grist Mill** (325 Hwy. 138, one block west of Mills

Junction, 435/882-7678, 10am-4pm Mon.-Sat. May-Oct., free), one of the oldest buildings in western Utah, eight miles north of Tooele in 1854. Wooden pegs and rawhide strips hold the timbers together. E. T. Benson, grandfather of past Mormon Church president Ezra Taft Benson, supervised its construction for the church. The mill produced flour until 1938, then ground only animal feed until closing in the 1940s. Local people began to restore the exterior in 1986. Much of the original machinery inside is still intact, and it offers a fascinating glimpse of 19th-century agricultural technology. Antique farm machinery, a granary, a log cabin, a blacksmith shop, and other buildings stand on the grounds to the east. Ruins of the Utah Wool Pullery, which once removed millions of tons of wool from pelts, stand to the west.

Donner-Reed Pioneer Museum

Early residents built this one-room adobe schoolhouse within the Grantsville fort walls in 1861. Today, the **Donner-Reed Pioneer Museum** (90 N. Cooley St., 10 miles northeast of Tooele in Grantsville, 435/884-3259, www.donner-reed-museum. org, open by appointment during the summer, free) honors the Donner-Reed wagon

Pioneers Museum in downtown Tooele

train of 1846. These pioneers crossed the Great Salt Lake Desert to the west with great difficulty, then became trapped by snow while attempting to shortcut through the Sierra Nevada to California. Of the 87 people who started the trip, only 47 desperate pioneers survived the harsh winter—by eating boiled boots and harnesses and the frozen flesh of dead companions. Museum displays include a large collection of guns and pioneer artifacts found abandoned on the salt flats, pottery, arrowheads, and other Native American artifacts. Outside, you can see Grantsville's original iron jail, an early log cabin, a blacksmith shop, and old wagons. Another adobe building across the street served as a church and dates from 1866.

Bonneville Seabase

Scuba divers can enjoy ocean-type diving in the middle of the mudflats. A natural pool at **Bonneville Seabase** (1600 N. Hwy. 138, 435/884-3874, www.seabase.net, 9am-3pm Thurs.-Fri., 8am-4pm Sat.-Sun., call for reservations) was found to have salinity so close to that of the ocean that marine creatures could thrive in it. Several dozen species have been introduced, including groupers, stingrays, triggerfish, damsel fish, clown fish, and lobsters. The springs are geothermally heated, so winter cold is no problem. The original pool has been expanded, and dredging created new pools. User fees run $15 per person; you can rent full equipment for scuba diving ($22) or snorkeling ($11). Bonneville Seabase is five miles northwest of Grantsville, or 15 miles northwest of Tooele. If you are coming directly on I-80, take exit 84, turn toward Grantsville, and drive five miles.

Accommodations

The **Oquirrh Motor Inn Motel & RV Resort** (8740 N. Hwy. 36, 801/250-0118, www.oquirrhinn.com, $65-68) is a comfortable motel north of town, near Great Salt Lake and I-80. If you are passing through, it's a good place to stay. In town, the ★ **American Inn and Suites** (491 S. Main St., 435/882-6100, www.americaninnandsuites.com, $109-119) offers full breakfasts, kitchenettes and efficiency kitchens, laundry facilities, a pool, and a spa. The **Hampton Inn** (461 S. Main St., 435/843-7700, $149-160) has a pool, a hot tub, and a free breakfast bar; each guest room has an efficiency kitchen.

Food

For a big breakfast anytime, head north to

Donner-Reed Pioneer Museum

Erda and hang with the locals at **Virg's** (4025 N. Hwy. 36, 435/833-9988, 7am-3pm Mon.-Thurs., 7am-9pm Fri.-Sat., 8am-3pm Sun., $6-8). **Thai House** (297 N. Main St., 435/882-7579, 10am-9pm Mon.-Sat., $8-9) is another good bet. If you're thirsty and looking for some good pub grub, head to **Bonneville Brewery** (1641 N. Main St., 435/248-0646, www.bonnevillebrewery.com, 10am-11pm daily, $7-13), a handsome brewpub with good burgers, pizza, salads, and such specialties as pork tenderloin topped with bourbon apples.

Information

The **Tooele Chamber of Commerce** (86 S. Main St., 435/882-0690 or 800/378-0690, www.exploretooele.com, 9am-4pm Mon.-Fri.) can tell you about the sights and services.

Getting There

Utah Transit Authority (UTA, 435/882-9031, www.rideuta.com) buses connect Tooele with Salt Lake City and other towns of the Wasatch Front Monday-Friday. The main bus stop is at Main Street and 400 South.

Great Salt Lake Desert

Lake Bonneville once covered 20,000 square miles of what is now Utah, Idaho, and Nevada; when the lake broke through the Sawtooth Mountains, its level declined precipitously, leaving the 2,500-square-mile Great Salt Lake and huge expanses of salt flats to the south and west. These salt flat remnants of Lake Bonneville in the western exurbs of Salt Lake City are almost completely white and level, and they go on for more than 100 miles. It is commonly said that one can see the earth's curvature at the horizon, although this apparently takes a very discerning eye.

You're most likely to visit the sites in the Great Salt Lake Desert if you're traveling along I-80 between Salt Lake City and the Nevada border, but it's good to know that towns like Wendover offer lodging and dining options, and that the surrounding deserts offer such curiosities as race tracks and scuba diving.

BONNEVILLE SALT FLATS INTERNATIONAL SPEEDWAY

A brilliant white layer of salt left behind by prehistoric Lake Bonneville covers more than 44,000 acres of the Great Salt Lake Desert. For much of the year, a shallow layer of water sits atop the salt flats. The hot sun usually dries out the flats enough for speed runs in summer and autumn.

Cars began running across the salt in 1914 and continue to set faster and faster times. Rocket-powered vehicles have exceeded 600 miles per hour. Expansive courses can be laid out; the main speedway is 10 miles long and 80 feet wide. A small tent city goes up near the course during the annual **Speed Week** in August; vehicles of an amazing variety of styles and ages take off individually to set new records in their classes. The salt flats, just east of Wendover, are easy to access: Take I-80 exit 4 and follow the paved road five miles north, then east. Signs and markers indicate if and where you can drive on the salt. Soft spots underlaid by mud can trap vehicles venturing off the safe areas. Take care not to be on the track when racing events are being held.

WENDOVER

Wendover began in 1907 as a watering station serving construction of the Western Pacific Railroad. The highway went through in 1925, marking the community's beginnings as a stop for travelers, and its population swelled during World War II, when the air base was active. Wendover now has the tacky grandiosity of a Nevada border town.

Wendover has a split personality—half of the town lies in Utah and half in Nevada. On both sides you'll find accommodations and

Out in the Desert

Two military installations, the Utah Training and Test Range and the Dugway Proving Ground, along with the Tooele Army Depot, a chemical and biological weapons storage area, occupy much of the land in the Great Salt Lake Desert. They are all extremely high-security areas.

UTAH TRAINING AND TEST RANGE

The Utah Training and Test Range (UTTR) provides the huge amount of land necessary to train military air crews and test weapons. It is, put simply, a bombing range, with many mock targets erected for fighter pilots and their crews to practice on. The UTTR was created in 1979 for cruise-missile testing. The large amount of land and airspace required for that purpose has made the UTTR a natural place to test smart munitions, long-range standoff weapons, remote-controlled or unpiloted air vehicles, boost-glide precision-guided munitions, air-to-air missiles, and autonomous loitering antiradiation missiles, as well as to dispose of unwanted explosives.

The UTTR also has the largest overland contiguous block of supersonic authorized restricted air space in the continental United States. The airspace is situated over 2,675 square miles of Department of Defense land, administered by the U.S. Air Force. The UTTR works closely with the U.S. Army at Dugway Proving Ground.

Although the UTTR quite obviously does not allow visitors, the Hill Aerospace Museum, located at the Hill Air Force Base just south of Ogden in the town of Roy, is open to the public and has many displays of military aircraft.

DUGWAY PROVING GROUND

The primary mission of Dugway Proving Ground is to evaluate, test, and develop chemical defenses; biological defenses; and incendiary, smoke, and obscurant systems and to conduct environmental technology testing. Dugway sells its services to all authorized customers, including the U.S. and foreign governments as well as nongovernmental organizations. In addition, Dugway is a major range and test facility for chemical and biological defense testing.

Dugway Proving Ground encompasses about 800,000 acres. In addition to chemical and biological defensive testing and environment characterization and remediation technology testing, Dugway is the Defense Department's leader in testing battlefield smokes and obscurants. The installation consists of more than 600 buildings.

As if all this weren't enough, Dugway has developed a following among ufologists, who suspect that the base's secret status, underground facilities, and low profile make it the perfect place for the sequestering of alien artifacts and other items of extraterrestrial origin.

TOOELE ARMY DEPOT

In the summer of 1996, the army began burning part of the nation's store of chemical weapons at the Tooele Army Depot, 10 miles south of the town of Tooele and 55 miles from Salt Lake City. The depot held the nation's single largest cache of chemical weapons, with 44 percent of the arsenal stored in underground bunkers called igloos. Part of the reason for burning the weapons, besides the requirements of treaties with the former USSR, was that there was a far greater risk of leakage and environmental damage in leaving the chemical agents in bunkers than there was in incinerating them. The chemicals destroyed include sarin, mustard gas, nerve gas, and lewisite, a skin-blistering agent. The last of Tooele Army Depot's chemical weapons were destroyed in 2007. The depot now tests and stores weapons for use in wars and for training.

restaurants where you can take a break from long drives on I-80. Six casinos on the Nevada side provide a chance to lose your money at the usual games. Most of the town's visitor facilities line Wendover Boulevard, also known as State Highway, which parallels the interstate. Lodgings are cheaper on the Utah side. The **Motel 6** (561 E. Wendover Blvd., 435/665-2267, $41-47) is one of the chain's better efforts.

Park City and the Wasatch Range

Look for ★ to find recommended
sights, activities, dining, and lodging.

Highlights

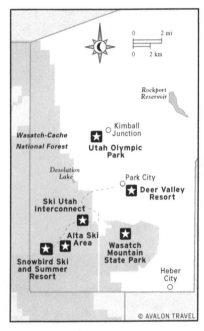

Lodge and indulge at the Cliff Spa, one of the nicest in the state (page 96).

★ **Alta Ski Area:** Here's where old skiers
come to...ski their tails off! Don't be surprised if
a 70-year-old helps you up from a fall. Alta is a
haven for skiers—no snowboarding allowed—
and the accommodations are homey and extra-
friendly (page 100).

★ **Deer Valley Resort:** When you need to
show off your new ski outfit, do it at Deer Valley.
Although you may ride the lift with a big-time
CEO, you're just as likely to cruise down a perfectly groomed run with the fun-loving members
of a blue-collar town ski club (page 109).

★ **Utah Olympic Park:** Bobsled, luge, and
ski-jump competitions were held here during the
2002 Winter Olympics. These days, winter or summer, come here to watch freestyle ski jumping or
take a bobsled ride. Guided tours of the competition sites are also available (page 114).

★ **Ski Utah Interconnect:** Learn the local
geography by skiing a challenging backcountry
tour among Snowbird, Alta, Solitude, Brighton,
Deer Valley, and Park City Mountain Resort (page
115).

★ **Snowbird Ski and Summer Resort:** In
addition to being a great place to ski (be sure to
make it over to Mineral Basin), Snowbird's summer activities mean that the adrenaline never
stops. If you want to relax, stay at the swank Cliff

★ **Wasatch Mountain State Park:** Along
with camping, hiking, and great scenic views,
Utah's largest state park has one of the best public golf courses you'll find anywhere (page 127).

Immediately east of Salt Lake City, the Wasatch Range soars to over 11,000 feet, and the steep canyons and abundant snowfall make for legendary skiing. Big Cottonwood Canyon, home to the Solitude and Brighton ski and snowboard areas, is just southeast of the city; the next canyon south, Little Cottonwood, has Snowbird and Alta, two world-class resorts. When the snow melts, the hiking is every bit as great as the skiing and boarding, and many of the resorts have summer operations, with lift-assisted mountain biking being the most popular activity.

About 45 minutes east of Salt Lake via I-80, Park City is home to three ski areas: Park City Mountain Resort, the Canyons, and Deer Valley. Park City is also the site of the annual Sundance Film Festival.

Although the entire northern Wasatch region is within commuting distance of Salt Lake City, skiers who can afford the somewhat pricey accommodations should try to spend at least a couple of nights at one of the many lodges, which range from Alta's friendly down-home places to Deer Valley's equally friendly but ultrachic digs.

PLANNING YOUR TIME

In the winter, if you have only a few days, it's best to pick an area—Big Cottonwood Canyon, Little Cottonwood Canyon, or Park City—and base yourself there for skiing and boarding. It's not really necessary to have a car, especially in the Cottonwood Canyon areas; if you want to explore another ski area for a day, it's generally cheaper to use a shuttle service than to rent a car. If not everybody in your group is interested in skiing all day long, Park City is the best bet—it's a real town with as much activity off the slopes as on them.

In the summer, it's nice to have a car (or a bike) and the freedom to poke around the mountains. Increasingly, the ski areas have structured summer activities, but there are also plenty of trails, and the summertime quiet of these canyons makes them good places to camp and hike.

Previous: Wasatch Mountains; Alta Ski Area. **Above:** Solitude lifts.

90

Park City and the Wasatch Range

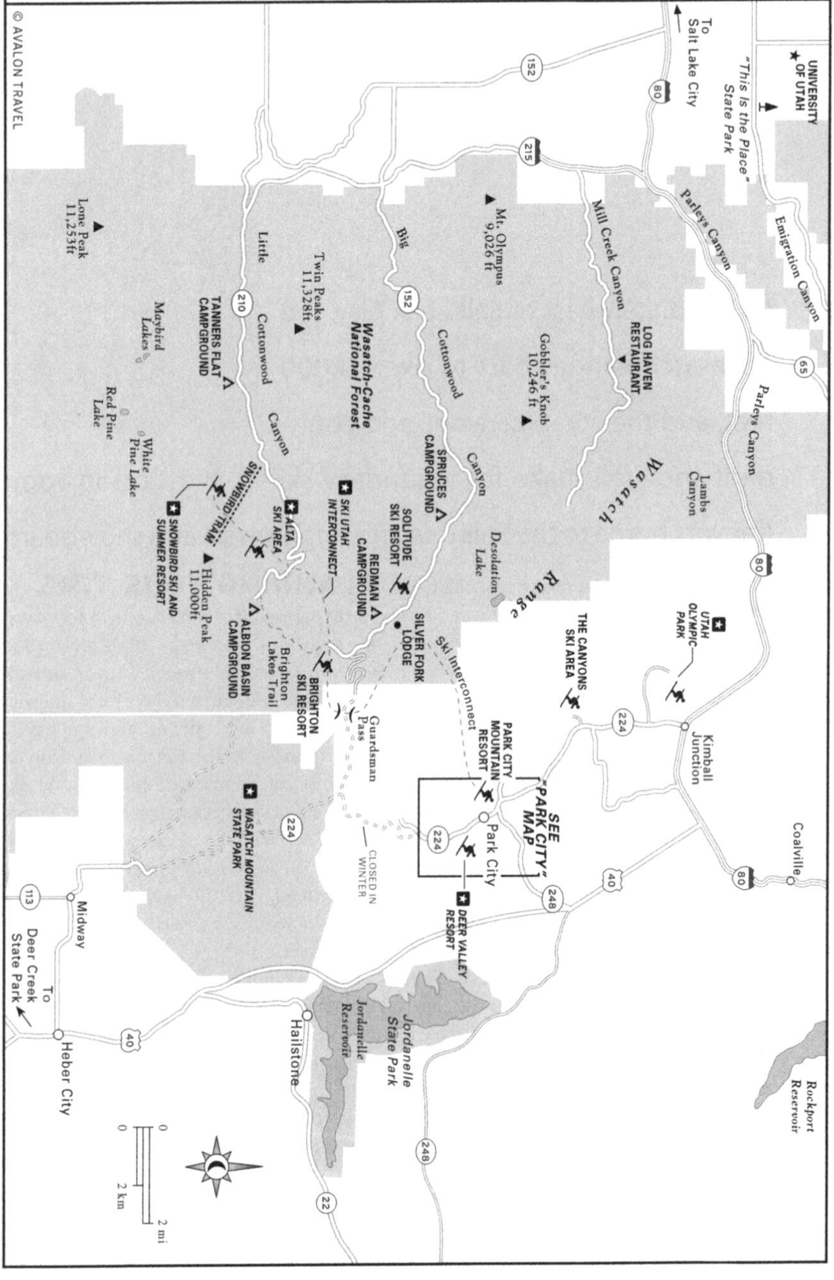

© AVALON TRAVEL

To Salt Lake City

"This Is the Place" State Park

★ UNIVERSITY OF UTAH

Emigration Canyon

Parleys Canyon

152

80

215

Mill Creek Canyon

LOG HAVEN RESTAURANT

Gobbler's Knob 10,246 ft ▲

▲ Mt. Olympus 9,026 ft

65

Parleys Canyon

80

Lambs Canyon

▲ Lone Peak 11,253ft

Little Cottonwood Canyon

210

Maybird Lake

Red Pine Lake

White Pine Lake

Twin Peaks 11,328ft ▲

Wasatch-Cache National Forest

Big Cottonwood Canyon

152

Desolation Lake

Wasatch Range

TANNERS FLAT CAMPGROUND ▲

SPRUCES CAMPGROUND ▲

SNOWBIRD TRAM

ALTA SKI AREA ✈

SNOWBIRD SKI AND SUMMER RESORT ✪

☀ SKI UTAH INTERCONNECT

SOLITUDE SKI RESORT ✪

REDMAN CAMPGROUND ▲

THE CANYONS SKI AREA ✪

✪ UTAH OLYMPIC PARK

224

Kimball Junction

▲ Hidden Peak 11,000ft

ALBION BASIN CAMPGROUND ▲

Brighton Lakes Trail

BRIGHTON SKI RESORT

SILVER FORK LODGE

Ski Interconnect

PARK CITY MOUNTAIN RESORT

SEE "PARK CITY" MAP

80

Coalville

Guardsman Pass

224

Park City

224

248

40

80

CLOSED IN WINTER

WASATCH MOUNTAIN STATE PARK ✪

224

✪ DEER VALLEY RESORT

113

Midway

40

To Deer Creek State Park

Heber City

Hailstone

Jordanelle Reservoir

Jordanelle State Park

Rockport Reservoir

248

22

0   2 mi
0   2 km

Big Cottonwood Canyon

Cliffs towering thousands of feet form the gateway to Big Cottonwood Canyon. Skiers come in season to try the downhill slopes at Solitude and Brighton and to cross-country ski at the Solitude Nordic Center or on snow-covered campground loop roads. Enter the canyon from Wasatch Boulevard and 7000 South, about 15 miles southeast of downtown Salt Lake City. The 14-mile road to Brighton Basin passes several summertime picnic areas and reveals splendid vistas at each turn while climbing to an elevation of 8,700 feet. The summertime-only Guardsman Pass Road turns off just before Brighton and winds up to Guardsman Pass (elev. 9,800 feet) at the crest of the Wasatches, then drops down into either Park City or Heber City on the other side; the mostly unpaved road is usually open late June-mid-October.

SOLITUDE MOUNTAIN RESORT

The best thing about **Solitude** (801/534-1400 or 800/748-4754, www.skisolitude.com) is reflected in its name—it's rarely crowded. The other thing that makes this ski area distinctive is the European-style village at the base area. The village square is closed to cars; day visitors park in a lot about a five-minutes walk away, and underground parking lots stow condo guests' vehicles. The inn and several condos face the pedestrian area. From all the lodgings, it's only a short walk to the lifts.

Ski season at Solitude runs from about Thanksgiving until the third week in April, depending on snow.

History

This area was originally called Solitude by silver miners in the early 1900s. It became a ski area served by two chairlifts in 1957, and in 1989 the Emerald Express became Utah's first high-speed quad lift. Until the Creekside condominiums opened in 1995, Solitude was entirely a day-use area. Solitude is privately owned by one family; Intrawest, which owns Steamboat in Colorado and several other resorts, was brought in to develop some of the lodgings but has no equity interest in the resort.

Terrain and Lifts

Skiers can choose from a wide variety of runs—there are plenty of nice wide blue cruisers and, when conditions are favorable, gates open to expert terrain, including Honeycomb Canyon, containing more than 400 acres of ungroomed powder skiing on the back side of the resort. The Honeycomb lift, a fixed quad, makes this challenging, largely natural area relatively accessible.

One of the nice things about Honeycomb Canyon is that, along with all the 50-degree-slope double-black-diamond tree runs, there's one run that's accessible to strong intermediate skiers and snowboarders. Woodlawn, a blue-black run, starts at the top of the Summit lift and goes right down the center of the canyon. There's one short steep section and a lot of moguls before it reaches the bottom of the Honeycomb lift, but on a clear day with good snow conditions, it's a great challenge for an advancing skier. In less than perfect conditions, it's terrifying and best left to the experts. Another good challenging intermediate run is Dynamite, also starting at the top of the Summit lift.

Day skiers (as opposed to resort guests) generally head out from the Moonbeam base area, where a quad lift shuttles skiers and boarders up to a network of green and blue runs. A large day lodge at the Moonbeam base has lockers, a café and bar, and a comfortable area where you can sit and wait for your die-hard companions to come off the mountain.

In all, there are more than 1,200 skiable acres, rated 20 percent beginner, 50 percent intermediate, and 30 percent advanced, served

Getting to the Slopes

Don't assume that you'll need a rental car for your ski trip to Utah, even if you want to visit more than one resort. The cheapest way to arrange a ski trip is to stay in Salt Lake City and take the UTA bus to the mountains.

UTA buses (801/743-3882, www.rideuta.com, $4.50 one-way in winter) run between Salt Lake City and Solitude and Brighton resorts, with stops at many hotels and park-and-rides. To reach Snowbird and Alta resorts, take the TRAX light rail from downtown south to the 7200 South station. Bus 960 travels up Big Cottonwood Canyon; bus 990 goes up Little Cottonwood. The bus ride from the 7200 South TRAX station to Alta takes a little over an hour. Buses run throughout the day daily in winter.

Even easier is taking a bus—either public or private—to a ski resort where you'll stay in resort lodgings. From the airport, **Canyon Transportation** (800/255-1841, www.canyontransport. com, $39 one-way, $76 round-trip) runs regular shuttles up Big Cottonwood Canyon, with stops at Solitude, Brighton, and Park City. **Alta Shuttle** (801/274-0225 or 866/274-0225, www.altas-huttle.com, any trip $37 one-way) runs shuttles among the airport, Alta, and Park City resorts.

Once you get to your destination, don't feel like you're tied to your chosen ski area. It's easy to take UTA buses between Snowbird and Alta or between Solitude and Brighton. For longer trips, private shuttle buses travel between Big and Little Cottonwood Canyons and the Park City resorts.

by eight lifts, including three high-speed quads. The green and blue runs are mostly clumped together, which makes it difficult for an expert and a novice to ski in the same area and meet up for lift rides together. Although Solitude does permit snowboarding and has a terrain park, most Big Cottonwood boarders head to Brighton.

Adult lift tickets cost $74, half-day tickets are $61, seniors over age 69 pay $52, lift tickets for ages 7-13 are $46; those under age seven ski free.

Lifts run 9am-4pm daily. For more information, check www.skisolitude.com. Solitude has a ski school, rentals, and kids' programs.

Solitude Nordic Center

Plenty of snow and nicely groomed tracks make Solitude's **Nordic Center** (Silver Lake Day Lodge, 801/536-5774 or 800/748-4754, ext. 5774, www.skisolitude.com, 8:30am-4:30pm daily mid-Nov.-mid-Apr., $18 adults, $14 after 12:30pm, free under age 11 and over age 69) one of the best places in Utah for both traditional cross-country skiers and skate skiers. The 12.4 miles of groomed trails are relatively easy to ski, with level loops for beginners and rolling

terrain for more experienced skiers. An additional 6.2 miles of trails are groomed for snowshoers. Don't hesitate to try the gentle, mostly downhill ski from the Nordic Center lodge to the downhill skiing base area at Solitude.

The Nordic Center is in the Silver Lake Day Lodge, about two miles up the road from Solitude's downhill area, almost all the way to Brighton. The shop's staff offers rentals (touring, racing, telemark, and snowshoes), sales, instruction, day tours, and advice on backcountry touring and avalanche hazards. Tickets can be purchased here or at Solitude's downhill ski area. The ski area is 12 miles up Big Cottonwood Canyon and only a 28-mile drive southeast of downtown Salt Lake City.

If you're not so fussy about skiing on groomed trails, explore the loop trails at **Spruces Campground,** 9.7 miles up Big Cottonwood Canyon. These trails are also popular with snowshoers.

Summer Activities

During the summer, the Sunrise lift operates 10am-6pm Friday-Sunday. A single ride costs $10 per person.

Mountain Biking

Twenty miles of single-track within the resort area, plus easy access to nearby Wasatch National Forest roads and trails, make Solitude a fun place to bike. Bicycles are permitted on the Sunrise lift (Fri.-Sun. summer, single lift ticket $10, full-day lift pass $20). Full-suspension mountain bikes ($39 for 2 hours, $49 full-day) are available for rent.

Disc Golf

The 18-hole course is free, although you may want to ride the Sunrise lift ($10 per ride) to get to the first hole, which is at 9,000 feet elevation, a pretty good hike up the mountain from the base area.

Accommodations

Most lodgings at Solitude are in the European-style ski village at the base of the slopes and are owned and managed by Solitude Mountain Resort (801/534-1400 or 800/748-4754, www.skisolitude.com). Rates at all of the Solitude-owned lodgings drop by at least half during the summer.

The **Inn at Solitude** ($269-449 winter, $149-164 summer) is a few steps from the base area lifts. As ski resort hotels go, it's rather intimate, with 46 guest rooms, a fancy restaurant and bar, a spa, and other amenities.

The **Village at Solitude Condominiums** offers condo units ($446-586 winter, $200-250 summer) in three different developments: Creekside is right next to the base area lifts; Powderhorn is only a few steps farther; and Eagle Springs, although a slightly longer walk to the lifts, has easy access to Club Solitude's indoor pool and exercise room. All have fireplaces, full kitchens, TVs and VCRs, and private decks, and come with 1-3 bedrooms. Just outside the main village area, find the **Crossings,** with three-bedroom town houses ($752-790 winter, $280 summer).

About one mile from Solitude, and not part of the resort village, is the **Silver Fork Lodge** (11332 E. Big Cottonwood Canyon, 801/649-9551, www.silverforklodge.com, $145-200 includes breakfast), which has eight rustic B&B

rooms without TVs or telephones. The Silver Fork is largely known for its restaurant.

Food

The Inn at Solitude's restaurant, **St. Bernard's** (801/535-4120, www.skisolitude.com, 7:30am-10am and 5pm-9pm Tues.-Sun. winter, $22-38), is the place to go for an elegant and expensive dinner. The menu leans toward country French; dinner reservations are recommended.

For a quick slice of pizza, an espresso, or good ice cream, stop by the **Stone Haus Pizzeria and Creamery** (801/536-5767, 7:30am-9pm Sun.-Thurs., 7:30am-10pm Fri.-Sat. winter, 9:30am-8pm Fri.-Sun. summer, $8-12), right in the village square. During summer, you'll be able to spot the distinctive grass roof; in the winter it's where cross-country skiers gather for a free shuttle back to the Nordic area.

Snowshoe (approximately 0.75 mile) to the trailside ★ **Yurt** (801/536-5709, 5:30pm Tues.-Sat., 5pm Sun.) for a five-course dinner ($125). Only 24 people are seated each evening; reservations are required, and it's best to make them well in advance. During the summer, dinner ($75) includes four courses and starts at 6:30pm Wednesday-Sunday July-September.

Outside the main resort complex, the **Silver Fork Lodge** (11332 E. Big Cottonwood Canyon, 801/649-9551 or 888/649-9551, www.silverforklodge.com, 8am-9pm daily, $12-36) has a friendly Western atmosphere. The restaurant uses a 70-year-old sourdough starter to make its pancakes. For dinner, go high-end with chateaubriand, or blue-collar with meatloaf; there's also brisket and ribs done in the smoker.

Getting There

From Salt Lake City, take I-80 east to I-215 south to exit 6 (6200 South); follow 6200 South, which becomes Wasatch Boulevard. Follow the signs to Big Cottonwood Canyon; Solitude is 14 miles up Big Cottonwood Canyon.

UTA buses and Canyon Transportation shuttles serve all resorts in Big Cottonwood Canyon.

BRIGHTON RESORT

Brighton (801/532-4731 or 855/201-7669, www.brightonresort.com, 9am-4pm daily mid-Nov.-mid-Apr., night skiing 4pm-9pm Mon.-Sat. early Dec.-Mar.) is a longtime favorite with local families for the excellent skiing and friendly, unpretentious atmosphere. There's no Euro-village resort here; it's all about being on the mountain. It's also the least expensive and most snowboard-friendly of the Cottonwood resorts and is the only place near Salt Lake with a real night-skiing program. The resort is in the Uinta-Wasatch-Cache National Forest and does not have a commercial summer season, but there are plenty of places to hike in the area.

History

This is Utah's oldest ski resort, dating from 1936, when ski-club members built a "skier tow" from half-inch wire rope and an old elevator drum. Two years later, a T-bar tow was erected, and in 1946, the area's first actual chairlift traveled up Mount Millicent.

Terrain and Lifts

Brighton skiers and boarders are serious about their mountain time, and the resort has cooperated by making all of its terrain accessible by high-speed quad lifts, which climb as high as 10,500 feet for a 1,745-foot vertical descent to the base. In addition to the 66 runs and trails at Brighton, you can hop on the Sol-Bright run to visit Solitude ski area; a lift there will put you back on a trail to Brighton. Although a lot of the territory is suitable for beginners and intermediates, Brighton does offer some difficult powder-bowl skiing and steep runs.

Absolute beginners can step onto the Magic Carpet and be gently carried up to the Explorer area, which is also served by a slow-moving (and thus easy to mount and dismount) lift. Beginners with a few runs behind them and cautious intermediate skiers

and boarders should venture onto the Majestic lift, which serves a good network of wide, tree-lined green and blue runs. More advanced skiers will prefer the bowls in the Millicent and Evergreen areas. One of the things that makes Brighton so popular with snowboarders (besides the fact that they're welcome here) is its lack of long run-outs. It also has an open-backcountry policy, although it's unwise to head off into the backcountry unless you're with locals who grew up skiing and boarding here.

Brighton's terrain parks are among the best in the West. Snowboarders looking for a challenge should head up the Crest Express quad and play around the My-O-My and Candyland terrain parks. Just down the slope from these areas are two more terrain parks and a half pipe.

Brighton has a ski and snowboard school, rentals, ski shops, a couple of cafeterias, and a sit-down restaurant in the lodge. Many Utah residents learned to ski at Brighton, and its snowboard classes are considered to be especially good.

Adults ski for $72 for a full day, $62 half-day (morning or afternoon), and $40 at night. Seniors over age 69 pay $42, ages 8-12 ski for $39, and children under age eight ski free with a paying adult. Cheaper prices may be available online.

Accommodations

Adjacent to the slopes is resort-owned **Brighton Lodge** (800/873-5512, $129-209), which offers accommodations with a heated outdoor pool and a spa adjacent to the restaurant. It's much smaller than most ski-resort lodges and very casual. A few hostel rooms (twin beds or bunks and shared baths, $129) are available along with regular guest rooms ($149) and suites ($209). If you want a more upscale setting, stay just down the hill at Solitude. A short walk from Brighton's lifts, off the Brighton Loop Road, **Brighton Chalets** (801/942-8824, www.brightonchalets.com, $295-1,150 winter) rents out a range of cottages and chalets. Each chalet comes with a furnished kitchen, a fireplace, and cable TV and sleeps at least four people.

Food

Slope-side restaurants include the cafeteria **Alpine Rose** (801/532-4731, ext. 252, 8am-9pm Mon.-Sat., 8am-4pm Sun. mid-Dec.-mid-Mar., 8am-4pm daily mid-Mar.-mid-Dec., $6-12), a good lunch spot; the **Millicent Chalet** (801/532-4731, ext. 219, 8am-4:30pm daily, $6-12) at the base of the Millicent quad; and **Molly Green's** (801/532-4731, ext. 206, 11am-11pm Mon.-Sat., 10am-8pm Sun. mid-Dec.-mid-Mar., 11am-8pm daily mid-Mar.-mid-Dec., dinner $9-18), a bar and grill with table service.

Getting There

Brighton is at the road's end, two miles past Solitude in Big Cottonwood Canyon. From Salt Lake City, take I-80 east to I-215 south. Take I-215 to exit 6 (6200 South) and follow 6200 South, which becomes Wasatch Boulevard. Follow the signs to Big Cottonwood Canyon; Brighton is 16 miles up Big Cottonwood Canyon.

UTA buses and Canyon Transportation shuttles serve all resorts in Big Cottonwood Canyon.

HIKING

Hikers in Big Cottonwood Canyon should leave their dogs at home; because of water purity concerns, dogs are prohibited in this watershed. A good map for hikes in the area is the *Trails Illustrated Wasatch Front North,* map 709.

Mineral Fork Trail

Mineral Fork Trail (5 miles one-way) follows an old mining road past abandoned mines, cabins, and rusting equipment to a high glacial cirque. Waterfalls, alpine meadows, wildflowers, and abundant birdlife make the steep climb worthwhile. The signed trailhead is on the south side of the road six miles up the canyon (0.8 mile past Moss Ledge Picnic Area). You'll climb 2,000 vertical feet in three miles

to the Wasatch Mine, whose mineralized water makes up much of the flow of Mineral Fork Creek. Another two miles and 1,400 vertical feet of climbing lead to the Regulator Johnson Mine. A loop trip can be made by climbing the ridge west of Regulator Johnson (no trail) and descending Mill B South Fork Trail to Lake Blanche and the main road, coming out 1.5 miles west of the Mineral Fork trailhead.

Donut Falls

The easy and popular hike to Donut Falls (0.75 mile one-way) starts just past the Jordan Pines campground and follows a trail that's partly through the woods and partly an old dirt road to the waterfall, which spurts from a "doughnut hole" in a rock. Rockfall and erosion have actually made the effect a bit less doughnut-like in recent years.

Brighton Lakes Trail

Brighton Lakes Trail (3 miles one-way) winds through some of the prettiest lake country in the range. Families enjoy outings on this easy trail, which begins in Brighton behind the Brighton Lodge. Silver Lake has a boardwalk giving full access to fishing docks. The first section follows Big Cottonwood Creek through stands of aspen and evergreens. The trail continues south across meadows filled with wildflowers, then climbs more steeply to Brighton Overlook, one mile from the start. Dog Lake, surrounded by old mine dumps, lies 200 yards to the south. Continue on the main trail 0.5 mile to Lake Mary, a large, deep lake below Mount Millicent. Lake Martha is another 0.5 mile up the trail. Another mile of climbing takes you to Lake Catherine, bordered by a pretty alpine meadow on the north and the steep talus slopes of Sunset and Pioneer Peaks on the south. Total elevation gain for the three-mile hike to Lake Catherine is 1,200 feet. Hikers can also go another 0.5 mile to Catherine Pass and descend 1.5 miles to Albion Basin in Little Cottonwood Canyon. Sunset Peak (10,648 feet) can be climbed by following a 0.5-mile trail from the pass.

CAMPGROUNDS

All Uinta-Wasatch-Cache National Forest campgrounds have water during the summer. Reserve at 877/444-6777 or www.recreation.gov ($9 reservation fee). Note that, in order to protect the Salt Lake City watershed, dogs are not permitted at these campgrounds, and this is strictly enforced.

At an elevation of 7,500 feet, **Spruces Campground** (9.7 miles up the canyon, late May-mid-Oct., $23) is the largest campground in the area. **Redman Campground** (13 miles up the canyon, mid-June-early Oct., $23) is located between Solitude and Brighton at an elevation of 8,300 feet.

Little Cottonwood Canyon

The road through this nearly straight glacial valley ascends 5,500 vertical feet in 11 miles. Splendid peaks rise to more than 11,000 feet on both sides of the canyon. In winter and spring, challenging terrain attracts skiers to the Snowbird and Alta ski areas. Enter Little Cottonwood Canyon from the junction of Highway 209 and Highway 210, four miles south of the entrance to Big Cottonwood Canyon.

Granite for the Salt Lake Temple came from quarries one mile up the canyon on the left. Here also are the Granite Mountain Record Vaults, containing genealogical and historical records of the LDS Church stored on millions of rolls of microfilm. Neither site is open to the public.

★ SNOWBIRD SKI AND SUMMER RESORT

When you drive up Little Cottonwood Canyon, **Snowbird** (801/933-2222 or 800/232-9542, snow report 801/933-2100, www.snowbird.com) is the first resort you get to. It's about a 40-minute drive from the heart of downtown Salt Lake City. Aside from sheer convenience, Snowbird is known for its great snow—an average of 500 inches a year, and much of that classified as "champagne powder." It's a big, fun place to ski or board, with lots of varied terrain.

History

Snowbird's owner and developer, Dick Bass,

The Albion Basin, at the head of Little Cottonwood Canyon, is a great place for summertime hiking.

is well known in mountaineering circles as the author of *Seven Summits*, his account of climbing the highest peak on every continent. He reportedly had the vision for this resort, including the deluxe Cliff Lodge, while he was holed up in a tent on Mount Everest. The soaring 11-story windowed atrium at the sturdy concrete Cliff imparts a sense of openness that was so sorely lacking in that Everest tent. Along with open space and light, Bass also had a vision of a spa.

It was important to Bass to build an environmentally friendly resort, and much effort was taken to preserve trees and improve the quality of the watershed, which had been degraded by mining. Mine tailings were removed and lodges built in their place to avoid harming existing trees and vegetation.

In 2014, Bass sold majority interest in Snowbird to Ian Cumming and his family.

Terrain and Lifts

Snowbird is on the west side of the Wasatch Range, with ski runs mostly on the north face of the mountains. There are three distinct areas to ski at this large and varied resort: Peruvian Gulch, Gad, and on the back side, Mineral Basin. And if 2,500 skiable acres aren't enough to keep you busy, you can buy a special lift ticket that allows skiing between Snowbird and neighboring Alta.

Plenty of lifts serve Snowbird, including six high-speed quads and a tram that can ferry up to 125 skiers at a time to the top of Peruvian Gulch. The runs here are also long (Chip's Run, from the top of the tram, is 2.5 miles), meaning that you don't have to hop a lift every few minutes. Unless it's a powder day, when locals call in sick and head for the mountains, lines are rarely a problem, especially midweek. The one place that does get crowded is the tram; lines can be quite long, especially first thing in the morning and just after lunchtime. But the tram really is the way to get up the mountain quickly, with access to the best territory.

Twenty-seven percent of the runs are classed as beginner, 38 percent intermediate, and 35 percent advanced. There are also plenty of ungroomed areas in the backcountry. Snowbird's ski and snowboard schools and separate "bunny hill" make it a good place to learn. The longest descent is 3.5 miles and drops 3,200 feet. Guided ski tours of about two hours (free with lift-ticket purchase) leave from the Snowbird Plaza deck at 9:30am and 10:30am daily and tour mostly blue runs.

Snowboarders can find a terrain park on the Big Emma run, under the Mid-Gad lift. The terrain, with lots of natural chutes, lends itself to snowboarding.

Skiers and snowboarders alike should be sure to check out the Mineral Basin area. Reach it by taking the tram to the top of Hidden Peak (11,000 feet) and then heading over to the back side of the mountain, or by riding the Peruvian Express lift and then riding a "magic carpet" through a 600-foot-long tunnel to Mineral Basin. Two high-speed quads serve a great network of runs on this side of the mountain.

Ski instruction and programs are available for both children and adults. Snowbird also offers a number of adaptive ski programs (801/933-2188, http://wasatchadaptivesports. org). Sit-skis, mono-skis, and outriggers make skiing possible for people with mobility impairments.

Standard lift tickets cost $92; add access to Alta's lifts and you'll pay $105. Seniors pay $75, youth (ages 7-12) tickets are $45; two children age six and under can ski free with each adult. Half-day and multiday passes are also available. The exceptionally long season at Snowbird runs mid-November-May, although many lifts close by May 1. Even confirmed Alta skiers head to Snowbird for their late-spring skiing.

Wasatch Powderbird Guides (801/742-2800, www.powderbird.com) offers helicopter skiing in the peaks above the regular runs. Rates start at $1,190 for six or seven runs; check the website for the rather complex rate and package information.

The Greatest Snow on Earth

What makes Utah's snow so great? In a word, geography. Storms come in from the Pacific, pushed by cold jet-stream air across the Great Basin. When these storm clouds encounter the Wasatch peaks, the jet stream forces them upward into even colder air, where they release their moisture. The extremely cold temperatures ensure that this moisture falls as light, dry snow.

Storm fronts often become trapped in the Salt Lake Valley, laden with moisture and too heavy to rise out of the Great Basin. These heavy clouds make it partway out of the basin, dump snow on the nearby mountains, then drop back to the Great Salt Lake where they pick up more moisture. This cycle continues until the storm weakens and the clouds release enough moisture to float over the tops of the mountains and continue eastward.

Summer Activities

Snowbird offers a full array of family recreation and resort facilities to summer visitors. All lodging, spa, and recreational facilities remain open, as do many restaurants and retail outlets.

A summer favorite is the tram ride to 11,000-foot Hidden Peak (11am-8pm daily) for a fantastic panorama of the Wasatch Range, the surrounding valleys, and the distant Uinta Mountains. Round-trip one-ride tickets are $17 adults, $15 children 7-16 and seniors, and free for children under age seven. The Peruvian chairlift also runs in the summer; jeep trails connect the two lifts, and a pass is good on either one.

Mountain bikers can ride the 7.5-mile Big Mountain Trail downhill from the top of the tram to the base; a special biking tram pass ($19 half-day, $29 all-day) is required.

The resort's summer commercial emphasis is on vaguely extreme sports, including the mountain coaster (think personal roller coaster, $15 per ride), although there are also plenty of general fitness and outdoor activities. An all-day pass for activities, including the coaster, jumping alpine slide, climbing wall, and more, goes for $42, or $32 for children under 48 inches tall.

The **Activity Center** (in the Snowbird Center, 801/933-2147) is the hub for summer activities. It also rents mountain bikes and can arrange horseback rides in Mineral Basin. A hiking map available at the center shows local trails and jogging loops. Guided hikes are available, and there's a nature trail adapted for guests with disabilities. If you're looking to relax, there's also the Cliff Spa and Salon, with beauty and massage treatments. Snowbird is also the site of frequent summertime musical and arts events.

Spa

The Cliff Spa (801/933-2225) offers all sorts of massage therapies, facials, manicures, yoga and Pilates classes, a weight room, cardio equipment, and its own rooftop outdoor pool. It's much nicer and more complete than most hotel spas. A day pass ($20) to the spa permits access to yoga classes and workout facilities; people who aren't staying at the Cliff are welcome. It's best to make an appointment for massages and other treatments at least a day or two in advance.

Accommodations

All of Snowbird's accommodations are run by the resort; the best way to find out about the many options is simply to call the central reservation line (800/232-9542) or check the website (www.snowbird.com). Rates vary wildly according to season, day of week, and view but are generally quite high during the winter, dropping to about half the winter rate during the summer.

The most upscale place to stay at Snowbird is the ski-in, ski-out ★ **Cliff Lodge,** with more than 500 guest rooms, scores of incredible Oriental rugs, four restaurants, conference facilities, retail shops, a year-round outdoor pool, and a top-notch spa. One very nice practical detail is the ground-floor locker (complete with boot dryer) assigned to each guest. The Cliff is swanky without being snobbish or stuffy—you don't have to look like the current season's Bogner catalog to fit in here (though many guests do). Standard winter room rates run about $390 (even the most basic rooms can sleep four), with many package deals available, including better rates on multiday packages that include lift tickets. The west wing of the Cliff has been remodeled as condo units; studios with kitchens and hot tubs at the **Cliff Club** condominiums run $360-380.

The **Lodge at Snowbird,** the **Inn at Snowbird,** and the **Iron Blosam Lodge,** which has timeshare units and requires a Saturday-Saturday stay, are the resort's three condominium complexes. Though they aren't quite as grand as the Cliff, they're perfectly nice and quite practical places to stay, and the three are pretty similar, with guest laundries, pools, steam and sauna areas, restaurants, and many kitchen units. All of these places are a short walk from the tram loading area. Most are one-bedroom units, with rates starting at $275.

More condos are available through **Canyon Services** (888/546-5707, www.canyonservices.com). These upscale accommodations are found between Snowbird and Alta, and they are available in several different complexes and in units with 2-7 bedrooms; winter rates are mostly $500-600 per night, with a five-night minimum.

If these prices seem prohibitive, remember that Salt Lake City is just down the hill, and city buses run up the canyon several times a day.

Food

Serious skiers will no doubt eat lunch either on the mountain at the **Mid-Gad Restaurant** or at the **Forklift,** a sandwich-and-burger joint near the base of the tram. While these places are perfectly acceptable refueling stations, be aware that there are a couple of very

good restaurants at Snowbird, and a new one planned to open in 2015 at the top of the tram.

The ★ **Aerie** (801/933-2160 or ext. 5500, breakfast and dinner daily winter, 5pm-9pm daily summer, $14-39) is the Cliff's fancy 10th-floor restaurant, offering excellent food with a slight Asian influence and fine sunset views of the mountains. If you'd like to partake of the Aerie's scenery but aren't up for the splurge, check out the **sushi bar,** open during the winter in the Aerie's lounge. It's a friendly, casual atmosphere with really good fresh sushi and live jazz drifting over from the bar area. The Aerie also serves a breakfast buffet in winter.

Another relatively elegant dinner restaurant is the **Lodge Bistro** (807/933-2145 or ext. 3042, 5:30pm-9pm Thurs.-Mon., $22-35), located in the Lodge at Snowbird. Dinners have a French influence, and it's easy to make a meal of small plates ($9-21).

The espresso bar in the Cliff's **Atrium** (801/933-2140, breakfast and lunch daily winter, breakfast 7am-10:30am daily summer, $4-6) has granola, bagels, and fruit. It's quick and has a splendid view of the mountain. The Atrium is also a pleasant place to relax at the end of the day, with a good après-ski menu of sandwiches, vegetarian chili, and other light snacks. For a not-too-extravagant dinner, the **El Chanate** (801/933-2025 or ext. 5100, 11am-9pm daily, $12-24) has reasonably priced (but not wildly exciting) Mexican food and an astounding array of tequilas. It's tucked away in the bottom of Cliff Lodge.

In the Iron Blosam Lodge, the casual **Wildflower Restaurant** (807/933-2230 or ext. 1042, 6pm-9pm Wed.-Sat. winter, $13-20) has good Italian dinners and good views.

Down at the bottom of the canyon, about 15 miles from Snowbird, the **Market Street Grill** (2985 E. Cottonwood Pkwy., 801/942-8860, www.gastronomyinc.com, 11:30am-2pm and 5pm-9:30pm Mon.-Fri., 11:30am-3pm and 4pm-9:30pm Sat., 9am-3pm and 4pm-9pm Sun., $20-50) is an excellent seafood restaurant and oyster bar with a classy, bustling atmosphere.

Getting There

The resort at Snowbird is six miles up Little Cottonwood Canyon and 25 miles southeast of downtown Salt Lake City. Snow tires are required November 1-May 1 with tire chains in the car. During extremely heavy snowstorms, the canyon may be temporarily restricted to vehicles with 4WD or chains.

UTA buses and Canyon Transportation shuttles serve all resorts in Little Cottonwood Canyon. Snowbird provides free shuttle service between the different areas of the resort during skiing hours.

★ ALTA SKI AREA

Alta (801/359-1078, snow report 801/572-3939 www.alta.com, $84 adults, $45 under age 13) has a special mystique among skiers. A combination of deep powder, wide-open terrain, charming accommodations, and the polite but firm exclusion of snowboards make it special, as does its clientele. Many Alta skiers have been coming here for years—it's not uncommon to share a lift with a friendly 70-year-old who, upon debarking the lift, heads straight for the steepest black run.

Do not come to Alta expecting to do anything but ski. There is no shopping, no nightlife, no see-and-be-seen scene. Unlike Park City's resorts, there are no housing developments surrounding the runs at Alta or Snowbird, which gives them a feeling of remoteness. The lack of development around Alta is largely thanks to the late Bill Levitt, owner of the Alta Lodge and mayor for 34 years, who fought developers all the way to the U.S. Supreme Court.

Dogs are not permitted in the town of Alta, unless they receive a special permit. Appeal to the powers-that-be at the town offices, if necessary.

History

The little town of Alta owes its original reputation to rich silver veins and the mining camp's rip-roaring saloon life. Mining started in 1865 with the opening of the Emma Mine and peaked in 1872, when Alta had a population of 5,000 served by 26 saloons and six breweries. Crashing silver prices the following year and a succession of deadly avalanches ended the boom. Little remains from the old days except abandoned mine shafts, a few shacks, and the cemetery.

By the 1930s, only one resident was left, George Watson, who elected himself mayor. In 1938 he deeded 1,800 acres to the U.S. Forest Service. There is some present-day

It's easy to find a challenge at Alta Ski Area.

speculation that Watson didn't ever really own the deeded land, but he did take advantage of the tax breaks he got by handing it over.

Ski enthusiasts brought Alta back to life. The Forest Service hired famous skier Alf Engen to determine Alta's potential as a site for a future ski area. In 1939 Alta's Collins chairlift became the second lift in the United States; detractors complained that the $1.50 per day lift tickets reserved the sport for the rich. Some of the original Collins single chairs are still around; look for them in the Wildcat Base parking lot near the Goldminer's Daughter Lodge.

Terrain and Lifts

The first thing to know about Alta is that it's for skiers; snowboards aren't allowed. And, even though it's right next door to Snowbird, it feels totally different. Whereas Snowbird feels big and brawny, Alta has an almost European quality. To keep the slopes from becoming too crowded, Alta limits the number of skiers allowed, although it's rare that anyone is turned away; this mostly happens during the holidays and on powder-filled weekends.

Alta's season usually runs mid-November-April. Average total snowfall is about 500 inches per year, and snow levels usually peak in March, with depths of about 120 inches. Lifts include two high-speed quads, a high-speed triple, four slower chairlifts, and several tow ropes. Even though Alta has the reputation of being an experts' ski area, there's a fair amount of very nice beginner territory. Of the 116 runs, 25 percent are rated beginner, 40 percent intermediate, and 35 percent advanced. The longest run is 3.5 miles and drops 2,020 vertical feet. Skiers should keep their eyes open as they ride the lifts—porcupines are a common sight in the treetops here.

A good strategy for skiing Alta's 2,200 acres is to begin the day skiing from the Albion Base on the east side of the resort, perhaps even warming up on the mile-long green Crooked Mile run near the Sunnyside lift before heading up the Supreme lift to fairly steep blue runs and some of Alta's famously "steep and

deep" black runs. Later in the day, move over to the Wildcat side, after the sun has had a chance to soften the snow there.

Holders of the Alta-Snowbird pass can cut over to Snowbird's Mineral Basin area from the top of Alta's Sugarloaf lift. The cut-across is not difficult, and Mineral Basin is a fun place to ski.

Alta's **Alf Engen Ski School** (801/359-1078) offers a wide variety of lessons; rentals and child-care services are also available. Guided snowcat skiing and snowboarding in the Grizzly Gulch backcountry is available for expert skiers and boarders with lots of off-trail experience. A two-hour beginner class costs $60; call the ski school to reserve a spot.

Cross-Country Skiing

Rent cross-country skis or purchase a trail pass ($10) from the ticket office at the base of the Wildcat lift, near the western end of groomed cross-country trails. This 1.9-mile (3-km) loop is groomed for both classic and skate skiing; it's not the world's most exciting trail—it essentially parallels the tow rope that runs between the Wildcat and Albion lifts—but it's a good place to learn cross-country techniques or get your legs in shape at the beginning of the season.

More ambitious cross-country skiers can head up the unplowed summer road to Albion Basin. Snowcats often pack the snow. The road begins at the upper end of the Albion parking lot, then climbs gently to the top of the Albion lift, where skiers can continue to Albion Basin. Intermediate and advanced skiers can also ski to Catherine Pass and Twin Lakes Pass. Cross-country skiers may ski the beginner (green) Alta trails.

Accommodations

Alta's accommodations are excellent, though pricey: Even bunk beds in a dorm room cost over $100. Note, however, that room rates at all of the lodges listed here include breakfast and dinner. In summer, room rates drop by nearly half. Note that there's an additional room tax of over 12 percent, and most lodges

Dealing with High Altitude

Suppose some skiers leave their sea-level hometown at 5pm on Thursday, fly to Salt Lake City, and get the first tram up from the Snowbird base area at 9am on Friday. By 9:15am, they're at 11,000 feet. No wonder they feel tired before they even start skiing.

It's hard to predict who will be immobilized by the altitude. Men seem to have more problems than women, and athletes often feel worse than more sedentary people. But the altitude (and the dry air that goes along with it) can have a host of effects.

EFFECTS OF HIGH ALTITUDE

- Sleeplessness.

- Increased drug potency, especially with tranquilizers and sedatives.

- Increased UV radiation. People taking tetracycline are especially sensitive to the sun.

- Stuffy nose. The dry air can make your sinus tissues swell and feel stuffy. Antihistamines or decongestants just make the tissues swell more.

- Increased sensitivity to MSG.

- Increased flatulence.

- Slightly decreased fertility (decreased testosterone production in men; delayed ovulation in women).

- Slow-drying, thick nail polish.

TIPS

- Don't expect to go full steam all at once. Day two can be particularly rough; don't feel bad about knocking off early and taking a nap. Rest is good, even when sleep is difficult.

- Don't take it too easy; it's best to get some light exercise.

- Drink lots of water and avoid alcohol for the first two or three days.

- Decrease salt intake to prevent fluid retention.

- Breathe deeply.

- Wear sunglasses or goggles. It is easy to sunburn your eyes and damage your corneas.

- Use a vaporizer at night; most ski resorts have them in the guest rooms.

- Try not to arrive with a cold. (Ha!)

- If you're seriously prone to high altitude's ill effects, consult your doctor before your trip. Diamox, a prescription drug, stimulates the respiratory system and decreases fluid retention, easing the effects of high altitude.

tack on a 15 percent service charge in lieu of tipping.

The easiest way to find a room is simply to call a reservation service: **Alta Vacations** (800/220-4067, www.altavacations.net) can make reservations at all lodgings and arrange transportation and ski packages.

In Alta, one of the most charming and most central places to stay is the **Alta Lodge** (801/742-3500 or 800/707-2582, www.altalodge.com, dorm bed $115-140 pp, standard room $336-503 includes breakfast, afternoon tea, and dinner), an old-fashioned ski lodge that oozes authenticity.

Rates include breakfast and dinner. Alta Lodge, built in 1939, is not fancy. In fact, descending the four flights of wood-plank stairs from street level is a bit like entering a mine. Fortunately, at the bottom of this shaft, guests are greeted by a friendly dog, engaging people, and a super-size bottle of sunscreen at the check-in window. The atmosphere is relaxed, and the Sitzmark Club, the lodge's bar, is lively. There are no TVs in the guest rooms at Alta Lodge, but a game room off the lobby has a big-screen TV. The lodge also has a good ski-and-play program for kids.

The most luxurious place to stay in town is **Alta's Rustler Lodge** (801/742-2200 or 888/532-2582, www.rustlerlodge.com, dorm bed $185 pp, standard room $460-750 d), with a heated outdoor pool, a fine-dining restaurant, and spacious guest rooms. But even here, there's no pretense. Après-ski, it's common to see guests wandering around the lobby swathed in their thick hotel bathrobes. The Rustler spa offers massage, facials, full-body skin care, and "altitude therapy"; call the lodge to book an appointment.

Alta's oldest, smallest, and most rustic place to stay is the **Snowpine Lodge** (801/742-2000, www.thesnowpine.com, dorm bed $144, standard room with private bath $395-509 d). It was built as a Works Progress Administration (WPA) project in 1938, and its original design was a smaller version of Timberline Lodge on Oregon's Mount Hood, another WPA ski lodge. Since then, the Snowpine has been extensively remodeled, but it is still small and cozy. Like Alta Lodge, the Snowpine is an easy place to make friends—the lobby area, the outdoor hot tub, and the dining room are all very convivial.

The **Alta Peruvian Lodge** (801/742-3000 or 800/453-8488, www.altaperuvian.com, men's dorm bed $150, standard room $329-609 includes breakfast, lunch, and dinner) is another good choice, with its large heated outdoor pool and grand lobby. Like most of the other local lodgings, the Peruvian has a

colorful history. In 1947 its owner acquired two hospital barracks from Brigham City, over 100 miles to the north, hauled them to Alta, and hooked them together. Although the original structure still stands, the lodge has been considerably updated and modernized.

The **Goldminer's Daughter Lodge** (801/742-2300, www.goldminersdaughterlodge.com, dorm bunk $168, private bedroom $378-516) is close to the base of the Wildcat lift, near the large parking area, with easy ski-in, ski-out access. (All of Alta's lodgings have easy access from the slopes, but most are up-slope from the lifts, meaning that at the end of the day, you've got to be hauled back to your lodge on a tow rope.) While the Goldminer's Daughter doesn't have quite the history or ambience of many of Alta's lodgings, it's plenty comfortable.

In addition to the traditional ski lodges, there are condos available for rent, including a wide range of properties through **Alta Chalets** (801/424-2426, www. altachalets. com). Be sure to pick up groceries in Salt Lake City; there are no food stores up here.

Food

Since virtually all of Alta's lodges include breakfast and dinner for their guests, Alta does not have a highly developed restaurant scene. All of the lodge dining rooms are open to the public; of these, the Rustler and Alta Lodge are particularly good places for dinner.

Stop for lunch on the mountain at **Watson Shelter** (801/799-2296, 11am-3pm daily, $7-13), mid-mountain beneath the top of the Wildcat lift. Upstairs, **Collin's Grill** (801/799-2297, 11:30am-3pm daily, $12-25) is a sit-down restaurant.

Alta's one real restaurant of note is the **Shallow Shaft** (801/742-2177, www.shallowshaft.com, 5:30pm-9pm daily, $18-40), across the road from Alta Lodge. Although the place looks a little dubious from the outside, the interior has great views of the ski mountain. Along with good steaks and chops, pizza is available to go; the wine list is as good as you'll find in Utah.

Getting There

Alta is eight miles up Little Cottonwood Canyon. Snow tires are required in the canyon November 1-May 1 with tire chains in the car. During extremely heavy snowstorms, the canyon may be temporarily restricted to vehicles with 4WD or chains; occasionally it shuts down entirely.

Parking can be difficult in Alta. Pay attention to the No Parking signs, as parking regulations are enforced.

UTA buses and Canyon Transportation shuttles serve all resorts in Little Cottonwood Canyon. **Alta Shuttle** (801-274-0225 or 866/274-0225, www.altashuttle.com, $37 one-way any trip) runs among the airport, Alta, and Park City resorts.

HIKING

Before heading up for a hike in Little Cottonwood Canyon, make sure that your dog is not along for the trip. Because this heavily used canyon is part of the Salt Lake City watershed, environmental regulations prohibit pets, even in the car.

White Pine, Red Pine, and Maybird Gulch

These trails lead to pretty alpine lakes. Red Pine and Maybird Gulch are in the Lone Peak Wilderness (www.fs.usda.gov/uwcnf). All three trails begin from the same trailhead and then diverge into separate valleys. On any one of them, you'll enjoy wildflowers and superb high-country scenery. This whole area is heavily used by hikers.

Start from White Pine trailhead (elev. 7,700 feet), 5.3 miles up the canyon and one mile beyond Tanners Flat Campground. The trails divide after one mile; turn sharply left for White Pine Lake or continue straight across the stream for Red Pine Lake and Maybird Gulch. Red Pine Trail contours around a ridge, then parallels Red Pine Fork to the lake (elev. 9,680 feet)—a beautiful deep pool ringed by conifers and alpine meadows. Maybird Gulch Trail begins two miles up Red Pine Trail from White Pine Fork and leads to tiny Maybird Lakes. From the trailhead,

The Shallow Shaft is Alta's only real restaurant.

White Pine Lake is 3.5 miles with 2,300 feet of elevation gain, Red Pine Lake is 3.5 miles with 1,920 feet of elevation gain, and Maybird Lakes are 4.5 miles with 2,060 feet of elevation gain.

Peruvian Gulch-Hidden Peak Trail

These trails give you the advantage of hiking just one way from either the top or bottom by using the Snowbird tram. From the top of Hidden Peak (elev. 11,000 feet), the trail crosses open rocky country on the upper slopes and spruce- and aspen-covered ridges lower down, then follows an old mining road down Peruvian Gulch. Elevation change along the 3.5-mile trail is 2,900 feet.

Catherine Pass

It's a lovely 1.5-mile hike to Catherine Pass (with 900 feet of elevation gain) and just under five miles to Brighton. After the big parking area just past the Snowpine Lodge, the road becomes dirt; follow it another two miles to a trailhead for Catherine Pass.

Cecret Lake Trail

At the end of the road past Snowpine Lodge is the Albion Basin Campground and Cecret Lake Trail, which climbs glacier-scarred granite slopes to a pretty alpine lake (elev. 9,880 feet) below Sugarloaf Mountain. Wildflowers put on colorful summer displays along the way. The trail is just one mile long and makes a good family hike; elevation gain is 360 feet. Continue another mile for fine views south to Mount Timpanogos from Germania Pass.

CAMPGROUNDS

Tanners Flat Campground (with water, mid-May-mid-Oct., $23) is 4.3 miles up Little Cottonwood Canyon at an elevation of 7,200 feet. **Albion Basin Campground** (with water, late June-mid-Sept., $21) is 11 miles up the road, near the head of the canyon, at an elevation of 9,500 feet; the last 2.5 miles are gravel road. Both campgrounds accept reservations (877/444-6777, www.recreation.gov, $9 reservation fee).

Park City

With three ski areas and the Utah Olympic Park, Park City (pop. about 7,800) is noted worldwide for its snow sports: The U.S. national ski team trains here, and many of the 2002 Winter Olympic competitions took place in the valley. In summer, guests flock to the resorts to golf and explore the scenic mountain landscapes on horseback, mountain bike, or foot.

However, there's a lot more to Park City than recreation: The well-heeled clientele that frequents the resorts has transformed this old mining town into the most sophisticated shopping, dining, and lodging center in Utah. However, such worldly comforts come at a cost. Condominium developments and trophy homes stretch for miles, encroaching on the beauty that brought people here in the first place.

Even if you're not a skier or hiker, plan to explore Park City's historic downtown. Late-19th-century buildings along Main Street and on the hillsides recall Park City's colorful and energetic past. Here you'll find a historical museum, art galleries, specialty shops, and fine restaurants. A busy year-round schedule of arts and cultural events (including the Sundance Film Festival), concerts, and sports also help keep Park City hopping.

Orientation

Park City is in a mountain valley (elev. 7,000 feet) on the east side of the Wasatch Range, 31 miles east of Salt Lake City via I-80 and Highway 224. The principal exit for Park City is called Kimball Junction, and although Park City proper is seven miles south, the condominiums and shopping centers begin immediately. Just south of Kimball Junction is the Canyons resort, with its mammoth lodges, and Utah Olympic Park, the ski-jump facility. In Park City proper, the Park City Mountain Resort is just west of downtown; most businesses stretch along historic Main Street. Two miles southeast of Park City is Deer Valley, the state's most exclusive ski resort and an upscale real estate development.

SIGHTS

No matter what else you do in Park City, spend an hour or two wandering along historic Main Street. Even with the influx of galleries, gift shops, and trendy restaurants, there's still considerable Old West charm here.

Park City Museum

Drop in to the renovated and expanded **Park City Museum** (528 Main St., 435/649-7457, www.parkcityhistory.org, 10am-7pm Mon.-Sat., noon-6pm Sun., $10 adults, $5 ages 7-17) to see historic exhibits on Park City's colorful past. In October 1868, with winter fast approaching, three off-duty soldiers from Fort Douglas discovered a promising outcrop

Park City

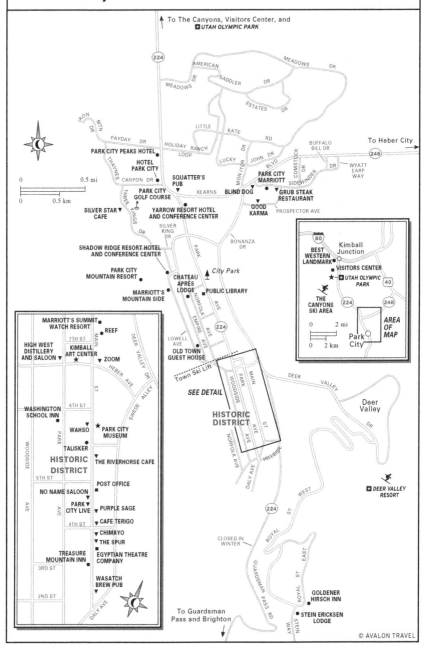

To The Canyons, Visitors Center, and
⊞ UTAH OLYMPIC PARK

224

MEADOWS DR

AMERICAN

SADDLER DR

MEADOWS DR

ESTATES DR

IRON MTN DR

PAYDAY DR

THAYNES

LITTLE

KATE

RD

HOLIDAY
RANCH
LOOP

LUCKY DR

MONITOR DR

JOHN DR

COMSTOCK BLVD

BUFFALO
BILL DR

SIDEWINDER DR

WYATT
EARP
WAY

To Heber City

248

PARK CITY PEAKS HOTEL

HOTEL
PARK CITY

CANYON DR

SQUATTER'S
PUB

KEARNS

PARK CITY
MARRIOTT

PARK CITY
GOLF COURSE

BLIND DOG

GRUB STEAK
RESTAURANT

THREE KINGS DR

SILVER STAR ▼
CAFE

YARROW RESORT HOTEL
AND CONFERENCE CENTER

GOOD
KARMA

PROSPECTOR AVE

SILVER
KING
DR

BONANZA
DR

SHADOW RIDGE RESORT HOTEL
AND CONFERENCE CENTER

PARK
DR

PARK CITY
MOUNTAIN RESORT

City Park

CHATEAU
APRES
LODGE

PUBLIC LIBRARY

NORFOLK AVE

EMPIRE AVE

224

MARRIOTT'S
MOUNTAIN SIDE

LOWELL
AVE

EMPIRE AVE

OLD TOWN
GUEST HOUSE

Town Ski Lift

SEE DETAIL

PARK AVE

WOODSIDE

MAIN ST

DEER VALLEY DR

HISTORIC
DISTRICT

NORFOLK AVE

DALY AVE

HILLSIDE

Deer
Valley

DEER VALLEY RESORT

224

ROYAL ST WEST

ROYAL ST EAST

CLOSED IN
WINTER

GUARDSMAN PASS RD

STEIN WAY

GOLDENER
HIRSCH INN

STEIN ERICKSEN
LODGE

To Guardsman
Pass and Brighton

0   0.5 mi
0   0.5 km

Detail (Historic District)

MARRIOTT'S SUMMIT
WATCH RESORT

REEF

7TH ST

MAIN ST

HIGH WEST
DISTILLERY
AND SALOON ▼

KIMBALL
ART CENTER

ZOOM

HEBER AVE

DEER VALLEY DR

SWEDE ALLEY

WASHINGTON
SCHOOL INN

6TH ST

WAHSO

PARK AVE

PARK CITY
MUSEUM

TALISKER

HISTORIC
DISTRICT

THE RIVERHORSE CAFE

WOODSIDE AVE

5TH ST

NO NAME SALOON

POST OFFICE

PARK AVE

PARK
CITY LIVE

PURPLE SAGE

4TH ST

CAFE TERIGO

CHIMAYO

THE SPUR

TREASURE
MOUNTAIN INN

EGYPTIAN THEATRE
COMPANY

3RD ST

WASATCH
BREW PUB

2ND ST

DALY AVE

To Guardsman
Pass and Brighton

Area of map inset

80

Kimball
Junction

BEST
WESTERN
LANDMARK

VISITORS CENTER

★ ⊞ UTAH OLYMPIC
PARK

THE
CANYONS
SKI AREA

224

40

248

AREA
OF
MAP

0   2 mi
0   2 km

Park
City

© AVALON TRAVEL

Historic buildings along Park City's Main Street house upscale shops and restaurants.

Kimball Art Center

The large civic **Kimball Art Center** (638 Park Ave., 435/649-8882, www.kimball-art.org, 10am-5pm Mon.-Thurs., 10am-7pm Fri., noon-7pm Sat., noon-5pm Sun., donation), at the corner of Heber and Park near the bottom of Main Street, exhibits works by noted artists and sponsors classes and workshops. Two galleries display monthly changing shows of paintings, prints, sculptures, ceramics, photography, and other media. Look for other art galleries along Main Street.

PARK CITY MOUNTAIN RESORT

The first great thing about **Park City Mountain Resort** (office 435/649-8111, www.parkcitymountain.com, lift tickets $105 adults, $68 seniors, $66 ages 7-12) is its convenience to downtown Park City: The Town Lift loads right above Main Street. The other thing skiers and snowboarders love about this place is its expanse. There's a lot of terrain, good bowl skiing for experts, and some of Utah's best terrain parks and pipes for snowboarders. In spite of all this space, the resort can get very crowded, especially on weekends and holidays.

The price of lift tickets varies depending on conditions and the time of purchase. Prepaying for a multiday pass offers the best deals. Purchase multiday tickets on the website or by calling guest services (800/227-2754).

Ski season usually runs mid-November-mid-April. Lifts operate 9am-4pm daily; night skiing runs 4pm-9pm daily late December-March.

History

Although Park City locals began messing around on skis and building ski jumps in the 1930s, the resort didn't open until 1963. Skiers and snowboarders can check out signs erected by the Park City Historical Society to mark old mining sites around the resort.

Park City Mountain Resort hosted all the snowboarding events and the men's and women's giant alpine slalom in the 2002 Winter

of ore on a hillside two miles south of the present town site. Their sample assayed at 96 ounces of silver per ton, with lesser values of lead and gold. Two years later, the Flagstaff Mine began operation, and development of one of the West's richest mining districts took off. What had been a peaceful valley with grazing cattle now swarmed with hordes of fortune hunters and rang with the sound of pickaxes. In 1898 a fire raced along Main Street, reduced 200 businesses and houses to ashes, and left much of the population homeless. Determined citizens immediately set to work rebuilding, and they constructed a new downtown within three months. Many of the businesses you see along Main Street date from that time. The museum is in the old City Hall Building, built in 1885 and rebuilt after the 1898 fire. There are great photos of skiers from the 1930s, and a car from an old underground chairlift (remember, this was a mining town). Go downstairs to see the original jail, known as the "dungeon."

Olympics. The resort was owned by Powdr Resorts, which also runs Mount Bachelor in Bend, Oregon, and Killington in Vermont. After a land-use dispute with Talisker, the resort's landowner, the Park City Mountain Resort was sold to Vail Resorts in the fall of 2014, with plans to combine operations with Vail's other resort in the area, The Canyons.

Terrain and Lifts

Many people access the ski area via the Town Lift, but the main base area is actually about 0.5 mile north, at the Resort Center. This is where the main resort parking lot is, and from here, lifts can get you to various points on the mountain.

Four high-speed six-passenger lifts, three high-speed quads, and nine slower chairlifts carry up to 20,200 skiers per hour high onto the eastern slope of the Wasatch Range. More than 100 trails range in length 0.25-3.5 miles (17 percent easier, 52 percent more difficult, and 31 percent most difficult). Three terrain parks and a super-pipe are part of Park City's successful effort to attract snowboarders. Experienced skiers and boarders can enjoy the powder in five open bowls near the top of the mountain on a total of 650 acres. The total vertical drop is 3,100 feet from the top of Jupiter Bowl to the Resort Center.

Blue runs dominate the lower and middle part of the mountain. Intermediate skiers and boarders will appreciate the hillside full of blue cruisers off the King Con high-speed quad; even beginners can get a nice long run from the mid-mountain (it's easy to get to by riding first the Town Lift, then Bonanza) by following the Home Run trail back to the Town Lift base. The Jupiter and McConkey's lifts ferry expert skiers and boarders to a series of steeper bowls. Actually, the lifts get you to only a couple of areas near the bowls; after getting off the lifts, many people hike along the ridges to find just the right run down.

Mountain hosts are posted around this sprawling resort, helping visitors find their way back to the Town Lift base or over to the challenging Jupiter Bowl area. Park City

ski area and the adjacent resort village offer night skiing, a ski school, rentals, ski shops, ice-skating, and restaurants (three are on the slopes).

Skiing at Park City Mountain Resort is one of several outdoor activities that people with disabilities can learn with the help of the **National Ability Center** (435/649-3991 voice or TDD, www.discovernac.org), located on the edge of town. The center provides special equipment and instruction at affordable rates, offers programs to people of all ages, and is open for summer programs as well.

Summer Activities

Although the Park City ski area shuts down most of its lifts for the summer, the resort remains open and maintains 30 miles of trails for mountain bikers, hikers, and horseback riders; you can ride up the Town or Payday Lift ($11) with your bike or picnic hamper. A free map of designated mountain biking trails is available from the resort and local bike shops.

Summertime thrill-seekers can ride the **Alpine Coaster** (11am-8pm Mon.-Thurs., 11am-9pm Fri.-Sat., 11am-6pm Sun. mid-June-Labor Day, shorter hours mid-May-mid-June and Labor Day-mid-Oct., noon-4pm daily winter, $20 driver, $7 youth passenger) through the aspen glades on an elevated track as it winds over a mile of curves, bends, and loops. Ride a lift to the top of the track, suck in your breath, and plummet downhill on this roller coaster-like ride.

In addition to the Alpine Coaster, which runs on tracks, the ski area has an **Alpine Slide** (11am-8pm Mon.-Thurs., 11am-9pm Fri.-Sat., 11am-6pm Sun. mid-June-Labor Day, shorter hours mid-May-mid-June and Labor Day-mid-Oct., $12 adults per ride, $3 under 48 inches tall and older than age 2), which is like a toboggan on a giant curving sliding board. A chairlift takes you to the start of a 0.5-mile track that twists and winds down the hillside. No special skills are needed to ride the little wheeled sled.

Even more frightening is the **zip rider**

(11am-8pm Mon.-Thurs., 11am-9pm Fri.-Sat., 11am-6pm Sun. mid-June-Labor Day, shorter hours mid-May-mid-June and Labor Day-mid-Oct., $20), a cable ride that makes a 60-second, 500-foot plunge along 2,300 feet. At its highest point, the rider is suspended 110 feet off the ground. Riders must weigh 75-275 pounds.

Other summer activities include a climbing wall, horseback rides, miniature golf, and hiking.

★ DEER VALLEY RESORT

Deer Valley Resort (435/649-1000 or 800/424-3337, ski report 435/649-2000, www.deervalley.com, lifts 9am-4:15pm early Dec.-mid-Apr., full-day $114 adults, $72 ages 5-12, $81 over age 64, afternoon $95 adults, $59 ages 5-12, $69 over age 64) is the crème de la crème of Utah ski areas. You'll find good, uncrowded skiing on immaculately groomed trails with all the extras of upscale accommodations, gourmet dining, attentive service, and polished brass everywhere. Lift operators steady the chairs as you plunk your bottom down, mountain guides lead free tours, and at the top of nearly every lift, a friendly green-parka-clad host points you to a run that's right for you. And in spite of its reputation as being a cushy, glitzy area for spoiled rich folks, the skiing here can be great, and the people riding the lifts are by and large friendly and interesting.

Deer Valley prohibits snowboards. The ski area is 1.5 miles south of downtown Park City (33 miles east of Salt Lake City), and free shuttle buses connect the resort and the town.

History

Although a small ski area called Snow Park operated in this area 1947-1965, Deer Valley did not open until 1981. The owners, Edgar and Polly Stern, wanted to provide a resort that was both easy to get to and more luxurious than other ski areas. The Sterns were soon joined by Roger Penske; the resort is still privately owned, with its longtime manager, Bob Wheaton, taking an active role. Like Park City's other ski areas, Deer Valley was built on private land (as opposed to the Cottonwood areas, which are on U.S. Forest Service leases) and is fueled by development. It's rather like the typical golf course development, where expensive homes are built immediately adjacent to the area, meaning that you're frequently skiing past incredibly huge, expensive homes. The 2002 Olympic

During the summer, the Town Lift ferries hikers and sightseers up the mountain.

slalom, mogul, and aerial events were held at Deer Valley.

Terrain and Lifts

Deer Valley spans six mountains: Bald Eagle Mountain, Bald Mountain, Little Baldy Peak, Empire Canyon, Lady Morgan, and Flagstaff Mountain. The main base area and parking is at Snow Park, but the mid-mountain Silver Lake area is much more of a hub. In fact, at the end of the day, you can't just ski straight down to the parking area; instead, you must make your way to Silver Lake, take a short ride on the Homestake lift out of the valley, then ski down Bald Eagle Mountain to the base.

The slopes are served by 21 lifts, including one high-speed four-passenger gondola and 12 high-speed quads, providing 100 runs, six bowls, and a vertical drop of 3,000 feet. The longest run is 2.8 miles. Twenty-seven percent of the skiing is rated easier, 41 percent more difficult, and 32 percent most difficult. Deer Valley has the reputation of coddling skiers (and it's true that the resort provides a green or blue way down from the top of every lift), but there's plenty of challenging territory for advanced skiers, especially in Empire Canyon, which has good access via the Lady Morgan lift.

Deer Valley is famous for its meticulously groomed trails. To find out what has been groomed, check the boards at the top of every mountain. Mountain hosts can also steer you to freshly groomed trails or onto ungroomed powder.

The majestic **Snow Park Lodge** (elev. 7,200 feet) contains the main ticket office, a ski school, rentals, a ski shop, child-care service, a gift shop, and a restaurant. You can drive three miles and 1,000 feet higher to **Silver Lake Lodge** (parking is more limited), a major hub of activity on the mountain, with more restaurants and luxury hotels.

Guides lead free tours of the mountain at 9:30am daily for advanced skiers and at 10am daily for intermediates from the Snow Park Lodge and at 1:30pm daily for intermediate and advanced skiers from the Silver Lake Lodge.

Bald Eagle Mountain, near the Snow Park base, contains the main beginners' area and served as a site for events in the 2002 Olympics. Aspiring slalom skiers can take a run on the Know You Don't slalom course; the Champion mogul course is also open to the public. At 9,400 feet, Bald Mountain is steeper and more exposed; its intermediate and advanced runs have spectacular views but often get skied out in the afternoon. Find steep, ungroomed trails in the Sultan and Mayflower areas.

On the right (west) side of Flagstaff Mountain (elev. 9,100 feet), the snow often holds up well, making its intermediate and beginner ski trails good bets for skiing later in the day. Blue runs off the Northside Express are good for intermediates. The Flagstaff area also has tree skiing and access to Ontario Bowl. Empire Canyon (elev. 9,570 feet) has skiing for all abilities, including a family ski area off the Little Chief lift, challenging but skiable intermediate terrain, and some of the most advanced skiing at Deer Valley, including eight chutes and three bowls. The classic last run of the day is Last Chance, which goes past stunning ski houses and some fairly amazing yard art all the way to the parking area. Tired skiers can also board the Silver Lake Express from the top and ride it back to the Snow Park base.

To prevent overcrowded trails, Deer Valley restricts the number of skiers on the mountain and often needs to restrict ticket sales during Christmas, New Year's, and Presidents Day weeks. If you're planning on skiing here during the holidays, reserve lift tickets at least a few days in advance.

Summer Activities

Hikers and sightseers can catch the Sterling and Silver Lake lifts (10am-5pm daily mid-June-Labor Day, full-day pass $23, scenic ride $15 children or seniors) to explore more than 50 miles of trails running from the peak. Rates for bike riders are $40 full-day, $29 single-ride; helmets are required. Mountain biking instruction, rentals, and tours are available; call the resort (888/754-8477) for more information. Summer is also the season for off-road cycling events, Utah Symphony concerts, and music festivals. For horseback rides, call Deer Valley Stables (866/783-5819). The resort is also the site of summertime stand-up paddleboarding classes (801/558-9878, www.supstats.com).

Accommodations

There are abundant condominium lodgings in Deer Valley, many almost immediately adjacent to the slopes. The best way to book lodgings is to contact **Deer Valley Central Reservations** (435/645-6528 or 800/558-3337, www.deervalley.com) and let them guide you through the process. The website has a good interactive map that will give you an overview of the accommodations and prices. Package deals are often available, but rates are still high—it's hard to find a condo for under $600 or a hotel room for less than $300 per night. But remember, you're only a couple of miles from Park City and about an hour from Salt Lake. It's worth skiing Deer Valley even if you can't afford to sleep here.

Accommodations are in two main areas: **Snow Park,** the Deer Valley base area, which is about one mile from downtown Park City, and the **Silver Lake** area, located mid-mountain approximately 3.2 miles from the Snow Park base area. A short distance past Silver Lake is the Empire Pass area, with a few condos. Both Snow Park and Silver Lake lodges are just day lodges.

Silver Lake

If money is no object, book a room at the luxurious **Stein Ericksen Lodge** (7700 Stein Way, 435/649-3700 or 800/453-1302, www.steinlodge.com, $750-2,200), mid-mountain in the Silver Lake area. The lodge is like a Norwegian fantasy castle built of log and stone. Guest rooms are exquisitely appointed, and there's a day spa with a pool and a fitness room. The restaurant here is one of the best rated in the area. You can book a guest room

here either through the lodge itself or through Deer Valley Central Reservations.

Another extremely comfortable place is the **Goldener Hirsch Inn** (7570 Royal St. E., 435/649-7770 or 800/252-3373, www.goldenerhirschinn.com, $529-1,139) in exclusive Silver Lake Village; it's a small Austrian-style ski-in, ski-out inn with beautifully furnished guest rooms (the gorgeous hand-carved beds were imported from Austria), hot tubs, a sauna, a lounge, meeting facilities, and underground parking. The restaurant is also extremely good.

Snow Park

At the Snow Park base, **The Lodges at Deer Valley** (435/645-6528 or 800/558-3337, www.deervalley.com, rooms $415-455, apartments $625-1,070) has hotel rooms, which have mini fridges and toasters, along with full-kitchen condos; the complex has a year-round outdoor pool and hot tub. These are joined by many, many other condos; central reservations can help you select a place.

Food

The mid-mountain lodges here are unique because you can actually drive to them.

Silver Lake

Several cafeteria-style restaurants make the Silver Lake Lodge a good spot for a quick lunch. On a sunny day, stretch out in the lawn chairs on McHenry's Beach, the big sunny spot in front of the lodge, with your meal. There are also a couple of small coffee shops on the mountain—they serve Deer Valley's trademark turkey chili and good cookies. At any of Deer Valley's restaurants, look for cheese from **Deer Valley Artisan Cheese**, made using cow and goat milk from the nearby Heber Valley.

For a sit-down lunch, après-ski snacks, or dinner, the **Royal Street Café** (435/645-6724, 11:30am-8pm daily winter, 11:30am-2pm daily summer, $12-28) in the Silver Lake Lodge is a good bet. For fine dining, the award-winning **Mariposa** (435/649-1000,

5:45pm-9pm Tues.-Sun. in ski season, $16-36) is a wonderful splurge, preparing "classic and current" cuisine; fresh fish, rack of lamb, steaks, chicken, and other meats receive savvy sauces and preparations. Reservations are recommended.

At the **Goldener Hirsch Inn** (435/649-7770, 7am-9pm daily, $28-50, reservations recommended) in Silver Lake Village, dishes reflect both an Austrian heritage and New World pizzazz: Wiener schnitzel ($38) is the house specialty, and fondue ($42) is a popular après-ski option.

At the Stein Ericksen Lodge, the elegant **Glitretind Restaurant** (435/645-6455, 7am-9pm daily, $27-39, reservations recommended) serves contemporary cuisine with a few Asian touches.

Snow Park

If you take an informal survey of lift riders here, the most popular meal in Deer Valley seems to be the **Seafood Buffet** at the **Snow Park Lodge** (435/649-1000, 6pm-9pm Mon.-Tues. and Thurs.-Sat. in ski season, $64 adults, $34 children). Both quality and quantity are unstinting.

From the base, take a funicular up to the massive St. Regis Resort to find Jean-Georges Vongerichten's ★ **J&G Grill** (2300 Deer Valley Dr. E., 435/940-5760, www.jggrill-deercrest.com, 7am-2pm daily and 5pm-9pm Mon.-Thurs., 5:30pm-9:30pm Fri.-Sat., $26-56), where the meats are grilled simply, but the quality of the ingredients and the elegance of the restaurant make it one of the area's finest. If you want to sample the atmosphere and have a drink and a burger ($18), head to the bar, but consider leaving your stinky ski parka in the car.

THE CANYONS

Talk about infinitely expanding ski areas: **The Canyons** (4000 The Canyons Dr., 435/649-5400, reservations 888/226-9667, www.canyonsresort.com), Utah's largest and fastest-growing resort, sports an entire city's worth of buildings near the bottom of the lifts. More high-speed lifts, including one with heated seats, than any other Utah resort reach nine separate peaks along the Wasatch Mountains, serving 4,000 skiable acres, making the Canyons one of the five largest ski areas in the United States. At the base of the slopes are three large lodge hotels. It's no surprise that, given all this development, ticket prices are pretty high.

The Canyons is 27 miles east of Salt Lake City via I-80 and Highway 224. A free shuttle bus runs between the resort area and Park City.

History

From a fairly small local resort called Park West, this area morphed into Wolf Mountain and then in 1997 became the Canyons. The Canyons is owned by Talisker Land Holdings and operated by Vail Resorts.

Terrain and Lifts

The Canyons (lifts 9am-4pm daily Nov.-Apr., lift tickets $107 adults, $69 seniors and ages 7-12, substantially cheaper online or at 877/625-1553 at least 14 days in advance) is the first Park City ski area you'll reach coming from Salt Lake City. Not counting the Cabriolet gondola from the day-use parking area, another gondola from housing to the base, and a couple of surface tows, the resort has 19 lifts, including an eight-passenger gondola, a detachable six-pack, and four high-speed quads. The 182 ski trails are rated 10 percent beginner, 44 percent intermediate, and 46 percent advanced and expert. The longest run is 2.5 miles and drops 3,190 vertical feet. For snowboarders, there are six natural half pipes and one terrain park. Many locals who once skied at Park City have shifted allegiances to the Canyons, mostly because of the less-crowded slopes here. However, if the snow is iffy, it's usually better to head over to the Cottonwood canyons; when conditions aren't absolutely favorable, the Canyons seems to have the worst snow of any of the Wasatch resorts.

To begin a day at the Canyons, ride the

Cabriolet from the parking area to the resort base. From the base, you'll have to wait in line for the Red Pine gondola, which soars over mountains, valleys, and terrain parks to the Red Pine Lodge, the mid-mountain base. From here, ski down to the Tombstone Express, ride that lift, and from there continue working your way south (left on the trail map) to the top of the Dreamscape lift, which lets out onto a mountainside full of nice blue runs.

Expert skiers and boarders can go from Tombstone to Ninety-Nine 90, a high-speed quad serving expert runs. The views from the top are breathtaking, and the trails there send you meandering through gladed steeps, open bowls, and narrow chutes. You could spend a whole day here, especially after a big snowfall. Also, from here, you can access backcountry skiing on huge bowls way above the tree line. There is a short hike, but it's well worth it.

At the end of the day, ride up on the Super Condor Express, then head home on Upper Boa to Willow Drain, a long easy cruise marred only by an uphill walk at the end. If you can't bear to walk, just ride the gondola back down to the base.

The resort offers day care, supervised lunches, ski lessons, and rentals for the younger set. The Canyons includes a ski school, a rental and sales shop, half a dozen restaurants (three mid-slope), and a free shuttle service from lodges and hotels in Park City.

Summer Activities

The **Red Pine gondola** (10am-6pm daily late June-Aug., 10am-5pm Thurs.-Sun. Sept., $18 adults, $13 ages 5-12) lifts you up to the Red Pine Lodge, where you can eat lunch or embark on a day hike or a mountain bike ride (bikes are permitted on the gondola, but dogs aren't). There's also a disc golf course (free) near the top of the gondola.

A mountain bike park has trails studded with features that demand good bike-handling skills. Two shorter chairlifts offer access to the bike park; a full-day lift ticket includes the gondola and goes for $32.

The resort can also arrange backcountry horseback rides and hot-air balloon rides.

Locals swing by the Cabriolet parking lot for a farmers' market (noon-6pm Wed. summer).

Accommodations

The Grand Summit Hotel, Sundial Lodge, and Silverado Lodge (reservations 866/604-4171, www.canyonsresort.com) are at the base of the ski slopes. Facilities at the **Grand Summit,** which directly fronts the gondola loading platform, include a full-service health club and a spa, including an indoor-outdoor pool, three on-site restaurants, a bar, and a brewpub. The **Sundial Lodge,** about 100 yards from the gondola, has an outdoor heated pool, a hot tub, and an on-site exercise facility. The **Silverado** is a few steps farther downhill, and it is the least expensive place at the resort. It has the requisite outdoor heated pool, hot tub, and exercise room. The Hyatt **Escala Lodges** are near the base of the Sunrise lift.

These enormous hotels are built on a scale unlike any other lodgings in Park City and vie with Canadian national park resorts in terms of grandness and scope. All of the lodges have a mix of hotel rooms and condos; expect to pay $380-550 for the most basic (though luxurious) guest rooms during ski season. However, if you book far in advance, it's possible to find rooms in the $200-250 range. Condos can get quite elaborate and expensive, topping out at more than $1,000 per night.

Just a little way downslope, and served by the Waldorf gondola, is the **Waldorf Astoria Park City** (2100 W. Frostwood Blvd., 435/647-5500, www.parkcitywaldorfastoria.com, from $659), the only lodge that's not booked through the Canyons. On top of the room rate, expect to pay an additional mandatory $35 resort fee.

Although the resort lodgings are prohibitively expensive for many travelers, two of Park City's least expensive hotels, the **Best Western Landmark** (6560 N. Landmark Dr., 435/649-7300, www.bwlandmarkinn.com, $170) and the **Holiday Inn Express** (1501

West Ute Blvd., 435/658-1600, www.holiday-inn.com, $155), are near Kimball Junction, about one mile from the Canyons.

Food

Mid-mountain, at the top of the gondola, the **Red Pine Lodge** (435/615-2888, 8:30am-4pm daily, $7-15) is a good place to grab a breakfast burrito or some lunch without having to disrupt a day on the slopes. It serves the typical pizza, burgers, soup, and salad. Better, indeed excellent, food is served at the ★ **Lookout Cabin** (435/615-2892, 11:30am-3pm daily, $17-22, reservations suggested), a sit-down restaurant just down from the top of the Orange Bubble lift. Warm up with a bowl of bison chili or stay light for afternoon skiing with an amazingly good salmon salad.

In the Grand Summit Hotel, **The Farm** (435/615-8080, 7am-2:30pm and 5pm-10pm daily, $18-38) uses locally sourced ingredients; you'll find an elaborate kale salad here, along with less usual farm-to-table fare such as artichoke stew.

RECREATION

Most sports stores in Park City (and there are lots of them) rent skis and related equipment in winter and bicycles and camping gear in summer. It's also easy to rent equipment, including mountain bikes in the summer, at the ski resorts.

White Pine Touring (1790 Bonanza Dr., 435/649-8710, www.whitepinetouring.com, 9am-6pm daily) rents cross-country skis, mountain-climbing equipment, camping gear, and mountain bikes.

Jans Mountain Outfitters (1600 Park Ave., 435/649-4949, www.jans.com) has downhill, telemark, and cross-country rentals, snowboards, mountain bikes, in-line skates, and fly-fishing gear.

Winter
★ Utah Olympic Park

Built for the 2002 Olympics, **Utah Olympic Park** (3000 Bear Hollow Dr., near the Canyons, 435/658-4200, www.

A freestyle skier jumps into a huge swimming pool at the Utah Olympic Park.

utaholympiclegacy.com, 10am-6pm daily year-round, basic admission is free) was the site of the bobsled, luge, and ski-jump competitions. It is now open to the public for guided tours ($10) of the competition sites, including visits to the top of the K120 ski jump and the bobsled run for panoramic views of the surrounding country.

The mission of the park now is to train aspiring athletes, and visitors can often watch them. During the summer, freestyle skiers do acrobatic jumps and plunge into a huge swimming pool. On Saturday afternoons in summer, there's a freestyle aerial show.

It's also possible to actually do something here, such as take a vigorous (some would say harrowing) bobsled run (summer $60, must be over age 13, winter rides $200, must be over age 15, reservations strongly advised) with a professional driver or ride a zipline ($20) or alpine slide ($15 adults, $5 children with paying adult). In the winter, adults can choose from a spectrum of bobsled, skeleton, luge, and Nordic jumping classes and workshops (from $75).

White Pine Touring

Park City's cross-country ski center, **White Pine Touring** (Park Ave. and Thaynes Canyon Dr., 435/649-6249, www.whitepinetouring.com, mid-Nov.-early Apr., $18 adults, $8 ages 6-12, free under age 7 or over 64), offers rentals, instruction, and guided snowshoe tours. It has a touring center and about 12.4 miles of groomed trails right in town. White Pine also has a yurt ($125-150) in the Uinta Mountains that's available year-round. There is a year-round office and shop (1790 Bonanza Dr., 435/649-8710).

★ Ski Utah Interconnect

If you look at the map, you'll see that Snowbird, Alta, Solitude, Brighton, Deer Valley, and Park City Mountain Resort are not that far from one another and can be linked by backcountry routes. Experienced skiers who are up for a challenging day can explore the backcountry among these ski areas in Big and Little Cottonwood Canyons and Park City with **Ski Utah Interconnect** (801/534-1907, www.skiutah.com, mid-Dec.-mid-Apr., $325, reservations required), which provides a guide service for extensive touring of Wasatch Front ski areas. Touring is with downhill equipment and requires legs of steel and the ability to ski ungroomed powder all day long and do a bit of hiking to reach those great bowls and chutes. Tours on Monday, Tuesday, Wednesday, Friday, and Sunday depart from Deer Valley and move on to Park City Mountain Resort, Solitude, Brighton, Alta, and Snowbird. On Tuesday, Thursday, and Saturday, tours start at Snowbird and visit Alta, Brighton, Solitude, and a lot of backcountry terrain. Rate includes guide service, lunch, lift tickets, and transportation back to the point of origin.

Sleigh Rides

Riding a horse-drawn sleigh to a Western dinner or an evening of entertainment is quickly becoming a Park City tradition. One of the more elaborate activities is offered by **Snowed Inn Sleigh Company** (435/647-3310, www.snowedinnsleigh.com, $89 adults,

$54 children, reservations required), which takes guests on a sleigh ride to a lodge where dinner is served; short rides without dinner are also available ($20 over age 1).

Summer
Parks and Rec Centers
Historic Union Pacific Rail Trail State Park (435/649-6839, http://stateparks.utah.gov, dawn-dusk daily year-round, free) consists of a multiuse nonmotorized trail built to accommodate hikers, bicyclists, horseback riders, and cross-country skiers. The trail parallels I-80 and runs 27 miles from Park City through the town of Coalville to Echo Reservoir. In Park City, from Park Avenue, turn onto Kearns Boulevard, then right onto Bonanza Drive. After about 200 yards, turn left onto Prospector Avenue, where you can catch the trail behind the Park City Plaza; the parking area is on the right.

The city-owned **Park City MARC** (1200 Little Kate Rd., 435/615-5400, www.parkcity.org, $10 visitors) features two outdoor pools, indoor and outdoor tennis, racquetball, basketball, volleyball, aerobics, and saunas.

Ballooning
A flight above Park City on a hot-air balloon is an exhilarating experience. Balloons take off in the early morning year-round, weather permitting, and trips typically include a continental breakfast and postflight champagne toast. The cost is $175-225 for one hour with either **Park City Balloon Adventures** (435/645-8787 or 800/396-8787, www.pcballoonadventures.com) or **Morning Star Balloons** (435/685-8555, www.morningstarballoons.com).

Fishing
Fly-fishing is a favorite pastime in the mountain streams and lakes of the Wasatch Mountains. The Weber and Provo Rivers are well known for their wily native cutthroat, wild brown, and rainbow trout as well as Rocky Mountain whitefish. Get your fishing license, supplies, and a guide at **Park City Fly**

Shop (2065 Sidewinder Dr., 435/645-8382 www.parkcityflyshop.com) or **Trout Bum 2** (4343 N. Hwy. 224, Suite 101, 435/658-1166 or 877/878-2862, www.troutbum2.com, 8am-6pm Mon.-Sat., 8am-5pm Sun. summer, 9am-5pm Mon.-Sat., 9am-4pm Sun. winter).

Golf

Park City has two 18-hole courses, including the city-owned **Park City Golf Club** (Park Ave. and Thaynes Canyon Dr., 435/615-5800, www.parkcitygolfclub.org, from $45). **Wasatch Mountain State Park** (435/654-0532, http://stateparks.utah.gov, $33-35), a short distance away in Midway, has two outstanding public courses.

Hiking

The ski areas open their trails to hikers in summer; pick up a trail map and just head out. **Deer Valley** (435/649-1000 or 800/424-3337, www.deervalley.com), **Park City** (435/649-8111, www.parkcitymountain.com), and **the Canyons** (4000 The Canyons Dr., 435/649-5400, www.thecanyons.com) all offer lift-assisted hiking that takes walkers up to the high country without a wind-sucking foot ascent; see individual resorts for information. From downtown Park City, follow trail signs to the slopes; well-marked trails start just on the edge of town and head uphill. Mountain Trails Foundation (http://mountaintrails.org), a trail advocacy organization, publishes a trail map, available at outdoor stores and the visitor center for a suggested $5 donation.

When hiking around Park City, stay clear of relics of the mining past that lie scattered about. You're likely to come across miners' cabins in all states of decay, hoist buildings, aerial tramway towers, rusting machinery, and great piles of mine tailings. Unlike other parts of the Wasatch Range, most of the land here belongs to mining companies and other private owners. Visitors need to keep a distance from mine shafts—which can be hundreds of feet deep—and respect No Trespassing signs.

Horseback Riding

Red Pine Adventures (2050 White Pine Canyon, 435/649-9445 or 800/417-7669, www.redpinetours.com, from $75) offers trail rides of varying lengths; 1.5-hour rides start several times a day.

Mountain Biking

This is a favorite summer activity in the Park City area, with more than 350 miles of mountain bike trails. Some of the local landowners, including ski resorts and mining companies, have offered access to their land and have even built trail sections at their own expense. Helmets are always required when riding on private land. All three Park City resorts keep a lift open for bikers and hikers during the summer. **Deer Valley** (435/649-1000 or 800/424-3337, www.deervalley.com) has 55 stunning miles of single- and double-track trails; **Park City** (435/649-8111, www.parkcitymountain.com) has 35 miles of trails. **The Canyons** (4000 The Canyons Dr., 435/649-5400, www.thecanyons.com) also offers mountain bikers gondola rides to the top of its lifts; from there they can access many trails. Check out Mountain Trails Foundation's online map (http://mountaintrails.org/map/) to plan a route.

Water Sports

Two-hour **rafting** trips down the Provo River Canyon are offered by **High Country Rafting** (435/649-7678, www.highcountryrafting.com, late Apr.-Oct., $49 adults, $29 under age 13). Trips start at Frazier Park, 30 minutes from Park City. Similarly priced white-water trips down the Weber River, north of Park City, are offered by **Park City Rafting** (435/655-3800, www.parkcityrafting.com). Hone your stand-up paddling skills with **PCSUP** (1375 Deer Valley Rd. S., 801/558-9878, www.parkcitysup.com); board rentals are available. **Boating, waterskiing,** and **stand-up paddling** are popular activities at the Jordanelle, Rockport, and Echo Reservoirs.

The trendy **Park City Live** (427 Main St., 435/649-9123, http://parkcitylive.net) is the largest music venue in town, with long lines at the door, a large crowded dance floor, and special VIP tables. The more down-home **No Name Saloon** (447 Main St., 435/649-6667, www.nonamesaloon.net, 10am-2am daily) is a sports bar with food, including what's often called the town's best burger; head up to the rooftop to spy on Main Street action. Duck into **The Spur** (352 Main St., 435/615-1618, www.thespurbarandgrill.com, 3pm-close daily winter, 5pm-close Wed.-Sun. summer) for rock, acoustic folk, or bluegrass and a friendly, convivial atmosphere. **The Sidecar** (333 Main St., 435/645-7468, 5pm-1am daily) is another low-key place with good live music most nights.

Jazz and pop singers entertain nightly at the **Riverhorse Cafe** (540 Main St., 435/649-3536, www.riverhorsegroup.com, 5:30pm-10pm daily). You can drink a microbrew and chat with friends at **Wasatch Brew Pub** (250 Main St., 435/649-0900, www.wasatchbeers.com, 4pm-midnight Mon.-Fri., 11am-midnight Sat.-Sun.) or, north of the Main Street neighborhood, at **Squatters Pub** (1900 Park Ave., 435/649-9868, www.squatters.com, 8am-10pm Sun.-Thurs., 8am-11pm Fri.-Sat.).

One of the best bars in town, **High West Distillery and Saloon** (703 Park Ave., 435/649-8300, www.highwest.com, 11am-9pm Sun.-Thurs., 11am-10pm Fri.-Sat.), is conveniently located at the bottom of Park City Mountain Resort's Quittin' Time run. Housed in a collection of historic buildings a block off Main Street, High West is classy in an old-fashioned Western ski town kind of way.

Park City's mining-town heritage is blended with a lively recreational scene.

Spas

Both Deer Valley and the Canyons resorts as well as the Waldorf Astoria hotel have full-service spas. There are also a number of spas in the old town area of Main Street.

Don't miss **Mountain Body** (825 Main St., near the Town Lift, 435/655-9342, www.mountainbody.com, 10am-10pm daily), a friendly family-run shop and spa offering locally made lotions and salves for dry high-altitude skin and a wide variety of spa treatments. At **Aura** (405 Main St., 435/658-2872), you'll find an eco-conscious salon and such treatments as hot stone, deep tissue, and sports massage in addition to facials.

ENTERTAINMENT AND EVENTS
Nightlife

As you'd expect in a ski resort, nightlife centers on bars and dance clubs. The principal hangouts are on Main Street, though all the lodges and resorts and most of the larger hotels have bars and clubs of their own.

The Arts
Concerts

Summer is music-festival time in Park City. The Utah Symphony and other classical performers take the stage at Deer Valley's outdoor amphitheater (2250 Deer Valley Dr. S., 435/649-1000, www.deervalleymusicfestival.org) from the third week of July to the third week of August for a summer concert series. The Canyons (801/536-1234, www.thecan-yons.com) offers rock, country, and jazz concerts on Saturday evenings late July-late August. The Park City Beethoven Festival (435/649-5309, www.pcmusicfestival.com) offers chamber music at various locations around town. Although the main concert series is in the summer, the season goes year-round. There are free concerts (6pm-8pm Wed. summer) at Deer Valley's Snow Park amphitheater (435/901-7664, www.deerval-ley.com).

Theater

The **Egyptian Theatre Company** (www.egyptiantheatrecompany.org) puts on dramas, comedies, musicals, and children's shows year-round in the historic Egyptian Theatre (328 Main St., 435/649-9371).

Cinema

Of course the big event is the annual **Sundance Film Festival** (www.sundance.org, mid-late Jan.), which spotlights more than 200 films from around the world and involves at least as many parties as films. Festival ticket packages range from $400 for 10 "nonpremium" films up to a $1,200 "premium" package for 20 films and a couple of parties. Buy these online, as the premium packages sell out early. Toward the end of the festival, individual tickets are often available for $15.

The **Park City Film Series** (435/615-8291, www.parkcityfilmseries.com, Sept.-June) offers art, foreign, and classic films. Check the website for location.

Festivals and Events

Contact the Park City Visitor Information Center (1794 Olympic Parkway, 435/658-9616, www.visitparkcity.com) for the latest news on happenings around town. The year's biggest event is in January, when the stars come to town for the **Sundance Film Festival** (www.sundance.org, mid-late Jan.).

In August more than 200 artists exhibit their work on Main Street for the **Arts Festival** (435/649-8882, www.kimballartcen-ter.org, $10). The **Summit County Fair** (202 E. Park Rd., Coalville, 435/336-3221, www.co.summit.ut.us, Aug.) has a parade, a rodeo, a horse show, roping, a demolition derby, entertainment, and exhibits.

Ski areas open in November. In celebration, there's a big street dance, ski racing, and fireworks, usually near Thanksgiving.

Park City's Egyptian Theatre Company stages plays year-round in this historic building.

Sundance Film Festival

Robert Redford began this noted festival in 1981 as a venue for independent films that otherwise had a difficult time reaching the screen or a mass audience. Since then, the **Sundance Film Festival** (435/658-3456, www.sundance.org) has become the nation's foremost venue for new and innovative cinema. The festival is held in the second half of January, at the height of the ski season, so Park City is absolutely packed and then some. As the festival has grown, some films are now shown at the Tower Theatre in Salt Lake City. Definitely make plans well in advance if you want to attend any of the screenings or festival activities.

Tickets to the screenings can be hard to come by, especially for films with advance buzz or big stars; if you can't get tickets, put your name on waiting lists or join the lines at the theaters for canceled tickets. However, tickets to less well-known films are usually available at the last minute. If you are coming to Park City expressly to see the films, inquire about package tours that include tickets.

Park City is exciting during the festival, as the glitterati of New York and Hollywood descend on the town. You'll see movie stars, some wild clothing, and lots of deal-making.

SHOPPING

Park City's primary shopping venue is historic **Main Street,** which is lined with upscale boutiques, gift shops, galleries, craft shops, and sporting-goods stores.

Markets

The open-air **Park Silly Sunday Market** (435/714-4036, http://parksillysundaymarket.com, 10am-5pm Sun. early June-late Sept.) takes over the lower stretch of Main Street. You'll find lots of arts and crafts, handmade clothing and hats, and at the bottom of the street, food carts and live music. It makes for agreeable shopping and fascinating people watching. The **Park City Farmers' Market** (noon-6pm Wed. early June-Oct.) is held at the Canyons resort's main parking lot (Canyon Resort Dr., 0.25 mile west of Hwy. 224).

Books and Cards

Dolly's Bookstore (510 Main St., 435/649-8062, http://dollysbookstore.com, 10am-10pm daily) has a good selection of books for all ages and interests. **Atticus** (738 Main St., 435/214-7241, www.atticustea.com, 7am-5pm daily) combines the virtues of a used-book store, tea and sandwich shop, and events center. It's

a fun place to hang out and catch Park City's subtle arty-alternative vibe.

Clothing

Panache (738 Main St., 435/649-7037, 10am-7pm Mon.-Sat., 10am-6pm Sun.) offers very stylish high-end women's clothing and jewelry. **Olive & Tweed** (608 Main St., 435/649-9392) is an artisans co-op featuring women's clothing, jewelry, and lots of gifts. **Cake Boutique** (511 Main St., 435/649-1256, 10am-7pm Mon.-Sat., 11am-6pm Sun.) is a fashion-forward clothing store that veers toward designer hipster wear, with lots of denim.

If you like the upscale Western look common in Park City, pick up some togs at **Park City Clothing Company** (558 Main St., 435/649-0555, 10am-6pm daily), with pearl-snap shirts, hats, boots, and jewelry amid the Coca-Cola memorabilia. If it's mostly boots that you're interested in, check out the walls of Western-style boots at **Burns Cowboy Shop** (363 Main St., 435/649-6300).

If your budget doesn't allow for shopping in Park City's high-end boutiques, check the good selection of pre-owned clothing at **Exchange Consignment** (350½ Main St., on Swede Alley beneath the Spur, 435/649-3360, noon-5:30pm daily).

Galleries

There are nearly as many art galleries in tiny Park City as in Salt Lake City; it's a major scene, with lots of high-end art. Most galleries are along busy Main Street, so they aren't hidden away. Here are some favorites.

Gallery MAR (436 Main St., 435/649-3001) represents a wide selection of mostly representational artists. The collection at **Coda Gallery** (804 Main St., 435/655-3803) includes sculpture, painting, and glass, much of it whimsical. **Julie Nester Gallery** (1280 Iron Horse Dr., 435/649-7855) represents a number of national contemporary artists, with more sophisticated works than you'd usually expect in a resort town. **Mountain Trails Gallery** (301 Main St., 435/615-8748) is Park City's top purveyor of Western and wildlife art, in both painting and sculpture. For trophy home-ready landscapes, check out the selection at **Montgomery-Lee Fine Art** (608 Main St., 435/655-3264). For Native American art, antiques, and collectibles, go to the **Crosby Collection** (419 Main St., 435/658-1813).

Park City's real jewel of a gallery is **Kimball Arts Center** (638 Park Ave., 435/649-8882, www.kimball-art.org, 10am-5pm Mon.-Thurs., 10am-7pm Fri., noon-7pm Sat., noon-5pm Sun., donation), a nonprofit community arts center where there's always interesting art to experience. It's an arts education hub plus a sales and exhibition gallery, and it's a great place to catch the spirit of the local artistic community.

ACCOMMODATIONS

Park City is awash in condos, hotels, and B&Bs; guest capacity far exceeds the town's permanent population. Rates peak at dizzying heights during the ski season, when accommodations may also be hard to find. Most lodgings have four different winter rates, which peak at the Christmas holidays and in February-March; there are different rates for weekends and weekdays as well. Many lodgings have rooms at a wide range of prices, from hostel rooms to basic hotel rooms to multiroom suites, so remember that the following price categories are for a standard double room in the winter high (but non-holiday) season. Summer rates are usually about half those given below. During ski season, many lodgings ask for minimum stays—sometimes a weekend, sometimes a full week. Park City's hotel tax is 10.35 percent; add this to any rate you're quoted.

The following accommodations are in addition to the lodges and hotels operated by

the Park Silly Sunday Market

and located at **Deer Valley** (435/645-6528 or 800/558-3337, www.deervalley.com) and **the Canyons** (reservations 888/226-9667, www.thecanyons.com).

Reservation Services

Undoubtedly the easiest way to find a room or condo in Park City is to contact one of the many reservation services; most also offer ski, golf, or other recreational packages. For general Park City lodging, try **Park City Lodging** (855/348-6759, www.parkcitylodging.com) and **Resort Property Management** (800/645-4762, www.resortpropertymanagement.com). **All Seasons Resort Lodging** (888/667-2775, www.allseasonsresortlodging.com) handles a vast number of condo units throughout the valley. For reservations in Deer Valley condos and private homes, contact **Deer Valley Central Reservations** (435/645-6528 or 800/558-3337, www.deervalley.com); it also represents some properties in Park City. The **Park City Area Chamber of Commerce** (www.visitparkcity.com) also has an online lodging locator.

If you're here to ski, and ski widely, ask about the Silver Passport when you book your room. The Silver Passport, a single lift ticket to all three resorts in the Park City area, must be purchased prior to arrival and in conjunction with lodging from participating lodging providers or **Park City Mountain reservations** (800/222-7275).

$50-100

You'll have to give up your privacy to get an inexpensive room in Park City, but it is possible to sleep cheaply at **Chateau Après Lodge** (1299 Norfolk Ave., 435/649-9372, www.chateauapres.com, dorm bed $45, private room $120 d), a short walk from the Park City Mountain Resort base. The lodge has a dedicated following among serious skiers; the guest rooms are far from elegant, but this is really Park City's best deal. The breakfast buffet is a great place to meet other skiers.

Although it's not in town, the **Best Western Holiday Hills** (200 S. 500 W., Coalville, 435/336-4444 or 866/922-7278, www.bwstay.com, $89-119), about 20 minutes northeast of Park City, is a reasonable bet for travelers who want a comfortable guest room (with continental breakfast included) that's only a few bucks more expensive than a lift ticket. It's located just off I-80 at exit 162.

It's also possible to find high-quality lodgings in this price range in Heber City, about 20 minutes from Park City.

$100-200

Out at the Kimball Junction exit on I-80 is the **Best Western Landmark Inn** (6560 N. Landmark Dr., 435/649-7300 or 800/548-8824, www.bwlandmarkinn.com, $169), with a pool, a spa, a breakfast buffet, and a free shuttle to ski areas and downtown Park City. If you want a high-quality reasonably priced (for Park City) hotel room and don't mind being a bit removed from the action, this is a good bet. During the summer, guest rooms are about $50 cheaper.

The **Holiday Inn Express** (1501 West Ute Blvd., 435/658-1600, www.hiexpress.com, $155) is located by the freeway and is close to the Canyons.

Prospector Accommodations (2200 Sidewinder Dr., 435/649-7100 or 800/453-3812, www.allseasonsresortlodging.com, standard rooms $149-159, 2-bedroom condos $249-269) is one of several hotel-condominium complexes managed by All Season Resorts. Several different room types are scattered through eight different buildings about one mile from Main Street and the main Park City lifts; the city's free shuttle bus stops here. Guests can use the adjacent Silver Mountain Sports Club.

A little ways from downtown is the **Park City Peaks Hotel** (2121 Park Ave., 435/649-5000 or 800/649-5012, www.parkcitypeaks.com, $169-219). It is an upscale hotel that is notable mainly because its summer rates are sometimes well under $100.

$200-300

A homey option for skiers and other outdoors enthusiasts is the ★ **Old Town Guest House** (1011 Empire Ave., 435/649-2642, www.oldtownguesthouse.com, $249-299, breakfast included), owned by a woman who leads backcountry ski tours with Ski Utah Interconnect. The old house is a comfortable, though not froufrou, B&B; the upstairs McKonkey's suite is most spacious and has the most privacy.

Adjacent to the Park City ski area is the **Shadow Ridge Resort Hotel and Conference Center** (50 Shadow Ridge St., 435/649-4300 or 800/451-3031, www.allseasonsresortlodging.com, $199-299). Shadow Ridge offers a mix of hotel-style guest rooms and kitchen-equipped condos with one or two bedrooms. Facilities include a heated outdoor pool, a sauna, and a fitness center. Park City has the **Park City Marriott** (1895 Sidewinder Dr., 435/649-2900, www.parkcitymarriott.com, $199-269), located in a business and condo development northeast of downtown. Designed with the small conference trade in mind, it offers swimming pool and spa facilities, two restaurants, and a lounge.

Right downtown is the ★ **Treasure Mountain Inn** (255 Main St., 435/649-7334 or 800/344-2460, www.treasuremountain-inn.com, $215-770). Treasure Mountain is a large complex of three buildings with several room types, all with kitchens. Newly refurbished guest rooms are large and beautifully furnished. If you want a quiet room in this extremely central locale, ask for one that faces the back pool and garden.

The **Yarrow Resort Hotel and Conference Center** (1800 Park Ave., 435/649-7000 or 800/927-7694, www.yarrowhotelparkcity.com, $299) is just below historic Main Street and close to the ski lifts. It's a little older than some other Park City lodgings, but the guest rooms are large and well kept; some have kitchens. There's also a restaurant, an outdoor heated pool, a hot tub, and an exercise room.

Over $300

Despite its pedestrian name, the **Hotel Park City** (2001 Park Ave., 435/200-2000, www.hotelparkcity.com, $449-1,749) is quite sumptuous, even by Park City standards. This all-suite hotel has deluxe in-room music players, comfy leather sofas, sumptuous baths, a heated outdoor pool, a spa and fitness center, and a good restaurant. It is a little too far to walk from the hotel to Main Street.

the Old Town Guest House

A landmark Park City boutique hotel just a block off Main Street is the **Washington School Inn** (543 Park Ave., 435/649-3800 or 800/824-1672, www.washingtonschoolinn. com, $850-4,000). The quarried limestone inn was built in 1889 as the town's elementary school; after a complete remodel in the 1980s, the old Washington School emerged as one of the most luxurious lodgings in Park City. There are four large standard guest rooms and four suites, a pool, hot tub, sauna, and ski lockers. During the summer it's possible to get a room for about $300.

★ **Marriott's Summit Watch Resort** (780 Main St., 435/647-4100, www.marriott. com, hotel room with kitchenette $369-479) is a cluster of condominium hotels at the base of Main Street near the Town Lift. They are some of the nicest lodging options in the downtown district, with lodgings ranging from studios to two-room villas. All guest rooms have kitchen facilities and luxury-level amenities; there's a central pool, and all the dining that downtown Park City offers is within a five-minute stroll.

Right at the main base of the Park City Mountain Resort and just a few dollars more expensive is **Marriott's MountainSide** (1305 Lowell Ave., 800/940-2000, www. marriott.com, hotel room with kitchenette $389-539); if you are looking for top-notch ski-in, ski-out lodging, this is a good choice. Although you can walk to town from here, it's a bit of a schlep in the winter.

Campgrounds

Park City RV Resort (2200 W. Rasmussen Rd., 435/649-2535, www.parkcityrvresort. com, tents $20, hookups $30-45) offers seasonal tent and year-round RV sites with showers and laundry. From I-80, take exit 145 for Park City and travel west one mile on the north frontage road. The campground is about six miles from Park City.

There are good public campgrounds in the Heber City area. **Jordanelle State Park** (435/649-9540 or 435/782-3030, http://state-parks.utah.gov, campsites $16-28, cabins $65) and **Wasatch Mountain State Park** (435/654-1791, http://stateparks.utah.gov, campsites $14-25, cabins $60) are both good places to pitch a tent in the summer. Both take reservations (800/322-3770, www.reserveamerica.com).

FOOD

Park City has the greatest concentration of good restaurants in Utah; the listings below are just a smattering of what you'll find in a very concentrated area. The five blocks of historic Main Street alone offer many fine places to eat, and each of the resorts, hotels, and lodges offers more options. Note that many of the restaurants close in May and November—the so-called mud season. During ski-season weekends, dinner reservations are strongly advised for all but the most casual restaurants.

Main Street and Vicinity

At the top of Main Street, **Wasatch Brew Pub** (250 Main St., 435/649-0900, www.wasatchbeers.com, 11am-10pm Mon.-Thurs., 11am-midnight Fri., 10am-midnight Sat., 10am-10pm Sun., $12-20) is a good place for a casual, inexpensive pub-style meal and excellent beers and ale; in good weather, there's a patio for outdoor dining.

Chimayo (368 Main St., 435/649-6222, www.chimayorestaurant.com, 5pm-10pm daily winter, hours vary in other seasons, $32-50) is the area's leading purveyor of contemporary Southwest cuisine, such as halibut encrusted with coconut and corn and served with wild mushrooms, spaghetti squash, and a citrus-infused chile sauce. One of the most romantic restaurants in Park City is ★ **Wahso** (577 Main St., 435/615-0300, www.wahso. com, 5pm-9:30pm Sun. and Wed.-Thurs., 5pm-10pm Fri.-Sat., $28-52). Its name is both Chinese and French (from *oiseau*, meaning "bird"), as is the cuisine at this stylish, slightly formal restaurant. French sauces meet Chinese cooking techniques and vice versa.

The inspiration for the food at pleasant **Cafe Terigo** (424 Main St., 435/645-9555, www.cafeterigo.com, 11:30am-2:30pm

Mon.-Tues., 11:30am-2:30pm and 5:30pm-10pm Wed.-Sat., $20-30) is Italian, but dishes such as porcini-dusted scallops on sweet corn risotto with roasted red pepper and arugula puree show that ingredients and techniques have been substantially updated. The atmosphere in the restaurant and on the side patio is simultaneously calming and fun.

Another signature Park City restaurant, **The Riverhorse on Main** (540 Main St., 435/649-3536, http://riverhorseparkcity.com, 5pm-10pm daily and 11am-2pm Sun., $32-60), in the old Masonic building, serves carefully prepared American standards with a few restrained flourishes; after a day of skiing, splurge on the trio of wild game. New American cooking is the order of the day at **Zoom** (660 Main St., 435/649-9108, www.zoomparkcity.com, 11:30am-2:30pm daily and 5pm-9:30pm Sun.-Thurs., 5pm-10pm Fri.-Sat., $16-38). The grilled meats are excellent, as are lunchtime sandwiches and burgers. Zoom has perhaps the nicest patio dining in Park City. Zoom is housed in an old railroad depot at the foot of Main Street and is owned by Robert Redford.

The traditional foods of the American West are celebrated and expanded on at the fun, stylish ★ **Purple Sage** (434 Main St., 435/655-9505, www.purplesageparkcity.com, 5:30pm-10pm nightly, $19-46), where such dishes as meatloaf, cowboy steaks, and sweet-corn-battered trout are prepared to exacting standards.

Although ★ **High West Distillery and Saloon** (703 Park Ave., 435/649-8300, www.highwest.com, 11am-9pm Sun.-Thurs., 11am-10pm Fri.-Sat., $14-34) is a great place to get an après-ski drink, it's also one of Park City's best restaurants. Try the three-bean bourbon chili topped with fried quinoa. Kids are welcome here, and there's a special menu with them in mind.

An opulent spot for fine dining is **Talisker on Main** (525 Main St., 435/658-5479, 5:30pm-10pm Tues.-Sat., $28-38), where seasonal local produce reigns supreme, with such

dishes as roast saddle of lamb with fresh garlic, chorizo, and sunchoke puree.

A nice change from Park City's upscale, meat-rich dining scene is the well-prepared eastern Mediterranean cooking at **Reefs** (710 Main St., 435/658-0323, www.reefsrestaurant.com, 5:30pm-10pm Mon.-Sat., $12-22), where you'll enjoy Lebanese and Turkish-style standards in addition to European classics such as chicken schnitzel and fusion dishes such as Moroccan salmon prepared with green chiles, cumin, cilantro, and tomatoes.

Prospector Square and Vicinity

A good, reasonably priced, and healthy bet for any meal of the day is **Good Karma** (1782 Prospector Ave., 435/658-0958, http://goodkarmarestaurants.com, 8am-9pm daily, $9-14), a sweet but tiny spot in Prospector Square with tasty Indo-Persian food (standard American fare is served at breakfast); sit out back in the courtyard.

One of Park City's best restaurants is the ★ **Blind Dog** (1251 Kearns Blvd., 435/655-0800, http://blinddogpc.com, 5pm-9:30pm Tues.-Sat., $20-34). Don't let its bland setting fool you; the food here is seriously good, and although crab cakes ($32) are favorites, the Dog also makes a mean meatloaf ($25), and the sushi is also top notch.

For a Western steak house atmosphere, go to **Grub Steak Restaurant** (2093 Sidewinder Ave., 435/649-8060, www.grubsteakrestaurant.com, 11:30am-2pm and 5pm-9pm Mon.-Thurs., 11:30am-2pm and 5pm-9:30pm Fri., 5pm-9:30pm Sat., 5pm-9pm Sun., $18-41) in the Inn at Prospector Square. The steaks, prime rib, grilled chicken, and seafood are excellent, and dinners come with a trip to the salad bar.

On Park Avenue at Kearns Boulevard is **Squatters Pub** (1900 Park Ave., 435/649-9868, www.squatters.com, 8am-10pm Sun.-Thurs., 8am-11pm Fri.-Sat., $10-20), a brewpub with above-average pub grub. Vegetarians should check out the charbroiled tofu tacos.

Luck into an outside table at **Silver Star Cafe** (1825 Three Kings Dr., 435/655-3456, www.thesilverstarcafe.com, 8am-9pm Sun.-Wed., 8am-10pm Thurs.-Sat., $18-27) and you'll have a great view of Park City. It's a favorite spot for brunch ($10-13) or a couple of small plates after hiking or skiing, or a dinnertime singer-songwriter concert, when the music complements the Silver Star's "American roots" food and easygoing atmosphere.

INFORMATION AND SERVICES

A number of Main Street storefronts advertise "visitors information"; these places are almost invariably real estate offices, although they do have racks of brochures. For the best selection of info and genuinely helpful staff, visit the **Park City Visitor Information Center** (1794 Olympic Pkwy., 435/658-9616, www.visitparkcity.com, 9am-6pm daily) near Kimball Junction at the turnoff to Utah Olympic Park. There's a branch office in the Park City Museum (528 Main St.).

GETTING THERE AND AROUND

Park City Transit (recording 435/645-5350) operates a trolley bus up and down Main Street (about every 10 minutes daily) and has several bus routes to other parts of town, including Park City, the Canyons, and Deer Valley ski areas (every 10-20 minutes daily). All buses are free; pick up a transit guide from the visitors center at Kimball Junction (1794 Olympic Pkwy., 435/658-9616), in the Park City Museum (528 Main St., 435/649-7457), on any of the buses, or by calling Park City Transit. Parking can be extremely difficult in downtown Park City, so it's a good idea to hop a bus.

All Resort (800/457-9457, www.allresort.com, $32-45 one-way, 24-hour advance reservations recommended) and **Canyon Transportation** (800/255-1841, www.canyontransport.com, $39 one-way) both make regular runs between Park City and Salt Lake City International Airport or downtown. All resorts also offer car rentals in Park City.

Parking can be tight in downtown Park City; hop the free trolley instead of driving.

Heber City and Vicinity

Its setting in a lush agricultural valley surrounded by high mountains has earned Heber City the title "Switzerland of America." Many of its people work at farming, raising livestock, and dairying, as their families have done since pioneer days, although it's also become the site of some fantastically expensive vacation homes. Heber City (pop. 17,600) makes a handy stop for travelers exploring the nearby Wasatch and Uinta Ranges or visiting the large Deer Creek and Strawberry Reservoirs. It also offers reasonably priced accommodations a short drive from Park City. Heber City merges almost seamlessly into the town of Midway, home to several upscale resorts.

SIGHTS

Heber Valley Historic Railroad

Ride a turn-of-the-20th-century train pulled by steam locomotive number 618 past Deer Creek Lake into scenic alpine Provo Canyon. The **Heber Valley Historic Railroad** (450 S. 600 W., 435/654-5601, www.hebervalleyrr.org, year-round, $20-30 adults, $15 ages 3-12) offers three different scenic tours, plus

a variety of dinner and adventure options as well, including a train ride to a zipline ($99 includes zipline and boxed lunch); check the website for details.

Soldier Hollow

Soldier Hollow (435/654-2002, www.soldierhollow.com, full-day trail pass $18 adults, $9 ages 7-17, $15 seniors), site of the 2002 Olympic and Paralympic cross-country skiing and biathlon events, offers roughly 20 miles of trails (including some easy ones added to the Olympic-level course) for cross-country skiing, snowshoeing, biathlon, and mountain biking. There's also a tubing hill ($20 for 2 hours over age 6, $10 ages 3-6). Rentals are available at the lodge. From Heber City, head west on 100 South to Midway. Take a left on Center Street (Hwy. 113) in Midway and head south for 3.5 miles to Soldier Hollow.

Homestead Crater

Just northwest of the town of Midway, on the grounds of the Homestead Resort, is a large volcanic-like cone called the Crater. This

The Homestead Crater is one of the odder swimming holes in the state.

geological curiosity is actually composed of travertine deposited by the local hot springs; water once flowed out of the top, but now it's piped to a 65-foot-deep, 95°F pool deep in the Crater's belly. **Homestad Crater** (435/657-3840, noon-8pm Mon.-Thurs., 10am-8pm Fri.-Sat., 10am-6pm Sun., $11 Mon.-Thurs., $16 Fri.-Sun., reservations required) is accessible for swimming, scuba diving ($22-27), and snorkeling. Scuba classes and guided dives are also offered, as are paddleboard yoga classes.

RECREATION
★ Wasatch Mountain State Park

Wasatch Mountain State Park (435/654-1791, tee times 435/654-0532, http://stateparks.utah.gov, day-use $5, 18 holes of golf $30-35), Utah's largest state park, encompasses 22,000 acres of valleys and mountains on the east side of the Wasatch Range. Unpaved scenic drives lead north through Pine Creek Canyon to Guardsman Pass Road (turn right for Park City or left over the pass for Brighton), northwest through Snake Creek Canyon to Pole Line Pass and American Fork Canyon, and southwest over Decker Pass to Cascade Springs.

The 1.5-mile **Pine Creek Nature Trail**

begins near site 21 in the Oak Hollow Campground. The vast park is also a popular place for off-highway vehicle riding, which is not always a rowdy and reckless pastime; in the fall, join a guided OHV leaf-peeping tour.

The excellent **Lake** and **Mountain Golf Courses** (975 W. Golf Course Dr., 435/654-0532) are in the main part of the park. The newer Gold and Silver courses are at **Soldier Hollow Golf Course** (1370 W. Soldier Hollow Ln., 435/654-7442), which occupies a corner of the park. A clubhouse includes a pro shop and a café.

Winter brings snow depths of 3-6 feet mid-December-mid-March. Separate **cross-country ski** and **snowmobile** trails begin near Soldier Hollow (435/654-2002, www.soldierhollow.com), which also has a tubing park and two lifts. **Homestead Cross-Country Ski Center** (Homestead Resort, 700 N. Homestead Dr., Midway, 435/654-1102) provides equipment for both sports.

To reach the main entrance of Wasatch Mountain State Park, drive west three miles from Heber City to Midway, then follow signs north two miles.

Jordanelle State Park

The large **Jordanelle State Park** reservoir

the clubhouse at Soldier Hollow Golf Course

(435/649-9540, http://stateparks.utah.gov), upstream of Heber City on the Provo River, provides recreation for boaters and anglers. It's east of U.S. 40, six miles north of Heber City. There are two recreation areas. **Rock Cliff Recreation Area** (435/782-3030, day-use $7) is at the upper end of the east arm of the reservoir and has restrooms, a nature center, boardwalks with interpretive displays, and pavilions for day use. **Hailstone Recreation Area** (435/649-9540 or 800/322-3770, day-use $10) has a large campground, restrooms and showers, day-use shaded pavilions, a marina with 80 boat slips, a general store, a laundry, and a small restaurant.

Deer Creek State Park

The seven-mile-long Deer Creek Reservoir in **Deer Creek State Park** (Midway, 435/654-0171, http://stateparks.utah.gov, day-use $10) lies in a very pretty setting below Mount Timpanogos and other peaks of the Wasatch Range. A developed area near the lower end of the lake has a campground with showers, a picnic area, a paved boat ramp, a dock, and a fish-cleaning station; elevation is 5,400 feet. **Island Beach Area,** 4.5 miles to the northeast, has a gravel swimming beach and a marina, open in summer, with a store, a snack bar, a boat ramp, and rentals of fishing boats, ski boats, and personal watercraft. Rainbow trout, perch, largemouth bass, and walleye swim in the lake. Good winds for sailing blow most afternoons. You'll often see a lineup of catamarans at the sailboat beach near the campground and crowds of sailboarders at the Island Beach Area. **Deer Creek Island Resort** (Island Beach Area, 435/654-2155, www.deercreekislandresort.com) has boat rentals.

Strawberry Reservoir

The 17,000-acre **Strawberry Reservoir** (435/654-0470), which is Utah's top trout fishery, lies on a high, rolling plateau 23 miles southeast of Heber City. Fishing is good all year (through the ice in winter) for rainbow and cutthroat trout and some brook trout

and kokanee salmon. The U.S. Forest Service maintains three marinas around the lake. Several winter parking areas along U.S. 40 provide access for cross-country skiing, snowmobiling, and ice fishing.

ENTERTAINMENT AND EVENTS

Horse shows and rodeos take place throughout the summer in the Heber City area (www.gohebervalley.com). The **Utah High School Rodeo Finals** are held in early June. A **powwow** (www.heberpw.com) in mid-June brings Native American groups to Soldier Hollow for dances and craft sales. **Wasatch County Fair Days** features a parade, a rodeo, exhibits, a livestock show, entertainment, and a demolition derby in early August. Labor Day weekend brings **Swiss Days** (www.midwayswissdays.com) to Midway as well as a huge gathering of border collies and their fans to Soldier Hollow for the **Soldier Hollow Classic Sheepdog Championship** (435/654-2002, www.soldierhollowclassic.com).

ACCOMMODATIONS

Heber City motels are generally well maintained and reasonably priced. A few miles west, in Midway, are several more expensive and luxurious resorts.

Heber City

The **Swiss Alps Inn** (167 S. Main St., 435/654-0722, www.swissalpsinn.com, $80-88) is a charming budget motel with an outdoor pool, a playground, and two suites with full kitchens.

The **Holiday Inn Express** (1268 S. Main St., 435/654-9990 or 800/315-2621, www.hi-express.com, $90-100), on the southern edge of town, is a good choice for those who don't appreciate the quirks of small-town budget motels.

Midway

Undoubtedly the truly unique place to stay in the Heber City area is the **Homestead**

Resort (700 N. Homestead Dr., 435/654-1102 or 800/327-7220, www.homesteadresort.com, $105-250). This hot-spring resort is three miles west of Heber City, near Midway, and features mineral baths, swimming, and accommodations. The natural hot-spring water is believed to be good for the skin, and if the water alone doesn't do the trick, the resort's spa services can probably help. The spacious grounds and stately buildings of the Homestead may remind you of grandma's house, and the guest rooms themselves are country-style but comfortable.

Golfers can play at the resort's 18-hole course (18 holes $49-59) but should also note that excellent golf courses are right down the road at Wasatch Mountain State Park. Stables offer horseback riding, hayrides (sleigh rides in winter), and bicycle rentals. Guest rooms should be reserved well in advance, especially for summer weekends. The **Blue Boar Inn** (1235 Warm Springs Rd., 435/654-1400 or 888/650-1400, www.theblueboarinn.com, $175-295) is right near an entrance to Wasatch Mountain State Park and the park's popular golf course. Each of the inn's 12 meticulously decorated guest rooms is devoted to a different poet or author; there's also a very good restaurant (7am-9pm daily, $26-38) and a cozy pub on-site.

The **Zermatt Resort** (784 W. Resort Dr., 435/657-0180 or 866/937-6288, www.zermattresort.com, $125-350) is an imposing Swiss-style lodge with restaurants, swimming pools, a spa, and its own travertine warm-springs plunge.

Sixteen miles southeast of Heber City, **Daniels Summit Lodge** (U.S. 40, 435/548-2300, www.danielssummit.com, $189-369) is located near the Strawberry Reservoir. This big country lodge offers plenty of activities, including horseback riding in the summer and snowmobiling in the winter. A restaurant is on-site, so you don't have to drive into town for dinner.

Campgrounds
Wasatch Mountain State Park (435/654-1791, http://stateparks.utah.gov, reservations 800/322-3770 or www.reserveamerica.com, day-use $5, campsites $14-25) has three campgrounds. The large Oak Hollow (tents) and Mahogany Campgrounds (RVs) are just north of the golf course (elev. 5,600 feet). Both have showers and hookups late April or early May-late October. Little Deer Creek Campground (water June-mid-Sept.) is a smaller and more secluded area, set in an aspen forest. Groups often reserve all the sites; check with the park office first.

From Heber City, drive west three miles to Midway, then follow signs north for two miles to the main park entrance. Little Deer Creek Campground is reachable by driving a seven-mile unpaved road to Cascade Springs, then turning north and going four miles on another unpaved road.

Jordanelle State Park (http://stateparks.utah.gov) offers walk-in camping at the **Rock Cliff Recreation Area** (435/782-3030, day-use $7, camping $16), at the upper end of the east arm of the reservoir. Facilities include restrooms and hot showers, a nature center, boardwalks with interpretive displays, and pavilions for day use. **Hailstone Recreation Area** (435/649-9540 or 800/322-3770, www.reserveamerica.com, day-use $10, camping $16-28) is a large campground with restrooms and showers, day-use shaded pavilions, a marina with 80 boat slips, a general store, a laundry, and a small restaurant. Facilities include wheelchair access with raised tent platforms. Jordanelle State Park is east of U.S. 40, six miles north of Heber City.

River's Edge at Deer Park (7000 N. Old Hwy. 40, 435/654-4049, www.riversedgeatdeerpark.com, year-round, RVs $38, yurts $90, cabins $110-130), a private resort about six miles north of Heber City, offers a variety of camping and cabin options just below the Jordanelle Reservoir dam.

Deer Creek State Park (Midway, 435/654-0171 or 800/322-3770, www.reserveamerica.com, day-use $10, camping $20-28) has a campground just off U.S. 189; it is 10 miles southwest of Heber City and 17 miles northeast of Provo.

The U.S. Forest Service maintains four campgrounds at **Strawberry Reservoir** (435/548-2321, www.recreation.gov, late May-late Oct., $17-34). **Currant Creek Recreation Complex** (435/654-0470, www.recreation.gov, late May-late Oct., $20) has a campground. **Currant Creek Nature Trail** begins from Loop D of the campground and climbs 400 vertical feet in a 1.25-mile loop. From Heber City, drive southeast for 42 miles on U.S. 40 (past Strawberry Reservoir), turn northwest onto Forest Road 083, and travel 19.5 miles along Currant Creek.

FOOD
Heber City

American-style cafés line Main Street, along with plenty of fast food to serve the skiing crowds. A fun, casual local place with good food is **Spin Cafe** (220 N. Main St., 435/654-0251, http://spincafe.net, 11:30am-8:30pm Sun.-Thurs. 11:30am-9pm Fri.-Sat., $8-19); the barbecue is a specialty.

The **Snake Creek Grill** (650 W. 100 S., 435/654-2133, www.snakecreekgrill.com, 5:30pm-9pm Wed.-Sun., $14-40), housed in a historic wooden building, is about as upscale as it gets in Heber City, with surprisingly well-prepared steaks, salmon, bison burgers, and pasta dishes and a friendly atmosphere.

Midway

In a little strip mall in Midway, find ★ **Tarahumara** (380 E. Main St., 435/654-3465, www.tarahumara.biz, 11am-9pm Mon.-Sat., $10-15), where the Mexican food is shockingly good; the salsa bar is a special treat. The dining room at the **Blue Boar Inn** (1235 Warm Springs Rd., 435/654-1400 or 888/650-1400, www.theblueboarinn.com, 7am-9pm daily, $26-38), which puts out elegant takes on standard dishes, is also highly regarded.

The casual restaurant at the Homestead Resort is **Fanny's Grill** (700 N. Homestead Dr., 888/327-7220, 7am-9pm daily, $10-15), and it's a good enough place to get a bite to eat after a swim in the Homestead Crater. **Simon's** (5pm-9pm daily, $12-27) is the Homestead's dinner restaurant, with an atmosphere and menu designed to bring comfort to those for whom turkey pot pie can provide it.

INFORMATION AND SERVICES

The **Heber Valley Chamber of Commerce** (475 N. Main St., 435/654-3666, www.gohebervalley.com, 9am-5pm Mon.-Fri.) dispenses information on businesses in Heber City and Midway. **Heber Ranger District Office** (2460 S. U.S. 40, 435/654-0470, 8am-4:30pm Mon.-Fri.) manages the Uinta National Forest lands east and southeast of Heber City.

The **Heber Valley Medical Center** (1485 S. U.S. 40, 435/654-2500) has 24-hour emergency care.

GETTING THERE

To reach Heber City, take I-80 (from about 25 miles east of Salt Lake City) to exit 146 and head 17 miles south on U.S. 40. No public transportation serves this area.

MAP SYMBOLS

═══ Expressway	★ Highlight	✗ Airfield	⚲ Golf Course
─── Primary Road	○ City/Town	✈ Airport	▣ Parking Area
─── Secondary Road	◉ State Capital	▲ Mountain	▰ Archaeological Site
∙∙∙∙∙∙ Unpaved Road	⊛ National Capital	✦ Unique Natural Feature	⛪ Church
------ Trail	★ Point of Interest		⛽ Gas Station
∙∙∙∙∙∙∙∙ Ferry	● Accommodation	↘ Waterfall	Glacier
------ Railroad	▼ Restaurant/Bar	♠ Park	Mangrove
═══ Pedestrian Walkway	■ Other Location	⬚ Trailhead	Reef
⊓⊓⊓⊓ Stairs	⋀ Campground	⛷ Skiing Area	Swamp

CONVERSION TABLES

$°C = (°F - 32) / 1.8$
$°F = (°C \times 1.8) + 32$
1 inch = 2.54 centimeters (cm)
1 foot = 0.304 meters (m)
1 yard = 0.914 meters
1 mile = 1.6093 kilometers (km)
1 km = 0.6214 miles
1 fathom = 1.8288 m
1 chain = 20.1168 m
1 furlong = 201.168 m
1 acre = 0.4047 hectares
1 sq km = 100 hectares
1 sq mile = 2.59 square km
1 ounce = 28.35 grams
1 pound = 0.4536 kilograms
1 short ton = 0.90718 metric ton
1 short ton = 2,000 pounds
1 long ton = 1.016 metric tons
1 long ton = 2,240 pounds
1 metric ton = 1,000 kilograms
1 quart = 0.94635 liters
1 US gallon = 3.7854 liters
1 Imperial gallon = 4.5459 liters
1 nautical mile = 1.852 km

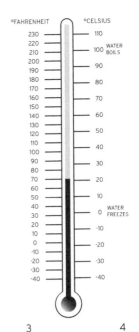

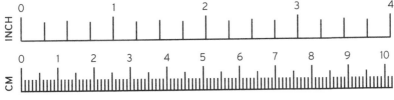

MOON SPOTLIGHT SALT LAKE CITY & PARK CITY

Avalon Travel
a member of the Perseus Books Group
1700 Fourth Street
Berkeley, CA 94710, USA
www.moon.com

Editor: Nikki Ioakimedes
Series Manager: Kathryn Ettinger
Copy Editor: Ann Seifert
Graphics Coordinator: Darren Alessi
Production Coordinator: Darren Alessi
Cover Design: Faceout Studios, Charles Brock
Moon Logo: Tim McGrath
Map Editor: Albert Angulo
Cartographer: Stephanie Poulain

ISBN-13: 978-1-63121-103-4

Title page photo: © © W.C. McRae
All photos © W.C. McRae, Judy Jewell and Paul Levy except page 87 and 100 © Alta Ski Area

Printed in the United States

ABOUT THE AUTHORS

W. C. McRae

Bill McRae has been exploring Utah for several decades, each time getting farther off the road and digging deeper into the landscape. Every trip has a different focus, whether it's hiking into a new and more remote canyon, fixating on ancient rock art, or going deluxe at guest ranches. Bill has written for Frommer's, Lonely Planet, and Mobil Guides, and has contributed to *1000 Places to See Before You Die*. He has also edited books for National Geographic and provided content for websites such as GORP.com and Expedia.com. When not fixing up his old house in Astoria, Oregon, Bill has a day job as a high-tech marketing writer.

Judy Jewell

While visiting Goosenecks State Park, Judy Jewell realized that, like the river below, she might be an example of entrenched meandering. Perhaps so . . . her work on Moon guidebooks to Utah, Montana, and Oregon has taken her to both the popular destinations and the remote areas in these states. In Utah, there's nothing she likes better than tromping through a dry wash in search of rock art or an old granary. When she's at home in Portland, Oregon, Judy works as a technical and scientific editor and a yoga teacher.

CPSIA information can be obtained at www.ICGtesting.com
Printed in the USA
LVOW01s1332260415

435959LV00004BA/14/P